LEADERSHIP IN CHRISTIAN PERSPECTIVE

Biblical Foundations and Contemporary Practices for Servant Leaders

JUSTIN A. IRVING
AND MARK L. STRAUSS

Baker Academic

a division of Baker Publishing Group
Grand Rapids, Michigan

From Justin:
To Tasha Irving, for your friendship and love.
I am so thankful to be sharing this journey of life with you.

From Mark:
To the memory of my father, Richard L. Strauss,
a consummate model of a servant leader.

Published by Baker Academic
a division of Baker Publishing Group
PO Box 6287, Grand Rapids, MI 49516-6287
www.bakeracademic.com

Printed in the United States of America

Library of Congress Cataloging-in-Publication Data
Names: Irving, Justin A., author.
Title: Leadership in Christian perspective : biblical foundations and contemporary practices for servant leaders / Justin A. Irving and Mark L. Strauss.
Description: Grand Rapids, MI : Baker Publishing Group, 2019. | Includes bibliographical references and index.
Identifiers: LCCN 2018043172 | ISBN 9781540960337 (pbk. : alk. paper)
Subjects: LCSH: Leadership—Religious aspects—Christianity.
Classification: LCC BV4597.53.L43 I78 2019 | DDC 253—dc23
LC record available at https://lccn.loc.gov/2018043172

ISBN 978-1-5409-6207-2 (casebound)

Contents

Contents

Figures

Figures

Introduction

A Fresh Look at Empowering Leadership

Introduction

In his 1978 book simply titled *Leadership*, James MacGregor Burns notes that leadership is "one of the most observed and the least understood phenomena on earth."[1] While such an observation can make writing and reading a book on leadership sound daunting, we see an opportunity in this observation.

Leadership affects all of us. For better or worse, our lives are and will be impacted by leadership done well or leadership done poorly. Because leadership has such far-reaching importance, we see in this reality an opportunity. It is an opportunity to bring health to teams and organizations. It is an opportunity to bring job satisfaction to leaders and followers working together. It is an opportunity to see the organizations and churches of our world flourish and become all that God intends for them.

Throughout this book we will be talking about leadership practices that focus on empowering others to grow and flourish in their service and work. Because the mission and effectiveness of most organizations matter, we want to see leaders learning to embrace this empowering approach to leadership practice.

Let's begin with our definition of empowering leadership:

Empowering leadership is a process by which leaders and followers partner together for the purpose of achieving common goals and shared vision.

1

This definition tells you about some of the values we bring to the table in this leadership book.

First, empowering leadership is about *empowerment* more than control. Although historical models of management and leadership often emphasized control, biblical principles and contemporary research point to the power and effectiveness of leadership focused on empowering followers rather than controlling followers.

Second, empowering leadership is about a *process* more than an event. Leadership is not about simple meetings and activities. Empowering leadership is about a leader-follower relationship over time. Leaders' modeling what matters, appreciating and valuing followers, and equipping and developing followers take time and investment in that core relationship.

Third, empowering leadership is about *shared* goals and vision more than it is about the leader's goals and vision. Although it can seem efficient for leaders to have a hands-on and highly directive approach to leadership, long-term effectiveness necessitates that both leaders and followers are owners of a common agenda.

Although models of directive and controlling leadership are often easier to find, throughout this book we will aim to highlight models of leaders focused on empowering and serving their followers. Increasingly, researchers are demonstrating that such empowering and servant-oriented practices are not only a good idea but also produce superior results.

As we begin our journey, we'd like to highlight the empowering leadership of Colleen Barrett, former president of Southwest Airlines. Barrett served as the president of Southwest Airlines from 2001 to 2008, after working in a variety of other roles with the company from 1978. Barrett had the same philosophy as the organization's founder—they viewed their primary job as working for their people and their customers. Barrett notes, "Our purpose in life as Senior Leaders at Southwest Airlines is to support our People. To us, that means treating People as family."[2]

The commitment of Barrett and other leaders at Southwest has been to make sure employees and the customers are the top priority—in that order. Barrett notes that their entire philosophy of leadership is quite simple: "Treat your People right, and good things will happen."[3] Barrett notes that when senior leaders talk to their employees at Southwest, their message goes like this:

> You are the most important Person to us. You are our most important Customer in terms of priority. Therefore, we're going to spend 80 percent of our time treating you with Golden Rule behavior and trying to make sure that you have an enjoyable work environment where you feel good about what you do, about

yourself, and about your position in the Company. But if we do that, what we want in exchange is for you to do the same thing by offering our Passengers— who are our second Customer in terms of priority—that same kind of warmth, caring, and fun spirit.[4]

This model of empowering and follower-focused leadership is compelling, and throughout the book we aim to provide you with biblical insight, research-based reflection, and practical recommendations for how you can grow as an empowering leader as well.

Leadership in Christian Perspective

Leadership in Christian Perspective is intentionally an integrative project. Although independent books could be written on effective leadership practice (based on current research and theory) or biblical reflections on leadership practice (based on thoughtful study of the Bible), we intentionally wanted to bring these disciplines together into a joint reflection.

Mark is a biblical scholar, with expertise in New Testament studies and Bible translation. Through his fifteen-plus books, Mark specializes in making sound biblical scholarship accessible to his readers. Justin is a leadership researcher and educator, with expertise in servant leadership and its application to team and organizational effectiveness. Justin has a passion for bringing sound research-based reflections on leadership to leaders in diverse sectors.

Though we could have simply engaged the topic of leadership from our respective disciplines, we desired to bring our disciplines together in this integrative project. Because of this, throughout the book we examine effective leadership practices in light of three primary areas of reflection: (1) biblical and theological perspectives, (2) theory and research-based perspectives, and (3) historic and contemporary examples and perspectives. In the end, we hope that drawing from these diverse and integrative sources of knowledge will provide rich and meaningful insight for you on what makes leaders effective and enables them to empower others.

As we consider the integrative nature of a project like this, some cautions are in order. It can be dangerous to use the Bible to support your pet theory. We groan when we see the latest self-help fad supported with a Bible verse taken out of context. Suddenly we have the "biblical view" of dieting, or dating, or exercise, or parenting, or financial investment. This book is about leadership; but we need to say right up front that the Bible is not a handbook on leadership. The Bible is a record of God's dealings with human beings: the story of their creation, their fall, and their redemption through the coming of Jesus the Savior. It is an invitation to find our place in the story and to come into a relationship with our Creator God.

So the Bible is not, first and foremost, a guide to leadership. Nor is every leader—whether in Israel or in the early church—a model to be imitated. There are some terrible examples of leaders and terrible models of leadership found in the Bible. We must also recognize that examples of leadership found in the Bible are deeply embedded in culture and so are not necessarily always "God's way to lead." For example, much of the Bible is set in highly authoritarian and hierarchical cultural contexts, where kings, emperors, governors, fathers, and husbands exercised absolute authority and dominance over their subordinates. Slavery was pervasive both in the ancient Near East and in the Greco-Roman world. Yet no one (we hope) would propose that this is a model for biblical leadership. So, again, caution must be used when drawing "biblical truth" about leadership from a cursory reading of the text.

With these caveats in mind, however, we can also assert that the Bible speaks a great deal about leadership. There are certainly positive models of leadership in the Bible worth emulating. We see leaders acting with discernment, wisdom, godliness, and compassion. We see courage in the face of adversity and perseverance in the face of trials. These leadership models appear in both the Old and New Testaments.

Yet the real revolution in leadership came in the teaching and example of Jesus. In the context of an authoritarian world—where power, dominance, and oppression were the order of the day—Jesus introduced a radical new model of leadership. This model has often been called "servant leadership." But it is anything but *subservient* leadership. A better description might be *empowering* leadership. It is a leadership that is other-centered, the goal of which is to enable others to fulfill their calling before God, to be all that God wants them to be. It is therefore also *equipping* leadership, with a focus on training up the next generation of leaders.

The radical premise behind this model is that the goal of leadership is not to promote the position, power, status, influence—or even the agenda—of the human leader. It is to accomplish *God's purpose* in the world. The leader is therefore more concerned with doing what is right than with personal success. He or she is focused more on the growth and success of those being led than on personal power or prestige.

Throughout this book we will pause in each chapter to take a biblical perspective on the topic at hand. The vast majority of these are taken from the example of Jesus himself and those who followed him, especially the apostle Paul. Paul perhaps sums up best this equipping model when he describes the reason Christ raises up leaders in his church: "So Christ himself gave the apostles, the prophets, the evangelists, the pastors and teachers, *to equip his people for works of service, so that the body of Christ may be built up until we all reach unity in the faith and in the knowledge of the Son of God and become mature, attaining to the whole measure of the fullness of Christ*" (Eph. 4:11–13).

The leader's role is to equip God's people for works of service, with the goal of spiritual maturity and a deeper relationship with Christ. We would assert that this should be the ultimate goal of all Christian leadership, whether of those in full-time Christian ministry in the church or those serving as Christian leaders in other sectors. The aim of empowering and equipping others to effectively engage God's purpose in the world, in diverse sectors, is vital for all seeking to lead in Christian perspective.

A Brief Survey of Leadership Study

Ancient Roots

Almost all models of "great leadership" from the ancient world were hierarchical and top-down. To lead meant to convince, cajole, coerce, or compel others to do your bidding. Indeed, most history writing—both ancient and modern—follows the exploits of rulers and their conquests. Leaders are extolled and remembered for the lands they occupied and the peoples they conquered.

This is not to say that rulers never served as benefactors for their nations and people. In the fourth century BC Alexander the Great, one of the great military geniuses of history, through his conquests spread Greek language and literature, art and architecture, philosophy and jurisprudence throughout the eastern Mediterranean and as far east as India. Three hundred years later the influential leadership of Caesar Augustus turned the Roman Republic into an empire and brought in the Pax Romana—an unprecedented period of peace and prosperity. The whole Mediterranean became a "Roman Lake," with open sea-lanes, a vast network of roads, and a good measure of law and order—all protected by the nearly invincible Roman legions.

Yet the Roman "peace" was not so peaceful for subject peoples and was often enforced with the sword. The Roman historian Tacitus quotes the Caledonian general Calgacus on the eve of a battle against the Roman legions. The Romans, he says, are "bandits of the world. . . . Robbery, butchery and pillaging they call government; they create a wasteland and call it 'peace.'"[5] One individual's peace is another's decimation.

When Jesus sees his disciples reflecting this kind of leadership by seeking the best positions in his kingdom, he sums up the world's model of leadership like this: "You know that those who are regarded as rulers of the Gentiles lord it over them, and their high officials exercise authority over them" (Mark 10:42). That pretty well epitomizes leadership through the centuries. Yet Jesus's next words turn the organizational chart upside down, representing a revolution in leadership theory: "*Not so with you*. Instead, whoever wants to become great among you must be your servant, and whoever wants to be first must be slave of all" (Mark 10:43–44).

In a world where the patriarch of the family has absolute authority over the household; where all of society is hierarchical, from the emperor at the top to the lowest slave at the bottom; where the wealthy exploit the poor with near impunity; where the powerful manipulate the court system for their own means; where slaves are viewed as mere property, not persons—it is in this world Jesus calls for "servant leadership"! This must have sounded like a strange oxymoron to his disciples. They would *not* hear it as the boss who "serves" the employees by bringing coffee to the office in the morning. They would hear it as "slave leadership," and a slave exists merely to serve the master, to do the master's bidding. This is the opposite of leadership!

Yet we would contend that Jesus is anything but nonsensical. He explains his model of leadership by pointing to himself: "For even the Son of Man did not come to be served, but to serve, and to give his life as a ransom for many" (Mark 10:45). Jesus demonstrated extraordinary authority and power during his public ministry—healing the sick, raising the dead, calming the storm, and so on. Yet his whole life was lived for the benefit of others—to bring them back into a right relationship with God. The leader who serves is not one who is weak and manipulated by others. Rather, he or she is other centered, taking the lead to equip and empower others to be all that God calls them to be. Many individuals throughout history have practiced this kind of empowering leadership. And a number of modern theorists have recognized its power and potential.

Leadership in the Past Hundred Years

While the practice of leadership has ancient roots, the contemporary study of management and leadership has taken place in a focused manner for the past 120 years. The intent of this book is not to provide an in-depth overview of every management and leadership theory over these years. Our intent is to provide practical and research-based insights on effective leadership practices *for the next hundred years*.

In order to do this well we must provide context for our reflections. Paying attention to core management and leadership theories from the past hundred years helps us see key advances over these years and how current practice stands on the shoulders of established theorists and researchers from the past.

In this section we provide an overview of four primary time periods and key leadership themes related to these periods. It will not be exhaustive—either in scope or depth. Other resources provide a more exhaustive overview of the history of leadership theory, and we recommend those desiring a more in-depth look at this history to explore these resources.[6] We do, however, want to highlight important leadership development and themes related to leadership practices we present in this book. We begin in the early 1900s.

TRAIT THEORY, SCIENTIFIC MANAGEMENT, AND HUMAN RELATIONS (1900–1940)

Based on this "great man" concept of leadership, leadership reflection in the early part of the twentieth century often focused on well-known historic leaders. The assumption was that leaders were primarily born, not made, and that the characteristics and traits of these leaders could be identified. Examples of traits studied include intelligence, self-confidence, integrity, extraversion, and determination.[7]

In addition to trait-based emphases, the early part of the twentieth century also emphasized two divergent themes: scientific management and human relations. *Scientific management* focused on minimizing human variance in the workforce through standardization practices.[8] This approach to leadership viewed organizations as machines. In this approach, human uniqueness is essentially a problem to be solved through standardizing practices. The heart of this approach is captured in a statement frequently attributed to Henry Ford: "Why is it that I always get the whole person when what I really want is just a pair of hands?"

By the 1920s there emerged studies focused on the sociopsychological dimensions of human work.[9] Building on the emphases of scientific management, the Hawthorne studies revealed the importance of manager care for and interest in workers and their work. Beyond financial motivations, the social and psychological dimensions of *human relations* were also motivating for workers.

LEADERSHIP BEHAVIORS AND SKILLS (1940–70)

Moving beyond and building on the trait, standardization, and human relations themes of the first forty years of the twentieth century, the next time period emphasized the skills and behaviors of leaders. Early work related to the skills of leaders highlighted the technical, interpersonal, and conceptual skills managers need at different levels of an organization.[10] While top-level managers need higher levels of conceptual skill, supervisory managers need high levels of technical skills. Managers across all organizational levels benefit from high levels of human or interpersonal skill.

The benefit of human interpersonal skills is also seen through research conducted on behavioral approaches to leadership. The Ohio State studies and the University of Michigan studies[11] identified the importance of leadership behavior focused on both task accomplishment and people orientation. Although task and production orientation produced results, absent of employee-oriented behaviors these results included negative factors such as increased absenteeism and turnover. When increased focus on employee-oriented behaviors was added, production was also high, but with higher levels of job satisfaction and lower levels of absenteeism and employee grievances. This line of research eventually resulted in something known as the *managerial grid*, which highlights the benefit of team management that has a high concern for people and a high concern for production.[12]

Theory X and Theory Y also emerged in this time period. Building on prior management ideas, Theory X and Theory Y emphasized important shifts in how followers in an organization were viewed and managed. *Theory X* emphasizes a pessimistic view of people and their commitment to work. In this approach, followers must be micromanaged due to the belief that workers will not produce results without extrinsic reward and punishment. Think of this as leaders primarily using a carrot-and-stick approach to managing others.

In contrast to Theory X, *Theory Y* emphasizes an optimistic view of people, maintaining that most people desire to take pride in their work when appropriately motivated. Participative management is used in place of micromanaging, and employee reviews are primarily used not for reward and punishment but rather for creating a leader-follower dynamic of open communication built on trust.[13]

FOLLOWER-CONSIDERATION AND MOTIVATION (1970–90)

The previous time period raised the value of leaders focusing on human skills and behaviors in leadership. These shifts served as a foundation for management and leadership theories in the 1970s through the 1990s to bring increased consideration to followers and how they are motivated.

One follower-considerate model of leadership—SLII®—emphasizes the importance of leaders adapting their behavior based on the needs of followers.

By assessing a follower's level of competence and commitment related to a task that needs to get done, leaders can apply the appropriate level of direction and support needed for individual followers in diverse situations.[14]

The *path-goal theory* of leadership was also developed in this time period.[15] At its core, path-goal theory is about leaders responding to follower needs in an effort to support goal accomplishment along defined paths. This leadership work involves defining goals, clarifying paths, removing obstacles, and providing support.

Building on these follower-considerate models of leadership, *leader-member exchange theory* emphasizes the relational interaction between leader and follower.[16] The quality of this relationship in the leader-follower dyad is seen as instrumental for influencing positive individual and organizational outcomes. When a high-level leader-follower relationship is present, this tends to result in positive outcomes such as higher organizational commitment and lower levels of employee turnover.

This time period also saw the formal introduction of two major leadership themes addressed in this book: servant leadership and transformational leadership. Although *servant leadership* has ancient roots, the contemporary study of servant leadership arose out of the work of Robert K. Greenleaf.[17] For Greenleaf, the servant leader ensures that other people's highest-priority needs are being served. Servant leaders put the needs of followers above the self-interest of the leader and engage followers with characteristics such as listening, empathy, and a commitment to the growth of people.

Transformational leadership is focused on organizational transformation and effectiveness through leader behaviors such as the intrinsic motivation of followers and the development of followers. As leaders and followers pursue organizational change and effectiveness, this is accomplished as people enter into a process of personal transformation. The theory is captured by the Four I's of transformational leadership: idealized influence, inspirational motivation, intellectual stimulation, and individualized consideration. In contrast to transactional leadership that is based on a quid pro quo leader-follower exchange, transformational leadership raises the motivation of leaders and followers to focus on mutually shared goals and aspirations for the organization.[18]

AUTHENTIC LEADERSHIP AND FOLLOWER EMPOWERMENT
(1990 TO 2020 AND BEYOND)

In the final time period we cover, many of the threads introduced in the past continue. For instance, an optimistic view of follower motivations, leaders' adapting their behavior based on needs of followers, a commitment to the transformation of organizations and people, and a commitment to serving the needs of followers all remain as key priorities for contemporary leaders. Building on these themes, greater definition has developed to assist leaders, particularly around the themes of emotional intelligence, authentic leadership, leader purposefulness, and servant leadership.

Emotional intelligence, applied to leadership, emphasizes the importance of the personal and social competence in the leader. This includes themes such as leader self-awareness and self-regulation (personal competencies) as well as leader empathy and social skills (social competencies). At its core, emotional intelligence is about recognizing and responding to emotion in oneself and in others, which is vital work for leaders.[19]

Authentic leadership emphasizes intrapersonal wisdom and an awareness of personal strengths and limitations. Core principles such as purpose, values, relationships, self-discipline, and leader heart characterize leadership done with authenticity. Authentic leaders are not simply committed to the organization's mission, they also bring personal passion and purpose to the table on behalf of the organization. While Henry Ford simply wanted "a pair of hands," authentic leaders recognize limitations when leaders do not bring their whole selves to the organization's needs and opportunities.[20]

Connected to themes identified in authentic leadership, *leader purposefulness* is also a priority for contemporary leaders. Rather than simply focusing on the "what" of leadership tasks and responsibilities, leader purposefulness encourages leaders to dig deeper into the "why" of leadership. While the reasons and purposes of organizations must be clear, followers likewise benefit from leaders who understand their personal sense of purpose and meaning. Leader purposefulness benefits followers and organizations by positively influencing variables such as higher levels of organizational commitment and higher levels of job satisfaction among followers.[21]

Finally, this recent time period has seen the *servant leadership* concepts introduced by Greenleaf developed into measurable theories and a growing research agenda. While it is easy to argue that servant leadership is a biblically consistent approach to leading, this contemporary study is demonstrating the positive effect servant leadership has on teams and organizations. Servant leadership is characterized by valuing people, developing people, building community, displaying authenticity, providing leadership, and sharing leadership. As leaders move beyond autocratic and paternalistic forms of leadership, followers and organizations benefit from leaders who place the needs of followers above the self-interest of the leader.[22]

Key Leadership Themes in the Book

As our reflections above clarify, leadership has been studied from diverse angles and perspectives down through the ages. While we will interact with some of these angles in this book, our discussion of leadership practice in light of the Bible and leadership theory will emphasize four major themes: (1) servant leadership and follower focus, (2) transformational leadership and organizational transformation, (3) team leadership and collaborative orientation, and (4) leader purposefulness and meaning-based work.

Servant Leadership and Follower Focus

How do you prioritize your commitments and practices as a leader? Servant leadership is an approach to leadership that prioritizes followers over leader self-interest. While many argue that a commitment to organizational goals must be prioritized over the people of the organization, a servant-leadership perspective argues that the most effective way to accomplish organizational commitments is through focus on followers. Barrett and the team at Southwest Airlines modeled this for us. By leaders focusing on followers, these followers are then able to deliver exceptional products or services to those the organization serves.

While the organization as a whole needs to be externally focused (serving its customers, constituents, or mission), the primary focus of the leader must be on serving and caring for the followers who are directly responsible for fulfilling the organization's mission. We prioritize such servant-oriented practice in our reflections on leadership in this book. This leadership commitment is about prioritizing follower focus and empowering followers for service of the team's mission.

Transformational Leadership and Organizational Transformation

Complementing the follower focus of servant leadership, transformational leadership is about creating broad and intrinsic ownership of the organization's mission by leaders and followers alike. Transactional leadership is primarily based on a leader-follower exchange that incentivizes followers through extrinsic motivators. In contrast, transformational leadership is based on a leader-follower engagement that motivates followers intrinsically. Transformational leadership is about engaging followers in such a way that leaders and followers are mutually committed to the organization's mission and are willing to undergo transformational change with organizational goals in view.

Team Leadership and Collaborative Orientation

In addition to servant- and transformational-leadership principles, we also advocate for collaborative and team-oriented approaches to leadership. Collaborative approaches to leadership and the use of teams recognize and affirm that great wisdom exists within the people of organizations. Rather than providing an overly directive or top-down approach to leadership, collaborative and team-oriented approaches to leadership harness the wisdom and insights of the people that compose the team. This leadership commitment is about leveraging team wisdom and utilizing collaboration toward the end of decentralizing authority and empowering people to carry out local work effectively.

Leader Purposefulness and Meaning-Based Work

Finally, we emphasize the importance of meaning and purpose in the work of leadership. On this point, Eric Eisenberg and Harold Lloyd Goodall write that "employees want to feel that the work they do is worthwhile, rather than just a way to draw a paycheck," and to see work as "a transformation of its meaning—from drudgery to a source of personal significance and fulfillment."[23] While employees bear responsibility for personally engaging their work with purpose, leaders play an important role in helping organizational members understand why the work they do matters. This leadership commitment is about leaders and followers alike seeing their personal work and the work of their colleagues as meaningful and significant.

Collectively, these four leadership priorities call leaders to see their role primarily as equipping and empowering the people they lead for effectiveness. Throughout the book, we argue that the most effective approaches to leadership move leaders from a focus on follower control to a focus on follower empowerment. Great things can be accomplished in and through teams and organizations when leaders and followers alike are empowered to accomplish great things in service of their mission and the people they serve.

How This Book Is Organized

In the remaining sections of the book, we present nine core leadership practices. These leadership practices cluster around three primary themes, which are the three main parts of the book: (1) beginning with authentic and purposeful leaders, (2) understanding the priority of people, and (3) navigating toward effectiveness (see fig. I.1).

Figure I.1

Empowering Leadership

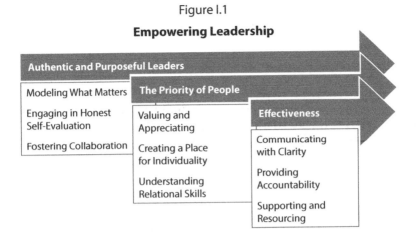

Part 1: Beginning with Authentic and Purposeful Leaders

Effective leadership begins with authentic and purposeful leaders. In a day when examples of ineffective and inauthentic leadership abound, it stands out when leaders truly understand their purpose and then authentically guide and empower others out of this sense of purpose. Three core leadership practices are highlighted in this part of the book: modeling what matters, engaging in honest self-evaluation, and fostering collaboration.

Part 2: Understanding the Priority of People

Premised on authentic and purposeful leadership, part 2 calls leaders to prioritize and focus on followers. Although leader service of self is common across diverse sectors and organizations, biblical wisdom and contemporary research support the priority of leaders focusing on followers as they seek to carry out team and organizational mission. Three leadership practices are explored in this part of the book: valuing and appreciating, creating a place for individuality, and understanding relational skills.

Part 3: Navigating toward Effectiveness

When authentic and purposeful leaders focus on the priority of the people with whom they work, great things can happen. Part 3 of the book emphasizes the importance of leaders and followers working together toward effectively accomplishing their shared mission. Toward this end, the final three leadership practices provide a pathway on which effective goal accomplishment may take place. These final leadership practices are communicating with clarity, providing accountability, and supporting and resourcing.

Organization of Chapters

The nine leadership practices selected for this book are not arbitrary. Although we personally believe in the power and effectiveness of these practices, you do not simply need to trust our judgment. These nine practices arise out of thoughtful research on which leadership behaviors contribute to effective teams and organizations. As previously noted, we unpack each of these nine leadership practices around three primary perspectives: (1) exploring the biblical foundations for the practice, (2) explaining the leadership research and theory that stand behind the practice, and (3) illustrating the practice with leadership examples and practical recommendations.

We count it an honor to share these reflections on effective leadership practice with you. It is our hope that your journey through this book will provide a vision for leadership that empowers others and transforms the teams and organizations within which you serve and work.

Part 1

Beginning with Authentic and Purposeful Leaders

THROUGHOUT THE BOOK, we emphasize the priority of leaders focusing on followers. In order for leaders to effectively nurture their other-centered orientation, they must begin the journey by fostering authentic and purposeful character. In part 1 of the book, we begin with the importance of leaders modeling what matters (chap. 1). It is not enough for leaders simply to tell followers what is expected. Leaders must model these priorities through their authentic example.

In order to effectively model expected team behavior, leaders must also be willing to engage in honest self-evaluation (chap. 2). Authentic and purposeful leaders are willing to see both their strengths and their weaknesses, and to practice their leadership with humble self-efficacy and humble self-confidence. Leaders who truly want to serve and empower followers are those who take time to understand themselves.

Finally, authentic and purposeful leaders recognize that they do not have all the answers that their teams and organizations need. Because of this, teams and organizations today need leaders willing to foster a collaborative and team-oriented environment (chap. 3). By beginning with authentic leaders— leaders who model what matters, engage in honest self-evaluation, and foster collaboration—there is a basis for understanding the priority of people and navigating the team to effective mission accomplishment.

1

Modeling What Matters

Introduction

The life and leadership of Lt. Col. Hal Moore are depicted in the movie *We Were Soldiers*. In the painful realities of war, the importance of leadership practices like modeling what matters is intensified. While training his officers, he communicated that he came from the paratroopers, where the officer was always the first man out of the plane. He argued that this was so officers could follow their instincts and inspire their soldiers by example—being with them in the intensity of battle.

The film illustrates this priority with Moore's speech to the Seventh Cavalry before going into the Battle of Ia Drang, where he makes this promise to his soldiers: "I can't promise you that I will bring you all home alive. But this I swear before you and before Almighty God: that when we go into battle, I will be the first to set foot on the field, and I will be the last to step off. And I will leave no one behind. Dead or alive, we will all come home together. So help me God."[1] This commitment to being the first into battle and the last to leave exemplifies the core of our focus in this first chapter—*modeling what matters*.

If leadership is primarily about control through positional power, asking followers to do what they are told regardless of the leader's example may work to a limited extent. However, if leadership is more about influence than control, the positive example and model of a leader is essential.

While it may be tempting simply to dictate to or tell followers what to do, the most effective leaders understand the importance of action. Leader behaviors provide a powerful example for followers. Leaders don't just use words in their communication. Leaders communicate, for better or for worse, through their actions. Are these actions communicating the right message? Are they supporting the stated values and vision of the leader and organization?

On this point, Ken Blanchard and his associates call leaders to embody the values and vision of their organizations: "[It] is all about walking your talk. The leader, above all, has to be a walking example of the vision."[2] Inauthentic leaders can demand of followers what they as leaders are unwilling to do. Authentic and purposeful leaders, however, must model what matters and be willing to practice what they preach when it comes to expected organizational behavior.

> *If leadership is more about influence than control, the positive example and model of a leader is essential.*

Although the wartime situations that Hal Moore faced intensify the need for leaders modeling what matters, any organization with a clear vision needs this leadership practice. Effective and empowering leaders set an example for others. Through this example, leaders build mutual trust and affirm the common values shared by the community. Regardless of your leadership context, learning the importance of modeling what matters as a leader is essential. In this chapter, we explore the topic through the following perspectives: (1) modeling what matters in biblical perspective, (2) modeling what matters in contemporary perspective, and (3) modeling what matters in practice.

Modeling What Matters in Biblical Perspective

When something is important to someone, they tend to repeat it a lot. Consider these statements by the apostle Paul, scattered throughout his letters:

"Therefore I urge you to imitate me." (1 Cor. 4:16)

"Follow my example, as I follow the example of Christ." (1 Cor. 11:1)

"Join together in following my example, brothers and sisters, and just as you have us as a model, keep your eyes on those who live as we do." (Phil. 3:17)

"Whatever you have learned or received or heard from me, or seen in me—put it into practice." (Phil. 4:9)

"You became imitators of us and of the Lord." (1 Thess. 1:6)

"For you yourselves know how you ought to follow our example." (2 Thess. 3:7)

Paul's leadership style is pretty obvious: "Follow my example"; "Imitate me"; "Put [what you have learned] into practice." It is *modeling*. The best way to lead is not to *tell* people what to do but to show them by example. And showing involves more than just a training session. It is a complete lifestyle that exemplifies what matters most in life. For Paul, it meant modeling *integrity, responsibility, investment,* and *equipping and empowerment.*

Modeling Integrity

The New Testament letters known as 1 and 2 Thessalonians were written to a community of Christian believers in the city of Thessalonica in northern Greece. Paul had established this church shortly before, during his first major missionary outreach into Europe (about AD 50–52). Paul always started preaching his message of salvation in the Jewish synagogue, and most of his converts came from the Jewish community and their Gentile benefactors (known as "God-fearers"). The larger Jewish community in Thessalonica was not happy with this. They viewed this new community of Christ-followers in the way we would view a cult—a dangerous and subversive threat to their religious tradition. Paul's life was threatened, and he was forced to flee Thessalonica (Acts 17:1–10). He continued his ministry, however, preaching in Berea, then in Athens and Corinth. Yet all along the way he was deeply concerned about this young church in Thessalonica. Would they abandon their newfound faith in the face of persecution? Were they strong enough to persevere?

Meanwhile, Paul's opponents in Thessalonica sought to undermine his credibility. They accused him of many things: seeking personal ambition and praise, starting the church out of greed and desire to "fleece" the flock, and abandoning the young church at their moment of need. These were not outrageous claims, since the Greco-Roman world was full of unscrupulous traveling philosophers and preachers—the snake oil salesmen of the first century—who were always trying to make a buck off gullible customers. In a letter to the church, Paul responds to these accusations by pointing to his lifestyle while among them:

> The appeal we make does not spring from error or impure motives, nor are we trying to trick you. . . . We are not trying to please people but God, who tests our hearts. You know we never used flattery, nor did we put on a mask to cover up greed—God is our witness. We were not looking for praise from people, not from you or anyone else. . . . Just as a nursing mother cares for her children, so we cared for you. Because we loved you so much, we were delighted to share with you not only the gospel of God but our lives as well. (1 Thess. 2:3–8)

Paul says, "you know" how we lived among you, modeling integrity in every way. Far from taking advantage of them, Paul and his fellow missionaries were like parents to the Thessalonian believers, nurturing and caring for them.

Confidence is inspired by congruence between our words and actions.

They shared with the Thessalonians not only their message but also their very lives. This is because they were accountable to a higher authority—God himself.

Integrity and authenticity are among the most important traits a transformational leader can model. Followers can sense hypocrisy a mile away. "Do as I say, not as I do" does not inspire transformed lives or motivated action. Confidence is inspired by congruence between our words and actions.

In addition to modeling integrity, a leader must model responsibility and competence, that is, the discipline and skills necessary to fulfill their responsibilities.

Modeling Responsibility

Throughout both 1 and 2 Thessalonians, Paul praises the believers at Thessalonica for their spiritual strength and maturity. Though young in their faith, this church was growing and thriving. Yet Paul also repeatedly tells certain members of the community to stop being idle or lazy and to get back to work (1 Thess. 4:11–12; 5:14; 2 Thess. 3:6–15). Scholars debate why these individuals were not working. Some think they expected Christ to return any day and so had quit their jobs and were living off the hospitality of others. Others think this has something to do with the Greco-Roman patronage system, where wealthy patrons would financially support clients in return for their loyalty, honor, and service. Since the church viewed itself as "family," perhaps poorer members now viewed themselves as clients of the wealthier members and were taking advantage of their generosity. Whatever the reason for Paul's concern, he takes these individuals to task for their irresponsibility and calls them to get back to work. He goes so far as to say that if someone refuses to work, they shouldn't be allowed to eat! (2 Thess. 3:10).

Yet Paul doesn't just give them orders, he points to his own example: "For you yourselves know how you ought to follow our example. We were not idle when we were with you, nor did we eat anyone's food without paying for it. On the contrary, we worked night and day, laboring and toiling so that we would not be a burden to any of you. We did this, not because we do not have the right to such help, but in order to offer ourselves as a model for you to imitate" (2 Thess. 3:7–8). Paul says the same thing in his first letter to the church: "Surely you remember, brothers and sisters, our toil and hardship;

we worked night and day in order not to be a burden to anyone while we preached the gospel of God to you" (1 Thess. 2:9).

As a full-time minister of the gospel, Paul could have lived off the support of others. But instead he set an example by taking responsibility for his own financial support. If we as leaders expect others to fulfill their responsibilities, we need to go above and beyond in our own duties and responsibilities.

Modeling Investment

In 1 Corinthians 11:1, Paul again emphasizes his modeling of leadership style: "Follow my example, as I follow the example of Christ." Here the example he is referring to has been set out in the previous three chapters (1 Cor. 8–10). The issue under debate at Corinth was whether Christians should eat food that had been sacrificed to idols. Most food in a Greco-Roman marketplace had been offered to a pagan god, and some Christians were claiming followers of Christ should abstain from such tainted food. Paul essentially responds that there is nothing wrong with eating such food, since an idol is nothing but wood and stone (8:4–6; 10:25–26). At the same time, Paul stresses his willingness to give up this right so as not to cause a Christian brother or sister—for whom that idol seems very real—to fall into sin. The cause of the gospel is so great that it is worth sacrificing everything for. Paul writes, "Though I am free and belong to no one, I have made myself a slave to everyone, to win as many as possible. To the Jews I became like a Jew, to win the Jews. . . . To those not having the law I became like one not having the law. . . . I do all this for the sake of the gospel" (9:19–23).

For Paul, the good news of salvation is worth any amount of investment, whether time, money, or resources. Leaders inspire others when they demonstrate true commitment to and investment in a shared vision. Consider entrepreneurs who might mortgage their own home or cash in their retirement to launch a business. Or the CEO who takes a reduction in salary to avoid laying off loyal workers during hard times. Such actions may be risky, but they model commitment and investment and so engender loyalty from others.

Modeling Equipping and Empowerment

Modeling relates not only to a leader's personal integrity, responsibility, and investment but also to the task of leadership training itself—reproducing yourself in others. When Jesus chose twelve of his followers to be his inner circle of disciples, he called them simply to "be with him" (Mark 3:14). They were to learn by living with him, watching his example, following his cues.

He then sent them out to replicate his ministry: preaching the gospel, healing the sick, casting out demons (Mark 3:14–15). In other words, he reproduced himself in them so that they would reproduce themselves in others. This is also evident from the Great Commission, Jesus's last instructions to his disciples to "make disciples of all nations" (Matt. 28:18–20). As disciples, they were to make disciples, reproducing themselves in others.

Paul had the same model, a ministry of spiritual replication. He makes this clear in his last letter, known to us as 2 Timothy, in which he instructs his assistant Timothy to carry on the task of leadership training after he is gone: "And the things you have heard me say in the presence of many witnesses entrust to reliable people who will also be qualified to teach others" (2 Tim. 2:2).

Paul has replicated his ministry in Timothy, and now he expects Timothy to do the same in others. A leader's primary role is to work him- or herself out of a job, to equip and empower others to utilize the gifts and abilities they have been given. A pastor is successful when the members of the congregation grow and thrive spiritually. A CEO is successful when workers are effective and satisfied in their vocations. A college president is successful when faculty, staff, and students achieve academic excellence and are fulfilled in their work. This is leadership as empowerment rather than coercion or control.

Success in this kind of leadership requires training/equipping, delegation of responsibility, accountability, and empowerment (providing appropriate resources to fulfill the task). This was Jesus's model. He trained the disciples by modeling servant leadership for them during his ministry. He delegated responsibility and held them accountable by sending them out to preach and to heal and, ultimately, by giving them the Great Commission. Finally, he empowered them with the presence of the Holy Spirit, their ultimate source of power and guidance (Luke 24:49; John 14:15–31; 15:26–16:15; Acts 1:8).

Modeling What Matters in Contemporary Perspective

Contemporary theory and research build on these biblical perspectives by providing additional insight into the importance of leaders modeling what matters for followers. In my (Justin's) research on the topic, leaders who "practice the same behavior they expect from others" were a statistically significant predictor of effectiveness within teams and organizations.[3] This expectation gets at the core of what leadership modeling is about.

In this section, we will highlight (1) modeling as a key to empowering followers, (2) modeling as a developmental approach to leadership, and (3) modeling as a transformational approach to leadership.

Modeling: A Key to Empowering Followers

Modeling what matters involves identifying priorities for the organization and then translating these priorities into meaningful action. Traditional models of leadership by command and control may have engaged organizational priorities in the past, but these models often neglected the more significant step of having leaders embody and model these priorities.

The proverbial statement that "actions speak louder than words" matters when it comes to leadership. By this we are not saying that words are unnecessary. We will discuss the importance of leaders communicating through their words in more detail in chapter 7. The emphasis here is that words alone are not enough. Leaders must not simply speak about the things that matter most for their organizations; leaders must also model these priorities in their actions.

To take this point a step further, it is not sufficient to say that words are not enough. In practice, if leaders fail to back up their words with action, then the words spoken could actually have a negative effect due to perceived inauthenticity or hypocrisy. On this point, one research participant noted that "leaders who don't authentically model the stated values are undeniable hypocrites. Their actions communicate much more loudly than words that these values are not really important."

Such incongruence between communicated and modeled values erodes the credibility and long-term effectiveness of a leader. Conversely, if a leader walks the talk when it comes to organizational values and priorities, modeling what matters becomes a powerful tool in the hand of an authentic and empowering leader. To this point, another research participant suggested that leadership modeling "is the primary and most effective way to communicate the organization's mission, values, and ethos."

Leaders desiring to engage their followers and communities in a compelling manner must not ignore the importance of modeling what matters most. Don Page and Paul Wong argue that leaders serving effectively in high-impact contexts provide a model for others. Leaders provide this model by setting a personal example of what it looks like to pursue high standards. This serves as a means for empowering others and fostering collaborative efforts as leaders pursue these standards together with their followers.[4]

In short, modeling what matters is a primary tool for leaders working to lead through influence rather than control. By leading through example, empowering leaders cast a vision for productive commitment to organizational outcomes. Such a model serves as a basis for followers responding with similar organizational commitment. Researchers argue that follower response to leader modeling is best explained by social exchange theory, since such action motivates followers to respond with extra commitment based on the example provided for them by leaders.[5]

Modeling: A Developmental Approach to Leadership

Modeling what matters is also important because it provides a pathway for engaging followers in their developmental journey. As noted earlier in the book, leadership by nature is more of a process than an event. Leadership is a process, in part, because followers are on a journey of developing as people and organizational members.

Effective leaders take this developmental approach to followers seriously. Contrasting self-serving leaders and called leaders, Blanchard notes that we can recognize called leaders by their willingness to develop others: "They thrive on developing others and the belief that individuals with expertise will come forward as needed throughout the organization."[6] Blanchard sees this rooted in the primary commitments of these leaders—a commitment to serve rather than be served and a deep desire to bring out the best in others.

SLII®

Blanchard is a primary theorist behind one of the well-known developmental models of leadership: SLII®.[7] This model emphasizes leaders interacting with followers in a dynamic and flexible manner. Based on an assessment of a follower's level of competence and commitment related to a task that needs to be accomplished, the leader provides a unique response.

This responsive approach is designed to bring out the best in others as leaders match their level of direction and support to the developmental level of the person being led. The approach "is based on the beliefs that *people can and want to develop* and *there is no best leadership style* to encourage that development."[8] Based on the model, leaders engage followers in a tailored manner that matches leadership style to the unique traits of the followers.

Leading with the aim of developing and empowering followers translates into leaders resisting traditional understandings of the organizational hierarchy. On this point, Blanchard and his associates write, "As a leader, once the vision and direction are set, you have to turn the hierarchical pyramid upside down and focus on engaging and developing your people so that they can live according to the vision."[9] Thriving organizations are populated with followers and leaders who are continually growing and developing. Leaders are responsible for nurturing this developmentally oriented culture, and modeling what matters is a core tool in fostering such a culture.

THE LEADERSHIP SQUARE

Offering a similar developmental orientation to leadership, some contemporary organizations utilize a model known as the leadership square.[10] This model follows a four-stage progression in which leaders intentionally model expected behavior and then provide opportunity for followers to take responsibility for this expected behavior. The four stages are (1) I do, you watch; (2) I do, you help; (3) you do, I help; and (4) you do, I watch (see fig. 1.1).

Figure 1.1
The Leadership Square

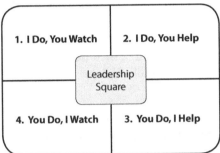

The leadership square provides a pathway by which leaders may move followers to a point of delegated responsibility. It is driven by the motivation to bring out the best in followers as they walk through the developmental journey in the leader-follower relationship.

EQUIPPING + EMPOWERMENT = EFFECTIVENESS

A commitment to developing followers requires leaders to both *equip* and *empower*. When one is present without the other, this inevitably leads to problems for the follower, leader, and organization alike. When I (Justin) teach on this theme, I share the following equations with students:

- empowerment − equipping = follower failure
- equipping − empowerment = follower frustration
- equipping + empowerment = follower flourishing

Those who are empowered but not equipped run the danger of failure. When followers have not been developed through proper direction and equipping, it is unreasonable to expect followers to perform as needed. Similarly, those who are equipped but not empowered run the danger of frustration.

When followers do not know they've been granted the freedom to enact their training, this communicates a lack of trust and results in equipped followers sitting on the sidelines when an important organizational mission needs to be accomplished. But when followers are both equipped and empowered, leaders and developed followers are able to work together in service of their shared organizational goals.

Modeling: A Transformational Approach to Leadership

Transformational leadership is a theory that includes an emphasis on leaders serving as models for followers. Bernard Bass and Bruce Avolio refer to this in their Four *I*'s of transformational leadership (see fig. 1.2). Regarding this dimension of transformational leadership they write, "Transformational leaders behave in ways that result in their being role models for their followers," and because of this example "followers identify with the leaders and want to emulate them."[11]

Figure 1.2
Four *I*'s of Transformational Leadership

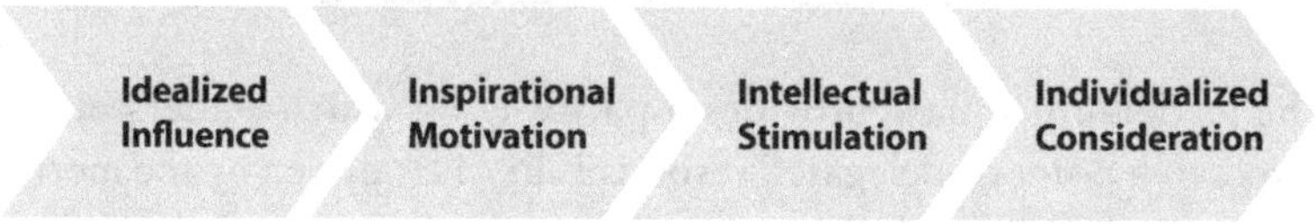

Richard Daft expands on this understanding of idealized influence, noting that leaders possessing this characteristic are trusted and respected by their followers. This trust finds its source not in position but rather in *who* these leaders are and the high standards they hold for themselves.[12] So what is the result of this idealized influence? When leaders model what matters, at least two outcomes may occur.

Transforming Follower Focus

First, leaders who model what matters for followers help to shift the focus of their followers based on the idealized influence they provide as leaders. What is the nature of this shift? First and foremost, it is a shift away from self-interest.

Peter Northouse expresses the change in the following manner: "[Transformational leaders] attempt to raise the consciousness of individuals and to get them to transcend their own self-interests for the sake of others."[13] As leaders model putting the needs of others over their own personal needs, followers tend to respond in kind. Followers become motivated and inspired intrinsically to pursue interests that move beyond self.

On this leadership dynamic, Francis Yammarino writes, "Instead of responding to his or her own immediate self-interests and those of followers, the transformational leader arouses heightened awareness and interests in the group or organization, increases confidence, and moves followers gradually from concerns for existence to concerns for achievement and growth."[14]

When teaching on this subject, I (Justin) talk about this as helping to move followers beyond the Ceiling of Self-Interest. The Ceiling of Self-Interest acknowledges the limitations in autocratic and leader-centered models. When the leader-follower relationship is based primarily on exchange, followers tend to relate to their leaders in a minimalistic manner. Rather than devoting discretionary effort to organizational goals, followers respond by giving only the necessary and required dimensions of their implicit or explicit leader-follower contract. In other words, when what is asked of them reaches the ceiling of their self-interest, extra effort is no longer given to required tasks.

When leaders model what matters for followers, the Ceiling of Self-Interest begins to erode.

Conversely, when the leader-follower relationship is based on a shared vision and mutual engagement around this vision, leaders and followers alike are willing to devote themselves to a cause bigger than any one person or any one person's agenda. When leaders model what matters for followers, the Ceiling of Self-Interest begins to erode. Leaders and followers mutually inspire one another to work toward a common and shared vision for the organization, even when extra and discretionary effort is required.

Transforming Followers into Leaders

The second result of idealized influence is that followers often move beyond their role as followers. As important as followership is to organizations, the new, emerging, and complex realities of our time require more expressions of leadership throughout an organization than ever before. Rather than leadership being the responsibility of only a select few at the top of organizations, leadership is a need throughout healthy and thriving organizations.

On this point Mark McCloskey writes, "Effective leadership in the New Normal is less and less about the charisma or competence of the few and increasingly about the collaborative effort of many."[15] He elaborates: "Organizations are best served not by an elite few doing all the important work, but by many member-leaders collaborating to get important things accomplished."[16] Seeing this shift toward increased leadership throughout an organization requires intentionality on the part of existing leaders as well as a willingness to release and empower followers.

In traditional models of leadership, the aim for the leader-follower relationship is largely control. Leaders are leaders, and followers are followers. Due to a pessimistic view of follower self-interest, classic management and leadership wisdom argue that followers need to be controlled in order to get them to do what they would not otherwise want to do. Because organizational goals are more about what leaders want accomplished, not what followers own and share as their own goals, leaders believe that extrinsic motivation—both positive and negative—is the key to motivating followers.

Under empowering models such as transformational leadership, the desired transformation is not simply about accomplishing organizational goals. The change is about people as well. The change is about moving followers from a place of compliance through extrinsic motivation to a place of mutual commitment through intrinsic motivation. As followers engage in this journey of personal transformation, leadership capacity and skills are developed.

As leaders model what matters through idealized influence, they serve as examples that inspire followers in their personal and professional development. Yammarino summarizes this concept well: "In short, transformational leaders develop their followers to the point where followers are able to take on leadership roles and perform beyond established standards or goals."[17] Success in leadership is not just about developing excellent followers but also about developing followers in their leadership capacity.

Modeling What Matters in Practice

As we have emphasized throughout this chapter, modeling is all about action on the part of the leader. Hearing a leader talk about what matters most for the organization is needed. But leaders' *demonstrating* what matters most is a powerful form of leader communication.

On this point, Daft writes, "Employees learn what is valued most in a company by watching what attitudes and behaviors leaders pay attention to and reward, how leaders react to organizational crises, and whether the leader's own behavior matches the espoused values."[18] Through observing leader priorities, members of a community learn what matters most in their organization.

Modeling: An Example from America's "Cheapest CEO"

When it comes to modeling organizational values, perhaps one of the most interesting examples comes from Bob Kierlin of Winona, Minnesota. Kierlin is one of the founders of the Fastenal Company and served as CEO through 2002 and chairman of the board through 2014.

Kierlin captured the heart of Fastenal's vision with four words: "Growth through Customer Service." Kierlin's commitment to growth through customer service ended up landing Kierlin with one of the most unique honors *Inc. Magazine* gave out in 1997: "The Cheapest CEO in America" recognition.[19]

Now, when *Inc.* says Kierlin is cheap, they are not saying he is poor. Around the final year of his role as chairman, the value of his Fastenal shares was over $500 million. But this type of wealth was generated over the years by a fierce commitment to being frugal on behalf of the company.

Though Kierlin and the team at Fastenal invested high quality in service of customers, their aim was to maintain a lean and efficient organization in this mission. Kierlin modeled some pretty extreme steps toward this goal. In the article reporting his prestigious Cheapest CEO award, we read several amazing steps Kierlin took to model his commitments to the company.

Kierlin kept the same $120,000 salary for over ten years, even though the board annually approved increases. He wore used suits bought for sixty dollars from a clothing store manager—not from the store of the manager. The company printed its annual reports in-house at a discount. On business trips, such as one to Chicago, Kierlin drove five hours rather than fly, ate at A&W for five dollars, and shared a room with Dan Florness, the company CFO, rather than pay for two rooms. Kierlin also insisted on not having a designated parking spot, and in the early days he jumped in to help shovel snow and sort mail at the headquarters.

By CEO standards, these behaviors may seem extreme and unnecessary. But to his employees, such things communicated volumes. Rather than viewing Kierlin as Scrooge, his employees saw Kierlin putting his behavior where his values were. Employees would state, "He never talks down to people, and he treats everyone with equal respect, whether they're a janitor or vice-president."[20]

Kierlin's cheapness in cost cutting allowed him and the company to serve others in powerful ways. Employees benefited from a generous profit-sharing plan. The community benefited from generous foundation giving. Investors benefited from a model focused on growth. And customers benefited by cost savings going to product and service excellence.

Kierlin's modeling what matters in service of his commitment to growth resulted in a powerful community of followers who understood that spoken values were owned by Fastenal employees at every level of the company.

Modeling what matters had bottom-line benefit. Fastenal's market capitalization, around $14.56 billion at the time of writing this chapter, testifies to Kierlin's vision and leadership example from the company's humble beginnings.

Modeling: Insights for Practice

Although Kierlin's story is likely enough to emphasize what modeling can look like in practice for leaders, here are a few quick principles for practice as you consider modeling what matters in your own leadership journey.

IDENTIFY WHAT MATTERS MOST

Modeling what matters begins with identifying what matters most for you and your organization. Peter Drucker would sometimes challenge leaders not to confuse motion with progress.[21] Perhaps you feel this temptation sometimes. Are you busy, but not being productive? Are you constantly in motion, but not making meaningful progress?

When it comes to modeling what matters, the first move is to take a step back and make sure we are focusing our attention on what our organizations actually need us to be doing. What matters most for our organizations and for the roles we serve in these organizations? What are the values to which we must hold on behalf of our organization and community? What is our primary mission? And what are our primary strategies for accomplishing this mission?

Once what matters most is identified, then the work of prioritizing can begin. Focusing on everything typically translates into making progress on very little. Significant progress occurs when we focus our attention on the right priorities. Begin your journey in modeling what matters. Identify what matters to you and your organization, and then make decisions to prioritize your most meaningful and strategic commitments. Take time to make a list of three core values in your organization. Consider how these should shape your daily work as a leader.

MODEL THE ENDS AND THE MEANS

After a leader identifies what matters most, it is time to move into action. As Max De Pree argues, "Clearly expressed and consistently demonstrated values" are often the most important factors in nurturing the sacred relationship between leaders and followers.[22]

When it comes to modeling what matters, leaders must prioritize both organizational *ends* and *means*. Leaders must be clear on what the organizational ends and goals are, but they also must be committed to the means by which these ends and goals will be pursued.

Bill George, former chairman and CEO of Medtronic, makes an important observation on this point. George notes that practicing solid values is not about simply identifying values but rather is about embodying and living them out. He writes, "Having found the purpose that ignites your passions, you then have to test your values in the crucible of life's experiences."[23] Applying this to our discussion of modeling what matters, followers do not simply need to hear what leaders personally and organizationally value; followers also need to see what these values look like in practice. George continues: "Only in the crucible will you learn how to cope with pressures to compromise your values and deal with potential conflicts between them. You have to put yourself in situations in which your values are challenged and then make difficult decisions in the context of your values."[24]

Another former CEO, Ralph Larsen of Johnson & Johnson, notes that it is when values pose a competitive *dis*advantage that these values become most clear in practice: "Core values embodied in our credo might be a competitive advantage, but that is not *why* we have them. We have them because they define for us what we stand for, and we would hold them even if they became a competitive disadvantage in certain situations."[25]

Consider the tragic story of Tylenol's contamination with cyanide in the early 1980s. In the face of competitive disadvantage, Johnson & Johnson and their CEO at that time, James Burke, made the bold but necessary decision to remove Tylenol from store shelves. Although the company was not directly responsible for the evil actions of the person who contaminated its product, it nevertheless took responsibility for the situation. This decision to voluntarily pull the product demonstrated a commitment to customer safety. The decision was not without cost, though; the company lost well over $100 million in that move.[26] However, it is in such crucible moments that deep commitment to values is modeled most for followers and organizational constituents. What are policies in your organization that either support or conflict with your core values? Take some time to list specific actions you will take to reach goals in a manner consistent with productive and healthy core values.

Don't Fake It

Finally, as we conclude our reflections on modeling what matters, an important caution is warranted: *don't fake it*. As followers observe leaders, inauthenticity is quickly exposed. Yes, followers need leaders who say and do the right thing. On this point, James Kouzes and Barry Posner write, "Leaders are measured by the consistency of deeds with words."[27]

But followers need more. They also need leaders who believe in what the organization is about. They need leaders who believe in what they say and do. This is an important thread emerging out of my (Justin's) research on leader purposefulness. Among dimensions of leader purposefulness, items such as "My leader believes in the purpose of our organization" significantly related to leadership effectiveness and important follower work outcomes like organizational commitment, job satisfaction, and person-organization fit.[28]

> *Followers need to understand that their leaders actually believe that what the organization does matters.*

In other words, followers need to understand that their leaders actually believe that what the organization does matters. When followers see a congruence between espoused and lived values, and when followers believe it is a real and authentic conviction on the part of the leader, this provides a leadership model that followers want to emulate. As Blanchard and his associates argue, embodying values and vision is all about walking your talk.[29]

So model what matters for the people of your community. Identify what matters most. Pay attention to both the goals and the means you use to accomplish these goals. And make sure the congruence of your words and actions flows from a place of authenticity.

Next Steps

- Take some time to make a list of three core values in your organization. Consider how these should shape your daily work as a leader.
- Take some time to list specific actions you will take to reach goals in a manner consistent with productive and healthy core values.
- Take some time to list specific steps that could move you and your organization toward greater transparency and authenticity.

Resources for a Deeper Look

Blanchard, Ken, et al. *Leading at a Higher Level.* Upper Saddle River, NJ: Prentice Hall, 2007.

Blanchard, Ken, Phil Hodges, and Phyllis Hendry. *Lead like Jesus Revisited: Lessons from the Greatest Leadership Role Model of All Time*. Nashville: Nelson, 2016.

Garland, David E. "Mark's Theology of Discipleship." In *A Theology of Mark's Gospel: Good News about Jesus the Messiah, the Son of God*, pages 388–437. Biblical Theology of the New Testament. Grand Rapids: Zondervan, 2015.

Kouzes, James M., and Barry Z. Posner. *The Leadership Challenge: How to Make Extraordinary Things Happen in Organizations*. 6th ed. San Francisco: Jossey-Bass, 2017.

Shogren, Gary S. *1 & 2 Thessalonians*. Zondervan Exegetical Commentary on the New Testament. Grand Rapids: Zondervan, 2012.

2

Engaging in Honest Self-Evaluation

Introduction

Peter Drucker, one of the top management consultants from the twentieth century, was once asked during an interview who the greatest leader was he had ever known. His answer: Frances Hesselbein, the former CEO of Girl Scouts from 1976 to 1990. That's quite an affirmation, considering the reputation of Peter Drucker.

Among her many qualities, one of the distinguishing marks of Hesselbein's leadership was the intentional effort she gave to honest self-evaluation. Consider Hesselbein's focus on values: "You have to have values that are the basis of all you do. You have to live your values. After all, *leadership is a matter of how to be, not how to do.*"[1] This is a difficult shift for leaders to make—moving from leadership as a matter of *doing* to leadership as a matter of *being*.

But when this shift can be made—leading out of one's being—a heart for serving others may truly emerge. Hesselbein puts it this way: "Every day I find a way to make a difference, to help someone, even if I don't know them. And then at night I ask myself, 'What did I do today that helped someone, some group or organization? In what ways did I make a difference in someone's life?'"[2]

In this chapter we explore this leadership practice of *engaging in honest self-evaluation*. If leadership is simply about managing processes and systems external to oneself, then avoiding and neglecting self-evaluation may be tolerable in theory. However, if leadership is a relational practice at its core—an argument we make in this book—then engaging leaders at the level of their being or personhood is essential.

Consider Paul's instructions in 1 Timothy 4:16: "Watch your life and doctrine closely. Persevere in them, because if you do, you will save both yourself and your hearers." Paul's charge to Timothy emphasizes that the nature of one's life and beliefs matters. It matters to leaders. It matters to followers.

> *"Leadership is a matter of how to be, not how to do."*
> —Frances Hesselbein

Christian leaders are encouraged to look to their own life and consider issues at the core of their personhood. They must consider their personal beliefs and values. They must consider their life and how they are living in light of their convictions and beliefs. For Paul, our convictions, and the way we live our lives based on these convictions, have eternal consequences—it matters deeply for leaders and followers alike.

At the end of the day, it is not ultimately self-centered to be self-focused around the right priorities. Leaders who truly want to serve and empower followers are those who take time to understand themselves. Such honest self-reflection and evaluation promote a pathway for leaders to become authentic and purposeful, surfacing potential blind spots and refocusing their leadership practice in a manner that brings health rather than dysfunction to the individuals and communities they lead and serve.

In order to bring such health to their followers and communities, leaders will increasingly need to nurture self-awareness through effective self-leadership and personal growth practices. In this chapter, we explore these themes and the topic of engaging in honest self-evaluation through the following perspectives: (1) self-evaluation in biblical perspective, (2) self-evaluation in contemporary perspective, and (3) self-evaluation in practice.

Self-Evaluation in Biblical Perspective

One of the most significant passages on leadership in the New Testament is found in Acts 20, the apostle Paul's address to the elders of Ephesus. Paul is on his way to Jerusalem, carrying a financial gift for the impoverished church there. Cognizant that great danger awaits him in Jerusalem (Acts 20:22–23), Paul stops at the port city of Miletus in Asia Minor and calls the elders of nearby Ephesus to meet him there. Paul had spent three years in Ephesus, so these are some of his closest ministry partners. He presents to them what he believes may be his final charge. His central message to these leaders is found in verse 28: "Keep watch over yourselves and all the flock of which the Holy

Spirit has made you overseers. Be shepherds of the church of God, which he bought with his own blood."

Paul reminds these Christian leaders that they are to be "shepherds" (the meaning of the Greek word often translated "pastor" [*poimēn*]), providing for and protecting the flock, which is the church. This is exactly what we would expect him to say. Be a faithful shepherd! Yet significantly, before Paul says to keep watch over the flock, he says, "keep watch *over yourselves*" (v. 28a). This is not a call for selfishness and egocentrism. Paul is not saying, "When the ship is sinking, forget everyone else and save yourself!" He is rather reminding them that *to serve others effectively, leaders must first take care of themselves.* Unless you maintain

> *To serve others effectively, leaders must first take care of themselves.*

your own spiritual, physical, and emotional health, you will be unable to serve others effectively. Self-care and honest self-evaluation are essential for success in leadership.

Leaders fail for a variety of reasons. But two of the most common are self-doubt and poor self-image on the one side, and pride and an overly exalted view of self on the other. Leaders plagued by self-doubts often find themselves paralyzed and constantly second-guessing their decisions and actions. Leaders filled with pride tend to abuse and exploit others in a constant drive to be on top. The remedy for both of these is a healthy, balanced, and realistic view of self.

Sober Self-Assessment (Romans 12:3)

The Letter to the Romans is Paul's greatest theological work. Chapters 1–11 represent a masterful description and defense of the gospel that he preached. This makes the twelfth chapter critically important, since it represents the application of all that came before. How ought Christians to live in light of God's incredible grace and mercy in providing salvation through Jesus Christ? How are they to respond to the empowering presence of his Holy Spirit now given to believers?

Paul's first answer is that his readers should offer themselves back to God as a "living sacrifice" (Rom. 12:1). Paul here uses the Old Testament image of an animal offered to God as a sacrifice to atone for sins. Such an offering was expensive—a significant sacrifice for the person bringing the offering. Yet it was an even greater sacrifice for the lamb or goat being offered! Paul essentially says, "You are that lamb!" Since Christ gave himself completely for us, we ought to give ourselves back to him as a "living sacrifice." By doing this, we will no longer be conformed to the sinful patterns of this world, but we will be transformed with a renewed mind, able to discern God's will (Rom. 12:2).

What does this transformation look like? Paul's answer is a realistic and balanced view of self: "For by the grace given me I say to every one of you: Do not think of yourself more highly than you ought, but rather think of yourself with sober judgment, in accordance with the faith God has distributed to each of you" (Rom. 12:3). Paul calls for neither an overly exalted nor a degraded view of self, but rather one based on "sober judgment." The Greek phrase used here can mean to be prudent, self-controlled, reasonable, or sensible. It often has the sense of "nothing to excess."[3] The point is to have a realistic view of self that enables the leader to function at maximum effectiveness. Just as the captain of a ship can operate a vessel best when fully aware of its strengths and weaknesses, and a race car driver can push the car to its maximum effectiveness by knowing its precise abilities and limitations, so leaders will be most effective when they are self-aware, fully cognizant of their strengths and weaknesses, their potential and limitations.

Christian Identity: Divine-Image Bearers Saved by Grace

This goal of sober self-assessment points to an important paradox in the Christian life. Salvation is gained only by recognizing our lowly status, that we are sinners undeserving of salvation, utterly bankrupt before God. It is only by his grace that we are saved, not by any goodness we have or merit we have earned (Eph. 2:8–9). In his famous hymn, John Newton expresses it this way: "Amazing grace! How sweet the sound that saved a wretch like me." Or, as Isaac Watts puts it in another well-known hymn: "Would He devote that sacred head for such a worm as I?"[4]

So are we "wretches" and "worms" in God's eyes? While it is certainly true that we are fallen creatures, sinful and unworthy of God's presence, "wretch" or "worm" theology is insufficient to describe our status. The Bible describes human beings as the pinnacle of God's creation, created in his image, deeply loved, and endowed with great honor by their Creator.

> LORD, our Lord,
>   how majestic is your name in all the earth! . . .
> When I consider your heavens,
>   the work of your fingers,
> the moon and the stars,
>   which you have set in place,
> what is mankind that you are mindful of them,
>   human beings that you care for them?
> You have made them a little lower than the angels
>   and crowned them with glory and honor.

You made them rulers over the works of your hands;
you put everything under their feet. (Ps. 8:1–6)

God's esteem and love for us as human beings motivated him to redeem us from our fallen state through the sacrificial death of Christ (1 John 4:9–10). This salvation transforms us into the glorified beings we were intended to be: children of God with extraordinary status and potential. As the apostle John reminds his readers: "Now we are children of God, and what we will be has not yet been made known. But we know that when Christ appears, we shall be like him, for we shall see him as he is" (3:2). This glorious position is not just a future inheritance; it is a present possession. We *are* children of God in the present: "See what great love the Father has lavished on us, that we should be called children of God! And that is what we are!" (3:1). Now endowed with the same Spirit of God that guided and empowered Jesus during his earthly ministry, we have extraordinary power and potential (John 14:12).

Humility Balanced with Self-Confidence

This paradoxical status of believers should instruct and motivate Christian leaders. We remain fully dependent on God for our salvation and for competence in our daily lives. Yet in his power we are adequate to accomplish anything he calls us to. Paul expresses this sentiment in 2 Corinthians 3, where he is defending his authority as an apostle by pointing to the good work he has accomplished in the lives of the Corinthians: "Such confidence we have through Christ before God. Not that we are competent in ourselves to claim anything for ourselves, but our competence comes from God" (2 Cor. 3:4–5). Notice that the *competence* he receives from God generates *confidence* in his abilities.

Leaders can be both humble and highly competent when they acknowledge that God is the true source of their competency.

Like Paul, the Christian leader should be both humble and confident. Humility is the recognition that we are inadequate and incompetent apart from Christ. Confidence comes from the recognition of his power at work within us. Later in this chapter, we will refer to this balance as humble self-efficacy. Leaders can be both humble and highly competent when they acknowledge that God is the true source of their competency.

Paul's humility came especially from the fact that earlier in his life he had opposed the work of God by persecuting the church: "For I am the least of the apostles and do not even deserve to be called an apostle, because I persecuted the church of God. But by the grace of God I am what I am, and his grace to me was not without effect. No, I worked harder than all of them—yet not I, but the grace of God that was with me" (1 Cor. 15:9–10). By identifying himself as the "least" of the apostles, Paul is not practicing false humility. He recognizes that his violent persecution against the church was a great evil, damaging lives and causing trauma, suffering, and even death. No doubt Paul still experienced guilt and bore emotional scars for his actions.

Yet Paul's consternation at his past is balanced by his affirmation of the present: "But by the grace of God I am what I am." God took an angry and violent persecutor and transformed him into a fearless proclaimer of the good news. Paul insists that none of this was through his own initiative or abilities. Three times in these two sentences he refers to the grace of God. It is only "by the grace of God" and "his grace to me" that "I am what I am." Even when he feels it necessary to defend his own authority against his opponents by quipping, "I worked harder than all of them," he quickly clarifies, "yet not I, but the grace of God that was with me." All of Paul's efforts and successes were ultimately the work of God.

Recognition of Gifts and Limitations

If the leader's humility and confidence have as their basis the status we have in Christ—as image bearers saved by grace—they express themselves through the leader's exercise of spiritual gifts. The "sober judgment" Paul refers to in Romans 12:3 comes, on the one hand, from the leader's recognition of their gifts and abilities and, on the other hand, from an acknowledgment of their weaknesses and limitations. It is no accident that immediately after referring to the need for sober judgment, Paul turns to the issue of giftedness: "For just as each of us has one body with many members, and these members do not all have the same function, so in Christ we, though many, form one body, and each member belongs to all the others. We have different gifts, according to the grace given to each of us" (Rom. 12:4–6).

Elsewhere Paul makes it clear that not everyone has every gift (1 Cor. 12:27–30). A leader may have extraordinary teaching gifts but poor administrative skills. Another may be an exceptional manager and organizer but not an effective teacher or motivator. Here, again, sober self-assessment is essential. Leaders who recognize their own gifts and limitations will build a team around them to fill in their gaps.

A comparison of two of Paul's assistants, Titus and Timothy, helps to illustrate this emphasis on unique gifts and abilities. It seems that when Paul needed an assertive person to take charge of a situation, he would send Titus.

For example, when Paul was at odds with the church at Corinth and his authority had been rejected by a group of renegade leaders, he sent Titus with a strong and severe letter calling for the church to repent and submit to his leadership (2 Cor. 2:4, 13; 7:5–7). Similarly, when Paul needed someone to put the unruly churches of Crete in order and appoint elders there, he again sent Titus (Titus 1:5, 10–16). Titus was Paul's tough guy.

Yet, when Paul needed someone to provide gentle love and encouragement, Timothy seems to have been the preferred choice. For example, when he wanted to send encouragement to the church in Thessalonica in the midst of their persecution and to remind them of his love and parental concern for them, he sent Timothy "to strengthen and encourage you in your faith" (1 Thess. 3:2; cf. 3:6–10). Timothy seems to have been a particularly sensitive and caring leader, with strong gifts of encouragement and pastoral care. As Paul writes to the Philippian church, "I have no one else like him, who will show genuine concern for your welfare" (Phil. 2:20). In both of these cases, awareness of and utilization of an individual's unique gifts led to successful ministry.

Self-Evaluation in Contemporary Perspective

Contemporary theory and research build on these biblical perspectives by providing additional insight into the importance of leaders engaging in self-evaluation. In my (Justin's) research on the topic, leaders who "honestly evaluate themselves before seeking to evaluate others" were a statistically significant predictor of effective leadership practice.[5]

Interestingly, this particular practice had the most dominant predictive effect on leadership effectiveness in the relevant studies. While honest self-evaluation may not immediately come to mind when thinking about effective leadership practice, sometimes it is the personal work that happens behind the scenes that is most important. From a research perspective, that certainly is the case with honest self-evaluation.

With this starting point in view, we will reflect on the following areas related to self-evaluation in this section: (1) self-evaluation and self-awareness, and (2) self-leadership and personal growth.

Self-Evaluation and Self-Awareness

Self-evaluation begins with honest self-awareness. For Christian leaders, this movement toward self-awareness necessitates being honest first and foremost with God and then having this honesty before God translate into honesty with self and others. As we engage the concept of self-awareness, we will do so by focusing on nurturing humble self-efficacy, leadership authenticity, and emotional intelligence.

HUMBLE SELF-EFFICACY

Increasingly, leadership researchers are recognizing the importance of humility for leadership effectiveness. One example of this comes from the work of Jim Collins. In his book *Good to Great*, Collins writes about the concept of Level 5 Leadership. Level 5 leaders uniquely embody a blend of professional will and personal humility. When we consider what followers and organizations need from their leaders, both sides of this leadership equation are a priority.

Humility. Organizations need leaders who possess humility and self-awareness. Followers, and the overall health of organizations, do not need leaders who are prideful and self-serving. Rather, they need leaders who are humble—leaders who truly believe that they are part of a larger team and are willing to serve that team beyond self-interest with broader organizational needs in view.

While humility is certainly about thinking beyond oneself, it is also important to recognize that humility is not primarily about thinking less of oneself. Blended with humility, there is also a need for leaders to bring confidence and determination to their work.

Although followers are not served well by prideful and self-serving individuals, neither are they served well by individuals who lack confidence and determination. Here is where the both-and approach of empowering leadership comes into play. It is about determination and ability coming alongside personal humility.

Challenging self-confidence. From a Christian perspective, it can be appropriate to challenge the notion of self-confidence. There are two basic grounds for such a challenge. First, for Christian leaders, our confidence resides primarily in God, not ourselves. He is our boast. He is the strength and power behind any confidence one possesses (see 1 Pet. 4:11).

A second ground for challenging an emphasis on self-confidence relates to the potential for having self-confidence that is disconnected from reality. When there is a disconnect between confidence and ability, confidence alone can lead to failure on the part of leaders and organizational members.

To illustrate this point, I (Justin) enjoy playing basketball regularly at our local YMCA. When it comes to pick-up basketball games at the local Y with my son or daughters, I feel fairly confident that I can usually be a positive contributor to the team at that level of play. If, however, I were offered a chance to play pick-up basketball with NBA stars like LeBron James and Stephen Curry, no amount of self-confidence would help me to succeed!

Self-efficacy. The key is to have confidence aligned with capacity in the life of a leader. Here is where the conversation of self-efficacy comes into the discussion. Self-efficacy involves an accurate perception of one's capacity to succeed in a situation given both strengths and limitations. While self-confidence may or may not be aligned with reality, we argue that self-efficacy is confidence aligned with an accurate self-assessment. A Christian view of self-efficacy would also emphasize the importance of being comfortable with the gifts, strengths, skills, and abilities God has placed in our care, and then learning to walk confidently in these along with not being anxious in the face of our limitations as well.

Such self-efficacy and self-awareness—learning to accurately evaluate one's strengths and limitations as a leader—is the foundation for both leader humility and leader confidence. More than ever, our organizations need leaders who embody both sides of humble self-efficacy.

LEADERSHIP AUTHENTICITY

Related to the leader's need for humble self-efficacy is a need for authenticity in leadership. As a leader nurtures a self-awareness that manifests itself in humble self-efficacy, this provides a basis for a leader's capacity to be authentic with oneself and others.

As evidenced by the growing focus on authentic leadership in the leadership literature, followers and organizational members are looking for an alternative to the cold and calculating managerial tactics of past decades. Authentic and purposeful leaders stand in stark contrast to these past strategies. They provide a model of leadership in organizations that emphasizes intrapersonal wisdom, including an awareness of personal strengths and weaknesses, along with an awareness of the impact these strengths and limitations have on others.

In his book *Authentic Leadership*, Bill George, former CEO of Medtronic, defines authentic leadership around core principles that are focused on internal dimensions of the leader. Authentic leaders must not simply look to organizational needs; they must also consider how their personal *purpose, values, relationships, self-discipline,* and *heart* relate to their organizations and the people they lead.

Taking authentic leadership's emphasis on purpose as an example, George argues that authentic and mission-driven organizations are guided by leaders with a deep sense of personal purpose. This sense of personal purpose is not just about adopting the purpose of the organization or adopting the purpose of someone else. Authentic leaders must also gain a clear sense of their personal purpose in life and leadership. This provides a foundation for authentically and effectively leading others out of this purposeful direction.

Leadership authenticity requires leaders to take time for self-evaluation in order to nurture an awareness of where ego and narcissistic impulse are pulling them away from a higher-order calling and purpose. While this may not be a concern for leaders who are interested only in serving themselves, for those wishing truly to serve and empower others, empowering leadership requires nurturing self-awareness and personal authenticity.

Emotional Intelligence

Self-awareness is also an important dimension of emotional intelligence. As we continue to reflect on the importance of self-awareness for effective leadership, we provide an overview of emotional-intelligence theory and how a leader's ability to recognize and respond to emotion contributes to effective leadership practice.

One of the earliest conceptualizations of emotional intelligence emphasized an individual's appraisal and expression of emotion in self and others, the regulation of emotion in self and others, and the utilization of emotion for positive ends.[6] At its core, emotional intelligence is about recognizing emotion and then responding to emotion in ways that limit its negative effects and maximize its positive effects.

It's easy to see how this is important for leaders. Take the first element of recognizing emotion in self and others. Emotion can have both verbal and nonverbal dimensions. Generally speaking, a person with higher levels of emotional intelligence would be able to notice in themselves or in others when there is continuity or discontinuity between the verbal and nonverbal dimensions of one's emotional expression.

Imagine, for example, if a person is asked, "How are you doing?" and then with crossed arms and furrowed eyebrows, the person answers simply, "Fine." An emotionally intelligent person might exhibit this type of discontinuity, but they would be able to recognize that discontinuity and respond accordingly to adjust either their verbal or nonverbal expression to bring this dual communication into alignment.

This is why self-awareness in leadership is so important. Leaders do not need to control their emotions perfectly. As we noted previously, authenticity in leadership is also vital. But leaders do need to be aware of their emotions and be able to utilize and regulate emotion in productive ways. Because empowering and servant-oriented leadership is more about caring for the needs of followers than it is about serving the needs of leaders, decisions to share or hold back emotion should be driven by consideration of what will best serve the needs of followers.

Leaders must be free to feel emotions from both their personal and professional lives, but at the same time must not, on the basis of those deeply felt emotions, cast an inordinately negative shadow on those they lead. Certainly there are times to let followers and organizational members be exposed to what you are feeling as a leader. But other times, these emotions need to be managed in different ways—acknowledging these emotions, processing them with those in a closer circle of trusted friends and counselors, and then regulating these emotions so they do not unnecessarily control interactions with followers.

For leaders, this work of emotional self-awareness and emotional self-management becomes the foundation for emotional social awareness and emotional social management (see fig. 2.1).

This foundation of recognizing and responding to emotion in one's own life becomes a basis for recognizing and responding to emotion in others and in those we lead. As many leadership theories emphasize, attending to the hearts of followers is vital. Learning to begin with attending to our own heart and emotions becomes a foundation for this work with others. Self-awareness and emotional intelligence are a starting point for this important work.

Figure 2.1
Emotional Awareness

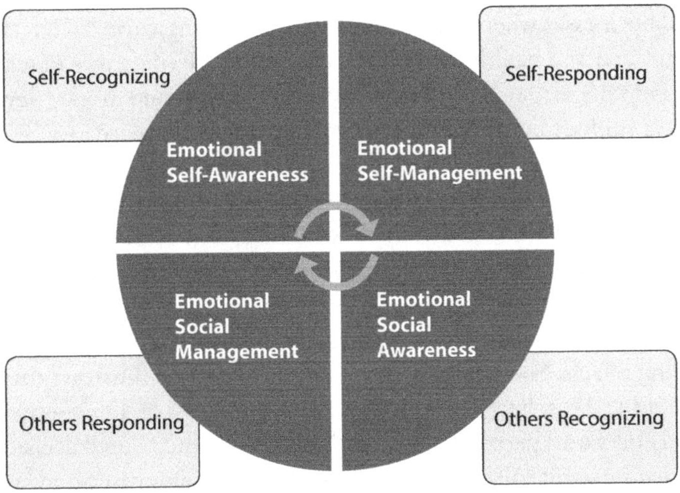

Self-Leadership and Personal Growth

As leaders build on self-awareness, self-leadership and personal growth become a possibility. Our former colleague Sam Rima engages the topic of self-leadership in his book *Leading from the Inside Out: The Art of Self-Leadership*. Rima asserts that "all effective, enduring leadership must be built on the foundation of effective self-leadership. It is our ability to successfully lead our own life that provides the firm foundation from which we can lead others."[7]

DIMENSIONS OF SELF-LEADERSHIP

If self-leadership is a priority for leaders seeking to lead themselves well, what are some of the core dimensions of self-leadership? Self-leadership requires looking at one's life in a holistic manner. While leaders may be known for their capacity for compartmentalizing dimensions of their professional lives, self-leadership requires leaders to resist the temptation to overly compartmentalize what is public and private in their lives. These leaders must intentionally draw from the multiple threads of their lives in a holistic manner.

So what are some of these threads? Though this is not an exhaustive list, self-leadership work draws from at least six areas: (1) spiritual well-being, (2) emotional well-being, (3) physical well-being, (4) intellectual well-being, (5) social and relational well-being, and (6) vocational well-being (see fig. 2.2). How we lead ourselves in each of these areas not only has an impact on us personally but also shapes the level of health, or at times dysfunction, we bring to others.

Kevin Harney points to the challenge of shipwrecked lives, families, ministries, and businesses when leaders avoid this important work: "What they lack is an examined and healthy inner life. This is the missing piece in leadership today. Too many leaders spend huge amounts of time and money developing a powerful skill set but forget to nurture and guard their own souls."[8]

For Christian leaders, this certainly includes attention to the spiritual dimensions of soul care. But attention to soul care necessarily relates to other areas, such as emotional, financial, physical, vocational, and relational health. Unhealthy self-leadership in any of these areas can have a lasting negative effect on the lives of those we lead.

Consider how lack of attention to simple dimensions in one's life can have devastating effects. Some use the acronym of HALT to illustrate this. Issues related to HALT—when one is Hungry, Angry, Lonely, or Tired—may have a profound effect on a person's emotional well-being and related decision making. For leaders and followers alike, personal struggles can often spring up

Figure 2.2
Some Dimensions of Self-Leadership

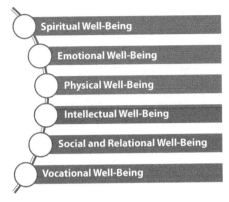

from very basic personal issues like these. For example, when we are hungry, angry, lonely, or tired, vulnerability to both blatant sin and general personal struggle becomes a pressing concern. Though the presenting sin or struggle need not be excused by the HALT issues at play, at times the solution to addressing these issues becomes quite straightforward.

Here is where the holistic side of self-leadership comes together in an important way. What may be an emotional or spiritual issue on the surface often finds its solution beyond those areas of life. For instance, practicing self-discipline in patterns of exercise and healthy eating has the capacity to nurture self-discipline in other areas of life. Or taking time to get a good night's sleep may provide a healthier emotional state for engaging the demands of leadership that arise on a particularly intense day.

We are whole beings. As life and leadership challenges often find their source in multiple domains of our lives, so do the solutions to these challenges. Self-leadership requires a broad look at our lives through a holistic lens. While this may be an intuitive process for some leaders, others will need to lean intentionally into the support of friends, pastors, coaches, and counselors to learn the art and practice of self-leadership. Whether accomplishing this intuitively or not, all leaders must nurture an intentional rhythm of self-leadership in their lives in order to bring health rather than dysfunction to those they lead.

SELF-DIFFERENTIATION

Related to the important work of self-leadership is a concept called self-differentiation. Self-differentiation is a concept arising out of family- and organizational-systems thinking that emphasizes the emotional capacity of an individual to engage with people in a manner that is not overly dependent on the opinion of others. One of the key presenting issues related to one's level of self-differentiation is a person's capacity for maintaining a non-anxious presence in the face of difference.

For example, if a person struggles with self-differentiation, intense criticism often leads to an anxious response. In this situation, criticism of one's ideas or behavior erodes one's sense of confidence and well-being, since this sense of well-being is dependent on rather than differentiated from others. One of the individuals who has emphasized self-differentiation from a leadership perspective is Edwin Friedman. In his book *A Failure of Nerve*, Friedman argues that leaders without appropriate levels of self-differentiation are held captive to models of leadership that are reactive in nature rather than proactive.[9]

From a positive perspective, this means that well-differentiated leaders maintain a proactive rather than reactive stance toward their leadership and are able to coexist with others and be okay with who they are in the face of difference and even criticism. The core of self-differentiation may be expressed in the following manner: *Leaders must care and not care at the same time. They must care deeply for the people they lead, but not for the shifting praise and approval of others.*

Self-differentiation has many benefits for leaders and the teams they lead. For instance, in my (Justin's) research on self-differentiation, we found that leader self-differentiation was positively related to resiliency.[10] Leaders in the study who engaged the challenges and obstacles of leadership with resilience and perseverance had a higher capacity for self-differentiation, which resulted in providing a non-anxious presence for those they led.

Such self-leadership and self-differentiation require leaders to live out an important paradox. Though not easy, the key to effective self-differentiated leadership is paradoxically to care and not care at the same time. When we are able to care truly for others by becoming less dependent on what others think of us as leaders, we are finally able to start acting on this love for others in a productive and other-centered manner.

A Commitment to Personal Growth

In all of these dimensions of self-leadership and self-differentiation, the answer is not for leaders to figure it all out before they start leading. Much of leadership is learned along the way in the journey of life together in organizations. What we are emphasizing in this chapter is the priority of leaders engaging in their leadership journey with a commitment to personal growth (see fig. 2.3).

In his book *The Making of a Leader*, J. Robert Clinton shares his theory of leadership development and emergence, which emphasizes themes such as inner-life growth and life maturing.[11] These themes capture Hesselbein's philosophy of leadership noted earlier. For the self-aware leader, inner-life growth becomes the occasion on which leaders begin to understand that effective leadership is much more about one's *being* than one's *doing*. Individuals who are unwilling to go through the hard work of inner-life growth and life maturing will not be ready to lead with effectiveness when the time is right. While those who do not engage this inner-life work may experience short-term effectiveness, it is only those willing to engage in sustained self-reflection and self-leadership who will be able to lead well over the long term.

> *Effective leadership is much more about one's being than one's doing.*

Figure 2.3
Some Dimensions of Personal Growth

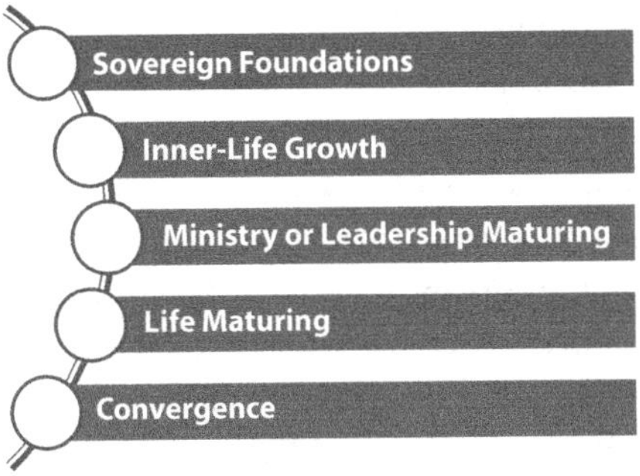

- Sovereign Foundations
- Inner-Life Growth
- Ministry or Leadership Maturing
- Life Maturing
- Convergence

Self-Evaluation in Practice

Throughout this chapter we have argued for the importance of honest self-evaluation in light of leader priorities such as humble self-efficacy, leadership authenticity, emotional intelligence, self-leadership, self-differentiation, and personal growth in the ongoing leadership-development journey.

For each of these priorities, honesty with increased self-awareness serves as the foundation for leaders wishing to engage in effective leadership practice. Building on these previous reflections, we conclude with a look at honest self-evaluation in practice. We begin with a reflection on how Bill George emphasized this movement toward the personal in his time at Medtronic.

Self-Evaluation and Authentic Leadership: Bill George

Bill George joined Medtronic in 1989 as the company's president and COO. Quickly, George also became the company's CEO and then its chairman. During his time of leading the company up until 2001, George and the team at Medtronic saw the company's annual sales grow from $755 million to $5.5 billion and saw its employee base grow from four thousand to twenty-six thousand employees.

The growth at Medtronic also translated into growth for shareholders. While Medtronic's market capitalization was $1.1 billion at the beginning of his time as CEO, the company's market cap grew to $60 billion by 2001, averaging growth of 35 percent per year.

While these metrics of recognizing company growth and value are impressive, from a leadership perspective the values and principles George brought to the table were equally impressive. Through his time at Medtronic, George began to embrace the priority of authentic leadership.[12] George also emphasized the need for leaders to find their unique voice and true north in the midst of competing voices and values.[13]

Illustrating this, George points out the dangers for CEOs when allowing one category of voices to drown out the leader's sense of purpose and value. For instance, when companies and their CEOs are overly focused on shareholders, this can create problems for all stakeholders—including shareholders. In extreme cases, this can lead to the corruption exemplified by the Enron, Arthur Andersen, and WorldCom stories. Even when CEOs are overly focused on shareholder value within the bounds of the law, this imbalance can have damaging effects.

George points out how cause and effect can be confused when it comes to increased shareholder value. Shareholder value is typically increased, not when a company focuses on increasing share value, but rather when a company focuses on increasing the value of their core products and services. On this point, George writes, "By striving so hard to please shareholders, [CEOs] often end up pleasing no one—not their customers, not their employees, not their communities, and ultimately not their shareholders."[14]

In the face of competing voices external to the leader, George argues that leaders must intentionally attend to personal issues. As noted above, such issues include purpose, values, relationships, self-discipline, and heart. This shift to a personal focus can be triggered by many things. Through interviews with 125 people, George identifies a pattern: this shift to the personal often was initiated (1) through their transformative experiences or crucible moments along the leadership-development journey, or (2) through the influence of key relationships and mentors in the leaders' lives.

As the demands of diverse voices press leaders, George calls leaders to a deep look within: "The test of leadership is ignoring those outside voices and learning to hear the one deep within. As a CEO, your attention ultimately has to be on the long run—and that is, of necessity, a lonely run. The voices clamoring for your attention will be many. Your job is to find your own."[15]

George was able to model this for us, and the work that he did paid off. As he gave attention to his own self-leadership, it paid off not only for him as a leader but also for Medtronic's diverse stakeholders, who benefited from his work of embracing authentic leadership. George lived out this journey of self-leadership, and it provided a sound basis for effective leadership at the highest corporate levels.

Self-Evaluation: Insights for Practice

As you consider your own process of nurturing honest self-evaluation, we offer the following principles for the next steps in your leadership journey.

GET THE SEQUENCE RIGHT

Part of the core lesson from the research supporting the priority of honest self-evaluation is a lesson in getting things in the right order. *Honest self-evaluation precedes evaluation of others.*

Followers can sense inauthenticity in leadership. When leaders are quick to evaluate others before—or in the absence of—evaluating themselves, this provides a powerful negative message for followers. As opposed to what we suggest in chapter 1, this practice communicates that followers should do what they are told, regardless of what their leaders model in their behavior.

When problems arise in an organization, leaders must model what matters when it comes to vulnerable self-evaluation. Ask yourself the tough questions:

- How am I contributing to this issue or problem?
- Are there areas of my inner life that adversely affect my work or those with whom I work?
- Are there any personal blind spots I'm missing in this situation? Do I need to seek out insight from anyone who could help me see these blind spots?

- To whom am I accountable as a leader? Who are the people helping me remain authentic and honest in my self-evaluation?
- What strengths and limitations am I bringing to this issue or process? How can I grow as a person or leader in order to contribute to the needed solutions in productive and healthy ways?

The list of questions could go on. Whether you use these specific questions or others, the key is to start looking at organizational challenges in a manner that includes self-evaluation as well. The work of self-evaluation, when done before evaluation of others, communicates authenticity to followers and provides the basis for leaders extending health rather than dysfunction to their followers.

Schedule Time to Rest and Reflect

While effective leadership includes honest self-evaluation, nurturing a rhythm of self-awareness and evaluation is difficult without a simple feature: time to reflect.

Do you intentionally create time in your schedule to think and reflect? In our day of continual connection to the world around us through technology, it is increasingly difficult for leaders to find time and space for deep reflection. Consider the ready access people have to us through smartphones, text messaging, a regular flow of emails, and meetings that are scheduled for us on shared calendars. While technology creates efficiencies in our work, this same technology also fills our lives in such a way that intentional reflection can be difficult.

On top of technology in the work environment, consider how technology in our personal lives also can work against time alone for reflection. For example, while there are many ways social media has the capacity to enrich our lives, social media also adds to already full schedules in ways that work against a reflective approach to life.

These realities mean that leaders need to be intentional in finding time and space in their lives to think and reflect. On this point, John Baldoni notes that organizations need leaders who first know themselves—leaders who "have an inner compass that points them in the right direction."[16] According to Baldoni, clarifying these dimensions of the inner life "begins with sound thinking—with taking time to think before we do."[17]

For Christians, time for reflection does not need to be an isolated activity. Through the practices of Sabbath and prayer, we are reminded that we are not alone in our work as leaders. Taking time for rest and prayer is a declaration of our trust in and dependency on God. Timothy Keller and Katherine Leary Alsdorf remind us that the practice of Sabbath is an act of trust, a reminder that God is at work even in the midst of our rest and that, ultimately, God is there—we are not alone in our work.[18] As we recognize that we are not alone in our work, we also may receive the invitation to seek out wisdom from God: "If any of you lacks wisdom, you should ask God, who gives generously to all without finding fault, and it will be given to you" (James 1:5). In our times of rest and reflection, we are able to not only lean into our own thoughts and convictions but we are also able to lean into God's wisdom.

So, are you making time to think and reflect in your life? Are you taking time for Sabbath rest and prayer? For those who have full calendars and high demands in their roles, this often means there is a need for scheduling time on their calendars for this important work. Remember, being busy does not always translate into being productive. As Keller and Leary Alsdorf remind us, "A deeply rested people are far more productive."[19] Sometimes pulling back from the intense pace of work is just the answer we need to the most demanding questions and challenges we face. Take time to rest, think, reflect, pray, and nurture a regular pattern of self-evaluation. Consider when this specifically will take place. When will it take place in the week ahead? When will it take place next month?

Seek Mentors and Coaches

Finally, while the focus of this chapter has been on *self*-evaluation, sometimes we need to press into the people around us in order to see new growth in these dimensions of self-leadership. Because we are relational beings at our core, we are designed to learn in the context of community.

Trusted friends, reflective mentors, and personal coaches can help us reflect on either areas for growth that do not come naturally for us or areas in which we exhibit potential blind spots. Although we do not want every voice in our lives providing personal feedback—both affirmation and critique—when it comes to friends, mentors, and coaches, we all need a core group of trusted individuals to whom we may turn for assistance in the reflective journey.

Engaging the topic of how people grow, Henry Cloud and John Townsend emphasize that mentoring is often a core feature. They note that when people succeed in life, the reality is that there are often many others who have taken these people under their wing, helped them along, and helped them develop in their careers.[20] Although this happens without our planning at times, usually we need to be intentional in seeking out time with trusted mentors and counselors.

Leaders must intentionally engage the work of self-reflection and self-evaluation. This work is typically most effectively carried out with wisdom and direction from trusted friends and mentors. Since blind spots are by definition most often unseen by us, sometimes we need the trusted people in our lives to help us see what we cannot see on our own. Find people who can speak into your life with honesty and help to spur you on in your work of honest self-evaluation. Your health and effectiveness as a leader depend on this vital work.

Next Steps

- Take some time to consider areas of your life that may be adversely affecting your work with others.
- Take some time to evaluate both your strengths and limitations, with a particular emphasis on how these influence others.
- Take some time to seek out input from a mentor or personal coach; ask a trusted friend or colleague about potential personal blind spots that may be negatively affecting your capacity to lead well.

Resources for a Deeper Look

George, Bill. *Discover Your True North: Becoming an Authentic Leader*. Rev. ed. Hoboken, NJ: Wiley, 2015.

Rath, Tom, and Barry Conchie. *Strengths-Based Leadership: Great Leaders, Teams, and Why People Follow*. New York: Gallup, 2008.

Rima, Samuel D. *Leading from the Inside Out: The Art of Self-Leadership*. Grand Rapids: Baker Books, 2000.

Skoglund, E. R. "Self-Esteem, Self-Love." In *Evangelical Dictionary of Theology*, edited by Daniel J. Treier and Walter A. Elwell, pages 1087–88. 3rd ed. Grand Rapids: Baker Academic, 2017.

Walton, Steve. *Leadership and Lifestyle: The Portrait of Paul in the Miletus Speech and 1 Thessalonians*. Cambridge: Cambridge University Press, 2004.

3

Fostering Collaboration

Introduction

Rock Church of San Diego has taken a focus on service and empowerment to a whole new level on behalf of its community. In 2009, the church approached the mayor of San Diego and pledged 100,000 hours of community service. Between 2009 and 2017, Rock Church served its city with 1,820,232 hours of community service.

Beyond being a compelling story of what embodied Christian love can look like in a community, this also is a story of collaborative and empowering leadership. Rock Church's senior pastor, Miles McPherson, has both an interesting life story[1] and a powerful leadership philosophy.

McPherson describes Rock Church's leadership culture this way: "That's the awesome thing about servant leadership: once it has become a fundamental component of organizational culture, it permeates every department, sneaks into every office, and defines every leader."[2]

Early on in McPherson's ministry with the church, he realized this commitment to serving others could not be accomplished simply by the work of an individual. It had to be a collaborative effort. He writes, "My reach and influence is tiny compared to the combined potential of all the people in our church. With a vision of pervasive hope, I had to become an *empowerer*. . . . I needed to make it my mission to serve, energize, and enable the people in the congregation to proclaim hope wherever *they* go."[3] In short, this commitment required a commitment to empowering servant leadership that fostered collaboration.

That is the focus of our chapter—*fostering collaboration*. If leaders hold a pessimistic view of follower motivation or capacity, collaboration becomes a low-order priority. If, however, leaders view followers as genuine partners in organizational mission, collaboration becomes essential for effective leadership practice.

Throughout the introduction and part 1 of this book, we have emphasized how leadership style is shifting from command-and-control approaches to styles of influence and empowerment. Along with modeling what matters and engaging in honest self-evaluation, this third leadership practice of fostering collaboration plays an important role in building a healthy organizational community where leaders and followers engage in authentic partnership in light of shared goals.

> *If leaders view followers as genuine partners in organizational mission, collaboration becomes essential for effective leadership practice.*

Commitment to collaboration is grounded in a fairly basic conviction—two are better than one (see Eccles. 4:9–12). Here, and elsewhere in the biblical Wisdom literature, the value of planning and working alongside others is affirmed: "Plans fail for lack of counsel, but with many advisers they succeed" (Prov. 15:22). Such wisdom is deeply compelling for leaders willing to listen and learn.

In this chapter, we explore the topic of fostering collaboration through the following perspectives: (1) collaboration in biblical perspective, (2) collaboration in contemporary perspective, and (3) collaboration in practice.

Collaboration in Biblical Perspective

The apostle Paul is sometimes portrayed as a lone wolf, a groundbreaking pioneer working tirelessly on his own to establish churches and write books of Christian theology. Yet our sources paint a very different picture. Paul was all about relationship, collaboration, and partnership. He always had assistants—missionaries in training—at his side. Several of his letters begin with statements like "Paul and Timothy, servants of Christ Jesus" (Phil. 1:1) or "Paul, Silas and Timothy, To the church of the Thessalonians" (1 Thess. 1:1). Though these letters are clearly from Paul himself, he includes his partners in ministry in the greeting. Paul was committed to joining with others to accomplish his mission.

Paul's pattern of ministry illustrates this. He would arrive in a major city, such as Ephesus or Corinth, and set up a base of operations. There he would not only preach the good news about Jesus in the synagogues and in the streets but he would also train other leaders to do the same, sending them out to the surrounding towns and villages. For example, when Paul wrote his letter to the Colossians, he apparently had never visited the church in Colossae. It was founded by one of his disciples, a man named Epaphras, whom Paul had likely sent from Ephesus (Col. 1:7; 4:12). Paul was constantly building networks of churches and of Christian leaders. He knew that the task he had been commissioned with—taking the message of salvation to the ends of the earth—was far too great for one man. It required a network of partnerships, collaboration, and shared leadership.

To get a taste of this collaboration, listen to some of Paul's closing comments in one of his letters, written late in his career to his assistant Timothy: "Crescens has gone to Galatia, and Titus to Dalmatia. Only Luke is with me. Get Mark and bring him with you, because he is helpful to me in my ministry. I sent Tychicus to Ephesus. . . . Greet Priscilla and Aquila and the household of Onesiphorus. Erastus stayed in Corinth, and I left Trophimus sick in Miletus. Do your best to get here before winter. Eubulus greets you, and so do Pudens, Linus, Claudia and all the brothers and sisters" (2 Tim. 4:10–12, 19–21). Get the picture? A bit of networking and collaboration going on here! If Paul had had a smartphone, it would have been full of contacts, appointments, notifications, and "to do" items. This is anything but ministry in isolation.

In this pattern of collaboration, Paul was not actually the innovator. His master, Jesus himself, had modeled it for him. As we saw in chapter 1, Jesus chose twelve disciples, trained and equipped them, and then sent them out to preach and to heal (Matt. 10:1; Mark 3:14–15; Luke 9:1–2). These were precisely the tasks that Jesus himself was performing. In other words, Jesus led by training others and partnering with them to get the message out. He knew he could never reach all of Israel alone, so he commissioned the Twelve to collaborate with him.

A Tale of Two Cities: Partners or Competitors?

Principles of collaboration can be seen by comparing and contrasting Paul's relationships with two of his churches, Philippi and Corinth. These two had much in common. Both were located in what is modern-day Greece, one in the north (Macedonia) and the other in the south (Achaia). Both cities were important metropolitan and cultural centers whose citizens took pride in their Greco-Roman heritage. Both churches were started by Paul during his second missionary journey. Paul dearly loved the members of both churches and viewed them as his spiritual children.

Yet apart from these similarities, there were striking differences between the two churches. The church at Corinth was an immature and struggling congregation. Its leaders tended to be arrogant and self-centered and often challenged Paul's authority. The church was divided into factions, centered on various leaders. By contrast, the church at Philippi viewed Paul as their partner in ministry. They shared a common vision and a common purpose, working together toward a common goal. The church considered Paul's mission to be their mission and their resources as his resources. They repeatedly supported him financially and in other ways. While by necessity Paul's leadership at Corinth tended to be authoritarian (and so less effective), at Philippi it was one of collaboration and partnership.

Collaboration Arises from a Shared Vision

At the beginning of his letter to the Philippians, Paul writes, "I thank my God every time I remember you. . . . I always pray with joy *because of your partnership in the gospel* from the first day until now" (Phil. 1:3–5). Paul rejoices that the church had not simply followed his leadership; they had become partners with him. They hadn't just followed a man; they had adopted a cause. Paul's mission became their mission, and his purpose their purpose. The best leaders do not sell themselves; they share a vision that is greater than any personality.

Paul continues, "It is right for me to feel this way about all of you, since I have you in my heart and, whether I am in chains or defending and confirming the gospel, all of you share in God's grace with me" (Phil. 1:7). The Greek word translated "share in" (*synkoinōnos*) in verse 5 is from the same root as the word translated "partnership" (*koinōnia*). Both here mean *participating together* for a common goal. Paul says that whether he is defending the gospel in the streets and assembly halls of Philippi or in chains under house arrest in Rome, the Philippians are there with him. His ministry is their ministry. His success is their success. His trials and suffering are theirs, because they are coworkers and partners in the gospel.

Contrast this with what is happening in the church in Corinth when Paul writes the letter we call 1 Corinthians. The church is being torn apart by divisions. Paul writes, "I appeal to you, brothers and sisters, in the name of our Lord Jesus Christ, that all of you agree with one another in what you say and that there be no divisions among you, but that you be perfectly united in mind and thought. My brothers and sisters, some from Chloe's household have informed me that there are quarrels among you" (1 Cor. 1:10–11). The root cause of these factions is that the church members are focusing their allegiance on different human leaders rather than a shared vision for the gospel. Paul continues, "What I mean is this: One of you says, 'I follow Paul'; another, 'I follow Apollos'; another, 'I follow Cephas'; still another, 'I follow Christ'" (1:12). Notice that Paul does not call for loyalty to himself. One of the factions supports him, yet he is equally critical of them! A truly effective leader is not concerned with self-exaltation or self-promotion. A servant leader calls others to embrace a cause greater than any personality cult. For Paul, that greater cause is the lordship of Jesus Christ and the establishment of the kingdom of God.

Collaboration Encourages Humility and the Valuing of Giftedness

Truly collaborative leadership has a cost, since a leader must relinquish power to those with whom they are collaborating. While authoritarian leadership seeks greater and greater power and influence, collaborative leadership empowers others to utilize their gifts and abilities.

Although the Philippian church did not have the level of division that the Corinthian church had, there was a simmering conflict that threatened the tranquility of the church. We don't know the exact nature of this conflict, but in Philippians 4:2–3 Paul pleads with two women, Euodia and Syntyche, to mend their fences and calls on another leader in the church to help them work out their differences. Before giving this counsel, however, Paul gives the whole church advice on how to maintain unity and resolve conflict. The key, he writes, is to "do nothing out of selfish ambition or vain conceit. Rather, in humility value others above yourselves, not looking to your own interests but each of you to the interests of the others" (2:3–4). A true servant leader puts the needs of others first. This can defuse the situation, since it is hard to stay angry with someone who is genuinely pursuing *your* best interests.

This can be costly for the leader, who must invest their time, resources, and abilities in developing others. The ultimate example of this kind of leadership, Paul says, is Jesus Christ himself. At this point, Paul cites an early Christian hymn (Phil. 2:5–11) describing the life and death of Christ as the model of sacrificial service for others. Though Jesus had all the position, power, and glory of God, he was willing to give all this up, to leave heaven's glory, to become a human being, and to suffer and die on the cross for our sins. This was the ultimate act of servant leadership (see also Mark 10:45). Yet through it, Jesus empowered and enabled us to become children of God (Phil. 2:15).

The opposite of humility and service is pride and self-aggrandizement, attributes more characteristic of the Corinthian church (1 Cor. 4:18–19; 5:2). This arrogance resulted in conflict with one another and with Paul. The two

New Testament letters written to the Corinthians bear witness to this conflict. In addition to the factions mentioned above, some of the Corinthian believers were suing one another (1 Cor. 6:1–11). There was also conflict between the rich and poor (1 Cor. 11:17–34) and between those who had greater or lesser scruples concerning food sacrificed to idols (1 Cor. 8–10). There were also tensions between Paul and the church (1 Cor. 4:18; 9:3; 14:37) that at times broke into open conflict (2 Cor. 2:1–4; 7:8). Such conflicts no doubt had a paralyzing effect on the church and reduced their ministry effectiveness.

Collaboration Results in Greater Effectiveness

It almost goes without saying that collaboration results in greater effectiveness and productivity. When followers do not take ownership, their interest in and passion for a project are diminished. The failure of communism worldwide testifies to this. Although the communist system was meant to be ownership by the workers, in fact it was ownership and control by the elite. Without a stake in the profits, workers were disincentivized and production suffered. A sense of ownership and an entrepreneurial spirit result in greater motivation toward success.

With their sense of partnership, the Philippian church contributed to Paul's ministry in positive ways. First, more than once they sent financial gifts to Paul (Phil. 4:14–16). These gifts would allow him to spend less time supporting himself in his trade as a tent maker and more time teaching and preaching the gospel. This assistance began very early on, shortly after Paul left Philippi for Thessalonica (4:16), so that Paul can speak of their "partnership in the gospel from the first day until now" (1:5). More recently, the Philippians had sent one of their own members, a man named Epaphroditus, to assist Paul during his house arrest (2:25–30). This kind of support enabled Paul to carry on a more extensive and effective ministry.

Collaboration Produces a Greater Sense of Community

Partnership results in loyalty to one another as well as to the shared vision, as the example of Epaphroditus shows. Paul also tells the Philippians that he is sending his assistant Timothy to them soon, so that Timothy can share news with Paul about how they are doing. He then praises Timothy for his loyalty to and love for the Philippians: "I have no one else like him, who will show genuine concern for your welfare. For everyone looks out for their own interests, not those of Jesus Christ. But you know that Timothy has proved himself, because as a son with his father he has served with me in the work of the gospel" (Phil. 2:20–22). Timothy's passion for the cause of Jesus Christ resulted in greater love for and loyalty to the Philippians, who were partners with him in that cause. As anyone who has participated in a successful team can testify, loyalty to a common cause tends to draw people together in a bond of loyalty to one another, creating a greater sense of community, collaboration, and mutual support.

Collaboration in Contemporary Perspective

Contemporary theory and research build on these biblical perspectives by providing additional insight into the importance of leaders fostering collaboration. In my (Justin's) research on the topic, leaders who encourage followers to "work together rather than competing against each other" were a statistically significant predictor of effective leadership practice.[4]

As we consider contemporary perspective on the topic, our engagement will include fostering collaboration both within teams and between leaders and followers. Because of this emphasis, it will be important to explicitly consider the theme of power. How leaders and team members use their personal and positional power is a vital factor that influences the degree to which collaboration may be fostered in meaningful ways in a community and organization.

With this starting point in view, we will highlight the following areas in this section: (1) collaboration and leader power, (2) collaboration and the development of authentic partners, and (3) collaboration and contextual considerations.

Collaboration and Leader Power

Leadership studies in the first half of the twentieth century often emphasized the importance of leaders controlling followers, due to a pessimistic view of employee commitments. Consider one of the leadership definitions offered in 1927: "the ability to impress the will of the leader on those led and induce obedience, respect, loyalty, and cooperation."[5]

From such a leadership perspective, power is a tool that resides with the leader and is used to bring followers in line with the leader's agenda. This approach to leadership emphasizes positional authority and aims to incentivize—or coerce in its negative forms—followers with extrinsic means of motivation. Although leadership in this approach may yield modest levels of achievement, these outcomes generally are not shared goals owned and valued by both leaders and followers. The emphasis is on leader outcomes rather than shared outcomes.

In the latter half of the twentieth century, leadership scholars introduced models that emphasized personal power over positional power and leadership influence over leadership control. One example of this comes from the writing of Robert K. Greenleaf. In his work with AT&T in the area of leadership development, Greenleaf formulated his conceptualization of servant leadership. Although servant leadership has ancient roots, the contemporary emphasis on servant leadership was influenced significantly by Greenleaf's reflections.

Greenleaf's understanding of servant leadership includes an important consideration around leadership power.

> A fresh critical look is being taken at the issues of power and authority, and people are beginning to learn, however haltingly, to relate to one another in less coercive and more creatively supporting ways. A new moral principle is emerging, which holds that the only authority deserving of one's allegiance is that which is freely and knowingly granted by the led to the leader in response to, and in proportion to, the clearly evident servant stature of the leader. Those who choose to follow this principle will not casually accept the authority of existing institutions. Rather, they will freely respond only to individuals who are chosen as leaders because they are proven and trusted as servants. To the extent that this principle prevails in the future, the only truly viable institutions will be those that are predominantly servant led.[6]

In Greenleaf's conceptualization of servant leadership, power resides more with followers than with leaders. As followers recognize the servant-oriented nature of their leaders, these followers are willing to recognize and respond to leaders as they utilize personal and positional authority in healthy ways.

Addressing this shift in leadership practice, Frank LaFasto and Carl Larson write, "There is clear movement away from understanding leadership as positional authority and toward understanding leadership in terms of the relationship."[7] Rather than power being viewed primarily in relationship to one's position, power in our emerging reality is more associated with personal authority.

This shift in power is important for anyone seeking to foster an authentically collaborative community. As leaders learn to draw increasingly on personal rather than positional power, coordination and collaboration between leaders and followers, as well as among team members, becomes a realistic vision. The aim is not to eliminate power in organizations. The aim is to recognize where power is present, and then to draw on healthy and empowering sources of authority rather than coercive sources that diminish others.

Collaboration and the Development of Authentic Partners

As leaders emphasize personal authority over positional authority, the development of a community with authentic partners becomes more of a possibility. Fostering collaboration in communities is best accomplished when individual team members are seen not as agents of the agendas of others but rather as partners in shared work and common agendas.

Humility provides a context where others may contribute.

The following quote attributed to Dwight D. Eisenhower captures the heart of partnership: "It is better to have one person working with you than three people working for you." A hunger for power feeds the desire of leaders to have people working for them. When leadership is more about accomplishing important work and serving others along the way, then leaders want authentic partners alongside them in this important work.

Humility

Once again this raises the importance of humility, a theme addressed in chapter 2 as well. Patrick Lencioni argues that humility is the greatest and most indispensable attribute for team players because humility provides the basis for healthy and collaborative engagement with others.

Here are a few of the characteristics Lencioni highlights that are related to humble team members. Humble team members

- Are quick to point out the contributions of others
- Are slow to seek attention
- Share credit
- Emphasize team over self
- Define success collectively rather than individually[8]

Humility provides space for others to enter into partnership together. Humility provides a context where others may contribute. Humility provides a healthy emotional culture where team members may offer their strengths in service of the common mission.

Presenting the core of collaborative engagement, Mark McCloskey notes that effective leaders recognize that each person is valuable, no one is sufficient, and all are required for the enduring success of the organization.[9] Leaders and organizational members can never own and embody such principles without humility. Humility is an essential foundation for effectively fostering a collaborative environment in our organizations.

BUILDING COMMUNITY AND PARTNERSHIP

Humility also provides space for building community. Addressing key servant-leadership behaviors, Jim Laub engages the priority of building community and displaying authenticity in leadership.

Laub argues that leaders build community and display authenticity by building strong personal relationships, working collaboratively with others, valuing the differences of others, being open and accountable to others, learning from others, and maintaining integrity and trust.[10] Such leader behaviors help to nurture an environment where team members shift from overly competitive leadership agendas to encouraging followers to work together in their common mission.

Further emphasizing the role that partnership plays in this approach to leadership, Laub highlights that servant-leadership practices stand against autocratic and paternalistic forms of leadership. While autocratic leaders treat followers as servants and paternalistic leaders treat followers as children, Laub argues that servant leaders treat followers as genuine partners.

If the mission matters, then so does authentic collaboration where followers are treated as partners. In multiple studies examining the effect of servant leadership on diverse outcomes, I (Justin) have repeatedly found in my research that servant leadership is not simply a good idea—it also works.

Servant leadership, which includes treating followers as partners, nurtures a collaborative environment with a greater sense of job satisfaction, higher levels of organizational commitment, a greater sense of person-organization fit, higher levels of team effectiveness, higher levels of organizational performance, and higher levels of overall leadership effectiveness.[11]

Although emphasizing practices such as community building can feel like a distraction from the work of an organization, these soft skills have solid results as employees become partners and followers become team members on a mission together.

SHARED VISION AND EMPOWERED TEAM MEMBERS

In their book *The Leadership Challenge*, James Kouzes and Barry Posner note that dreams don't become realities through the actions of a single person. The task of envisioning and implementing these dreams must include empowered partners.

Because of this, Kouzes and Posner highlight the priority of leaders inspiring a shared vision and enabling others to act on this shared vision. Leaders in the past likely viewed the task of casting a vision as primarily their own responsibility, but as power is being pushed out of the front office into the lives of partner-employees, formulating and casting vision must include the voices of these vital partners.

Leadership in our emerging environment is not just about vision; it is about *shared* vision. Kouzes and Posner note, "No matter how grand the dream of an individual visionary, if others don't see in it the possibility of realizing their own hopes and desires, they won't follow."[12] In healthy organizations, vision is owned by both leaders and followers.

> *Leadership in our emerging environment is not just about vision; it is about* shared *vision.*

As leaders foster collaboration through a shared vision, this provides a basis for empowering team members to act on these visions. The vision in this model is not merely the leader's vision, but rather a vision owned by leaders and followers alike. Because of this, when it comes time to enact the vision, followers have a vested interest in the vision's successful implementation. This is where the concept of enabling others to act comes into play in collaborative processes.

Kouzes and Posner write, "Exemplary leaders *enable others to act.* They foster collaboration and build trust." Because command-and-control techniques of the past no longer apply or work, Kouzes and Posner affirm the importance of enabling others: "Leaders make it possible for others to do good work. They know those who are expected to produce the results must feel a sense of personal power and ownership."[13]

Vision is vital to any leadership process, but vision birthed in isolation dies in isolation. Leaders today must build community around a shared vision, and then empower this community of partners to own and enact the vision together.

TEAM STRUCTURES AND PROCESSES

This emphasis on fostering collaboration, community, and shared vision calls for a better understanding of what contributes to effective teams and teamwork.

Addressing the shift toward more decentralized structures, John Gardner notes, "Most leadership today is an attempt to accomplish purposes through (or in spite of) large, intricately organized systems." Gardner's point is that as organizations and society grow increasingly complex, "there is no possibility that centralized authority can call all the shots," and that "individuals in all segments and at all levels must be prepared to exercise leader-like initiative and responsibility, using their local knowledge to solve problems at their level."[14] This is a call for increased collaboration and for effective team processes.

Tuckman's model. One of the early models providing insight into how teams work well is Bruce Tuckman's theory of the normal developmental sequence in groups. His model includes the four stages of forming, storming, norming, and performing (see fig. 3.1).[15]

Figure 3.1
Tuckman's Model of Team Development

| Forming | Storming | Norming | Performing |

The forming stage is a time for orientation, with members getting to know one another and the leader serving as a facilitator of both social interchange and helping to establish relevant group norms.

The storming stage helps teams recognize that disagreement and conflict are a normal part of group processes. In this stage the leader encourages participation from multiple parties, helps to surface differences, and seeks to empower the group in healthy conflict-management strategies.

The norming stage is about the establishment of cohesion and order. Although some norms are introduced in earlier steps, the norming phase further reinforces and normalizes these as the leader helps the team clarify values, norms, and team roles.

Finally, the performing stage is about realizing the benefits of the team's investment in the earlier stages. As the team moves into the performing stage, the team experiences deeper levels of collaboration and cooperation and leans into problems together as they seek creative solutions. The leader's role at this stage emphasizes facilitation of task accomplishment as team members work together in their common responsibilities.

The priority of collaborative climate and trust. A successful journey in teamwork is premised on a collaborative climate and mutual trust. On the first point of collaborative climate, Larson and LaFasto note that "Collaborative climate refers to the extent to which members communicate openly, disclose problems, share information, help each other overcome obstacles, and discover ways of succeeding."[16] Such a climate provides the context where individual members of the team learn to work effectively with and trust one another.

Noting that trust is the mainstay virtue for the commerce of humanity, Larson and LaFasto further note that "[trust] is the bond that allows any kind of significant relationship to exist between people," and that "once broken, it is not easily—if ever—recovered."[17] For better or worse, trust—and lack of trust—affects team performance.

Larson and LaFasto see trust produced in a climate where honesty, openness, consistency, and respect are present. Not only are leaders responsible for managing the objective parts of organizations—such as budgets, processes, and systems—they also must attend to the climate of their organization. Healthy and collaborative dimensions of the organizational climate help foster an environment within which team members trust one another and maintain a focus on what matters most to the team and organization.

Collaboration and Contextual Considerations

As leaders and organizations consider increased emphasis on collaborative and team-oriented practices, attending to generational and cultural considerations is vital.

GENERATIONAL CONSIDERATIONS

Individuals in the Generation X and Millennial segments of society—those born in the late 1970s through the early 2000s—often have a strong preference for collaborative models of leadership. Val Nordbye and I (Justin) found this to be true in our study of a US nonprofit drawing on employees from this demographic.[18]

In this study, young adult employees demonstrated a strong preference for styles of leadership that provide room for decision making by those most qualified to make the decision, not simply those in positional authority. These employees also demonstrated a strong preference for styles of leadership that view staff as partners in the work.

The study not only looked at generational preferences toward collaborative styles of leadership over autocratic styles but also demonstrated that such collaborative and servant-oriented styles of leadership led to higher levels of performance across multiple organizational measures. Such research points toward a reality that many leaders already observe in practice: young organizational members value and appreciate collaborative practices over more command-and-control styles of directive leadership.

CULTURAL CONSIDERATIONS

Beyond generational shifts, it also is important to consider collaborative and team-oriented practices in light of cultural differences. One of the largest leadership studies ever conducted is the Global Leadership and Organizational Behavior Effectiveness research project, known as the GLOBE studies.[19]

Drawing on responses from over seventeen thousand managers across sixty-two countries, the GLOBE studies provide key insight into conversations surrounding leadership and cultural differences in the global context. Among many dimensions of the project, the GLOBE studies highlight six leadership behaviors and compare these across cultures (see fig. 3.2). Relevant to our discussion of collaboration is GLOBE's examination of participative leadership.

Figure 3.2
Types of Leadership Behaviors

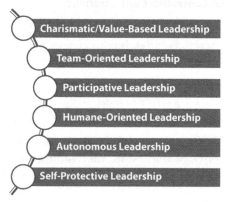

In the GLOBE research project, participative leadership pertains to a leader's inclusion of others in decision making and implementation. This can be quite different across cultures. As an example, the Anglo and Nordic cultural clusters in the study have higher levels of participative leadership, while the Confucian Asia and Eastern Europe cultural clusters have lower levels of participative leadership.

Such differences relate in part to what some students of culture call power distance. The cultural variable of power distance relates to the degree to which a culture shares power unequally. A culture with higher power distance exhibits strong lines separating leaders and followers. A culture with lower power distance exhibits flatter organizational structures, where employees can approach and even disagree with leaders.

Variables like power distance need to be considered as leaders work to foster collaboration in our increasingly globalized world. In cultural contexts with lower power distance, collaborative structures may be received more naturally. In cultural contexts with higher power distance, leaders implementing collaborative approaches in organizations may need to work at a slower pace of change. Along with generational considerations, these cultural considerations are also a high priority for global leaders wishing to foster collaboration.

Collaboration in Practice

Throughout this chapter we have argued for the priority of collaboration as demonstrated in authentic partnership and team-oriented practices. But if collaboration is to take hold in a community, fostering collaboration must begin with those possessing organizational influence. On this point, McCloskey observes that "collaborative engagement typically begins and ends with the attitudes and behaviors of those with formal authority."[20] Above, we considered the priority of collaboration in light of its biblical and theoretical roots. In this final section, we provide recommendations for practice, starting with a case on nurturing shared vision in a community.

Collaboration: A Case for Shared Vision

Earlier in this chapter we highlighted that vision birthed in isolation dies in isolation. One expression of collaborative leadership is the importance of building community around a shared vision and then empowering the community to own and enact the vision together.

Pastor Dave Ridder and the community at Grace Point Church in Newtown, Pennsylvania, provide a helpful example of how shared vision may be effectively nurtured in an organization. Ridder served as pastor of Grace Point from 1984 to 2007. About ten years into his ministry at Grace Point, Ridder was learning about the importance of vision and recognized this was a necessary emphasis for the community. With the guidance of a consultant, Ridder gathered with the church staff and board members for an intentional time of strategic planning and vision casting over a weekend retreat.

Coming out of this retreat, the leadership team developed their *Vision 2000* statement and associated strategic priorities. *Vision 2000* was brought to the full congregation at a quarterly business meeting, where it was unanimously passed. In the five years leading up to 2000, though the church experienced some successes, such as a fruitful capital campaign for a new building, overall the ministry was facing a lack of momentum, and the goals of *Vision 2000* were largely unrealized or at least under-realized.

In 2001 this led Pastor Ridder and the leaders of the church to reconsider how the church could approach the process of vision formation and casting. For nearly a year the leaders and members of the church pursued a renewed sense of spiritual vitality in the congregation as they sought God through extended seasons of prayer, confession, and worship. Ridder describes this season as a time when a fresh wind of the Spirit was blowing through Grace Point.

By 2002 there was a sense that the time was right to think intentionally through their vision again, but this time in a much more collaborative way. This collaborative process included monthly Vision Team gatherings—meetings that were open to any in the congregation wishing to participate. The Vision Team intentionally thought through the results of church surveys, community demographic studies, and other important insights, helping the team better understand the core DNA of the church and community.

By 2003 the Vision Team had pulled together multiple drafts of their 2.0 vision statement. By the time they had come to a sixth draft, a group of forty ministry leaders and members from the church gathered to speak into the emerging vision. The church elders used this input to refine a seventh draft, and then this version was presented to the full congregation early in the summer. The congregation was asked to mull it over during the summer months and pray that God would direct Grace Point through this process.

After the summer, Pastor Ridder and other team members preached through a series of eight messages focused on biblical perspectives related to the emerging vision. Following this series in the fall, small groups in the church were asked to discuss the vision and bring feedback to the leaders. An open town hall meeting was provided for small group leaders to report their findings to the wider congregation.

Significant changes were made in the final draft—the eighth draft—based on the feedback, and the community expressed gratitude for having had the opportunity to shape the vision directly. In addition to the vision statement's unanimous approval at a congregational meeting, well over one hundred people had directly contributed in some way to writing the final vision statement.

In contrast to the initial *Vision 2000* work, this vision 2.0 work was owned widely by the congregation. In *Vision 2000*, members were largely renters of the vision. In vision 2.0, the members were owners of the vision. For some, this work of fostering shared vision may seem like too much effort. But it is the extra steps in a shared process that solidify a deep sense of investment on the part of community members. It is this effort that moves community members from renting to owning when it comes to the organization's mission and vision.

Collaboration: Insights for Practice

Whether it is engaging a community with shared vision or embracing more team-oriented practices in your organization, fostering collaboration is an important factor contributing to effective leadership. As you consider your own collaborative processes, here are three quick principles we offer as you take the next step in your leadership journey.

Lead with Humility

Healthy collaboration begins with humility. In order to effectively collaborate with others, there needs to be an authentic belief that you do not have all the answers and that other people bring value to the table that complements you and the value you bring.

In his book *Good to Great*, Jim Collins engages the concept of Level 5 Leadership.[21] Level 5 leaders possess a unique blend of professional will and personal humility. Although they are driven to get things done for the organizations they serve, their drive is accompanied by humility. Leaders possessing this humility are quick to acknowledge their own limitations and quick to celebrate the contributions of others. Such humility is vital for collaborative work to thrive in the face of tough organizational challenges. In the week ahead, take time to intentionally find areas where you see and acknowledge your reliance on others in the organization.

Celebrate the Contributions of Others

With a leader's willingness to think of oneself less comes an increased capacity to see and celebrate the contributions of others. In chapter 4 we take up the practice of valuing and appreciating in more detail. But celebrating others is relevant to our conversation here as well.

In order to foster authentic collaboration, leaders must first recognize the contributions of team members and then be willing to step back and provide space for team members to thrive in these contributions. Some servant-leadership researchers describe this as the leader's role of standing back.[22] Standing back relates to a leader's giving priority to the interests of others first and then retreating into the background in order to see the success and contributions of others celebrated.

The concept of standing back presses this important question: *Are you okay with your team members being smarter than you and better than you at something?* Leadership driven by ego will struggle with this. However, through embracing humility and a willingness to stand back, the work of fostering collaboration provides a pathway for team members to become authentic partners in the mission of your organization. Take time in the week ahead to celebrate the significant contributions of your team members. Celebrate these partners who are serving in the shared mission of your organization.

Embrace What Is Better Together

When considering collaboration and the practice of teams, an African proverb captures the heart of teamwork: "If you want to go fast, go alone. If you want to go far, go together." Engaging in collaborative teamwork is typically not the easiest or the fastest approach, but we contend that it is the more effective option.

Teams are more helpful for bigger projects over a longer period of time. When the outcome requires coordinated work being brought together to advance collective goals that will be collectively evaluated, then a team is the most effective approach. Although teamwork done well tends to take more time than working as an individual, this extra time investment pays off in the quality of the team's performance. Teams are best when the stakes are high and quality is more important than speed.

Teams provide a context for better ideas and increased insight. Teams provide a context for idea generation and for increasing insight for complex problem solving. Teams provide a place for multiple perspectives to emerge, and teams facilitate creativity as members bounce new ideas off one another. Further, teams provide a context for *more* ideas to be generated, which generally leads to better ideas being generated so long as groupthink is proactively addressed.

> *Teams are best when the stakes are high and quality is more important than speed.*

Teams provide increased courage to face challenges. Being alone can be a challenge in calm organizational seasons, but being alone can be a major challenge during turbulent organizational seasons. Teams provide a context for facing problems together and an esprit de corps—the feeling that we are in this together. Teams provide a context for the collective group taking bigger risks than individuals, because when we are in it together there is a courage that is infused into the group that most individuals do not experience in isolation. Together, teams are able to face challenges that feel too big for any one individual.

Teams provide a natural presence of peer support. Because teamwork is done with others, it provides the opportunity for increased peer support. Teams provide a context for improved morale because teams provide space for mutual encouragement among members. Teams also provide a context for support and mutual accountability—accountability that facilitates collaboration in working toward goal accomplishment on behalf of the group and organization.

Teams provide a context for mentoring and training. Teams provide a unique opportunity for organizations to develop younger or newer talent, because the teams provide an organic environment for leadership development. Teams provide a natural context for modeling preferred organizational behavior and a place for both formal and informal mentoring to occur. Rather than providing leadership development and mentoring as a side program, teams provide a natural environment in which emerging team members and leaders can observe and interact with tenured team members and leaders in the normal flow of work life. Teams provide a context for members to be valued, developed, and released as partner-contributors.

Conclusion

Whether working directly in the context of teams or bringing a spirit of collaboration to a variety of organizational structures, leaders who nurture an environment where team members work together rather than compete against one another are vital to effective organizational leadership. Fostering collaboration is a biblically consistent and research-based practice that leaders may utilize to engage authentic partners in the important mission their organization is serving.

Next Steps

- Take some time to observe intentionally areas where you see and acknowledge your reliance on others in the organization.
- Take some time to celebrate the significant contributions of your team members; celebrate these partners who are serving in the shared mission of your organization.
- Take some time to consider how this proverb applies to your organization: "If you want to go far, go together." Consider how a collaborative process could yield superior performance in your organization.

Resources for a Deeper Look

Asumang, Annang. "Modelling the Gospel in Joyful Partnership: Exemplars and the Uniting Theme of Philippians." *Journal of the South African Theological Seminary* 13 (March 2012): 1–50.

Jennings, Mark A. *The Price of Partnership in the Letter of Paul to the Philippians: "Make My Joy Complete."* New York: Bloomsbury T&T Clark, 2018.

LaFasto, Frank, and Carl Larson. *When Teams Work Best: 6,000 Team Members and Leaders Tell What It Takes to Succeed.* Thousand Oaks, CA: Sage, 2001.

Lencioni, Patrick. *The Five Dysfunctions of a Team: A Leadership Fable.* New York: Wiley, 2007.

Osborne, Larry W. *Sticky Teams: Keeping Your Leadership Team and Staff on the Same Page.* Grand Rapids: Zondervan, 2010.

Part 2

Understanding the Priority of People

PART 1 OF THIS BOOK focused on beginning with authentic leaders. Based on this foundation of authentic and purposeful leaders, we now turn to understanding the priority of people in part 2. In this part of the book, we emphasize the importance of leaders prioritizing and focusing on followers. This focus on followers begins with the leader's role in valuing and appreciating (chap. 4). Although it is important to appreciate the contribution that individuals make to the team and organization, the chapter begins with a more basic affirmation of the intrinsic value of people made in God's image. Leaders see this inherent value and find ways to communicate the care and value they have for the people with whom they work.

Based on this leadership practice of valuing and appreciating people, we turn in our next chapter to the leader's work of creating a place for individuality (chap. 5). In the twentieth century, approaches like scientific management aimed to standardize work and minimize human variation. Treating organizations and people like machines has some degree of efficiency, but this approach sacrifices the uniqueness of human creativity—creativity that provides real value to organizations. We call leaders to see and create a place for follower individuality in their work.

As leaders understand the priority of people, it becomes a top priority for these leaders to understand effective relational skills as well (chap. 6). As leaders foster collaboration, value and appreciate followers, and create space for follower individuality, all of this work necessitates effective relational skill on the part of the leader. In this chapter we engage the relational and intercultural skills needed to work effectively with followers in today's organizations.

4

Valuing and Appreciating

Introduction

In the introduction to this book we shared the story of the empowering leadership of Colleen Barrett, former president of Southwest Airlines. Part of her commitment included prioritizing and valuing people.

For Barrett, the people of Southwest Airlines were not simply cogs that made the organizational machine move; rather, they were valued members of the team who were to be treated as family. Barrett and her team would say to Southwest employees, "You are the most important Person to us. You are our most important Customer in terms of priority."[1]

Southwest Airlines has been very successful as a company. In an industry that historically has lost money, Southwest Airlines has continued to turn a profit year after year. But Barrett and the team at Southwest understand the real source of this success. They prioritize and value their people.

This is the focus of our chapter—the leadership practice of *valuing and appreciating*. Because leaders work with people, understanding the value of people and their contribution is a vital part of leadership. Leaders who understand the practice of valuing and appreciating people for who they are and what they contribute will be positioned well for effectively leading in their organizations.

If, deep down, leaders see followers as problems to be controlled and managed, positive leadership behaviors like valuing and appreciating are likely not a priority; in these negative leadership models, the focus is on control and fear. If, however, leaders see followers as the organization's number-one asset—an asset to be empowered and released in the organization's mission—valuing and appreciating are vital.

David Gergen captures the essence of this shift and the importance of seeing followers in such a light: "Increasingly, the best leaders are those who don't order but persuade; don't dictate but draw out; don't squeeze but grow the people around them. They push power out of the front office, down into the organization, and become a leader of leaders. Most important, as Peter Drucker insisted, they understand that the people in an organization are its No. 1 asset."[2]

Do you believe that the people of your organization are your number-one asset? Leaders who see this reality recognize that taking time to express value and appreciation of followers is not wasted time. As James Kouzes and Barry Posner argue, "Leaders get the best from others not by building fires under people but by building the fire within them."[3] This means learning to lead with love over fear. This means learning to express value and appreciation in tangible ways.

In this chapter, we explore the topic through the following perspectives: (1) valuing and appreciating in biblical perspective, (2) valuing and appreciating in contemporary perspective, and (3) valuing and appreciating in practice.

Valuing and Appreciating in Biblical Perspective

If, as we have said, servant leadership is focused first on people rather than on tasks, then valuing and appreciating those people should be among the highest priorities of the leader. It is interesting that in the letters of the apostle Paul, he does not refer to those he works with as his "disciples" (*mathētai*) or "followers." To be sure, he often calls on those to whom he is writing to follow his example or to imitate him (1 Cor. 4:16; 11:1; Phil. 3:17; 4:9; 1 Thess. 1:6). As we saw in chapter 1, modeling or teaching by example was his primary means of training others. But instead of "disciple" or "follower," he uses terms like "brother/sister," "co-worker," "partner," and "fellow soldier."[4] These are terms of partnership and teamwork, rather than authority and subordination.

We touched briefly on Paul's appreciation for two of his coworkers in chapter 3. In Philippians 2, Paul commends both Timothy and Epaphroditus for their loyal and faithful service. Epaphroditus had been sent by the Philippian church to care for Paul's needs. He had done so faithfully, despite a severe illness that almost killed him. Paul has now sent him back to Philippi with a strong commendation, telling the church there to "welcome him in the Lord with great joy, and honor people like him" (Phil. 2:29). In a culture like that of the Greco-Roman world, where honor and shame were among the most important social values, such a public statement of commendation would bring great honor to Epaphroditus.

Paul's praise for Timothy is even more lavish. Paul tells the Philippian church that since he is under house arrest and unable to come himself, he is planning to send Timothy in his place. Paul then warmly affirms that he has no one like Timothy, who genuinely cares for them. While so many are motivated by selfishness and self-interest, Timothy passionately pursues the cause of Christ (Phil. 2:19–23). It is significant that Paul's appreciation for Timothy as a person is based on Timothy's own love and appreciation for the Philippians. This is leadership motivated by a genuine love for people, not by a desire to be first or even a desire to get things done.

The Example of Barnabas

While we see the leadership quality of valuing and appreciating people in Paul and in Timothy, another character in the book of Acts provides a repeated and consistent example of this. This is a man from Cyprus named Joseph, who is nicknamed "Barnabas," meaning "Son of Encouragement" (or, in contemporary idiom, "Mr. Encourager"). Barnabas could be called one of the "minor characters" in Acts, since he doesn't play as prominent a role as people like Peter and Paul. Yet he keeps showing up in the story, and each time he's doing the same thing: bringing people together and building bridges of understanding. These episodes point to Barnabas's character as a leader who particularly values and appreciates people, bringing out the best in them.

VALUING BY SEEING THE NEEDS OF OTHERS (ACTS 4:36–37)

The first mention of Barnabas is in a summary of the church's unity and generosity (Acts 4:32–35). The narrator tells us that there are no impoverished people in the Jerusalem church because whenever there were needs, someone would step forward to meet those needs. The specific example of Barnabas is then given: "Joseph, a Levite from Cyprus, whom the apostles called Barnabas (which means 'son of encouragement'), sold a field he owned and brought the money and put it at the apostles' feet" (4:36–37).

The first thing we learn about Barnabas is that he is concerned enough about the needs of others to sell his own property. In the narrative of Acts, this account of Barnabas's generosity is contrasted with the deceit and hypocrisy of Ananias and Sapphira, who are judged by God for lying about the money they give for the poor (5:1–10). The implication is that Barnabas has given from pure motives. His motivation was not praise or prestige but love and concern for those in need. A servant leader sees people not simply as resources to be utilized but rather as valued human beings made in God's image.

Valuing by Seeking Reconciliation (Acts 9:26–27)

The next time we meet Barnabas in Acts, he is again seeking to bring about reconciliation. The episode occurs several years later, after the conversion of Saul (Paul). As a zealous and committed Jewish leader, Saul considered the fledgling Christian movement to be a false religion, a cult undermining Judaism. Following the execution of Stephen, the first Christian martyr, Saul began going house to house, arresting and imprisoning Christians (Acts 8:1–3). With letters of reference from the high priest in Jerusalem, he headed to Damascus in Syria to arrest Christians there (9:1–2). On the way, however, a light from heaven blinded him, and a voice from heaven announced, "Saul, Saul, why do you persecute me?" (9:4). The speaker identified himself as the resurrected Jesus, and Saul's life was radically transformed. The great persecutor of the church became its greatest defender.

Three years after his Damascus road experience, Saul came to Jerusalem to meet the apostles. He no doubt wanted to learn the stories of Jesus from these original disciples. Yet the Jerusalem apostles feared it was a trap, thinking Paul was seeking to lure them out of hiding and arrest them. Luke writes, "When he came to Jerusalem, he tried to join the disciples, but they were all afraid of him, not believing that he really was a disciple" (Acts 9:26). Yet, true to form, one man was willing to take a risk: "But Barnabas took him and brought him to the apostles. He told them how Saul on his journey had seen the Lord and that the Lord had spoken to him, and how in Damascus he had preached fearlessly in the name of Jesus" (9:27).

Again, we see Barnabas willing to take a risk to bring about reconciliation. This time the threat was not a loss of wealth but the risk of arrest, imprisonment, and even execution. But for Barnabas reconciliation was worth the risk. The apostle Paul would become the first great theologian and most effective church planter in the early church. But it was Barnabas who opened the way for Paul.

Effective servant leaders value relationships enough to take risks to bring about reconciliation. And, historically, peacemaking can be risky business. Consider Egyptian president Anwar Sadat. In a historic visit to Jerusalem in November 1977, Sadat acknowledged the State of Israel's right to exist, a first for an Arab leader. Though widely denounced by his Arab colleagues, in 1979 he signed a peace treaty with Israel, a treaty that still holds today. But

in October 1981, while reviewing a military parade in Cairo, Sadat was assassinated by Muslim fundamentalists. Peacemaking can cost you your life.

Or consider Israeli prime minister Yitzhak Rabin. Rabin was awarded the
Nobel Peace Prize in 1994 for the Israeli-Palestinian peace accord with Yasser
Arafat. A year later, in November 1995, Rabin was assassinated by a right-
wing Israeli nationalist. Of course, US history has its own examples. Most
famously, Martin Luther King Jr. was silenced by an assassin's bullet on April
4, 1968, for seeking racial reconciliation and justice for all. Peacemaking is
risky business, since the forces of evil in this world profit from hatred and
conflict. Servant leaders don't pit followers against one another but rather
encourage cooperation, unity, and reconciliation.

Valuing by Promoting Diversity and Crossing Cultural Barriers (Acts 11:19–24)

The third reference to Barnabas in Acts appears in chapter 11. It is sparked
by a shocking development in the church. Following the stoning of Stephen,
many from the Jerusalem church fled. Luke reports: "Now those who had
been scattered by the persecution that broke out when Stephen was killed
traveled as far as Phoenicia, Cyprus and Antioch, spreading the word only
among Jews. Some of them, however, men from Cyprus and Cyrene, went
to Antioch and began to speak to Greeks also, telling them the good news
about the Lord Jesus. The Lord's hand was with them, and a great number
of people believed and turned to the Lord" (Acts 11:19–21).

When news reached the church in Jerusalem about this development, they
were no doubt uncertain about what to do. The question of how Gentiles
could be saved was one of the most chal-
lenging issues the early church faced. Did
Gentiles first need to become Jews (the true
people of God) before they could become
followers of Jesus (the Jewish Messiah)? To
check out the situation, the church sends
the man with a proven track record of resolving conflicts: Barnabas (Acts 11:22).

*Leaders who value people look
beyond external differences
of gender, ethnicity, and
cultural heritage, valuing
people . . . as human beings
created in the image of God.*

Some leaders would no doubt have come
to Antioch and demanded change before
allowing Gentiles to enter the church. Get
them on the good kosher diet; teach them
the stories of Jewish heritage; and circumcise the men (!). Then we'll see. But
this was not Barnabas's attitude: "When he arrived and saw what the grace

of God had done, he was glad and encouraged them all to remain true to the Lord with all their hearts. He was a good man, full of the Holy Spirit and faith, and a great number of people were brought to the Lord" (Acts 11:23–24).

Barnabas looked past cultural differences and saw straight into their hearts ("he . . . saw what the grace of God had done"). Leaders who value people look beyond external differences of gender, ethnicity, and cultural heritage, valuing people for their inherent worth as human beings created in the image of God.

Valuing by Seeing and Encouraging the Strengths of Others (Acts 11:25–26)

Another example of valuing and appreciating others comes at the end of this episode. After working in Antioch for a time, Barnabas heads north to Tarsus in Cilicia to look for Saul. After his visit to Jerusalem in chapter 9, Saul had returned to Tarsus (Acts 9:26–31). This was prompted by attempts on his life in Jerusalem, since he was viewed as a traitor by many Jews there. Saul's presence in Jerusalem created such a volatile situation that the apostles sent him back to Tarsus, both to protect his life and to bring stability to the Jerusalem church (9:28–31). Barnabas, knowing that Saul has been called to preach to the Gentiles, now goes and brings him from Tarsus to Antioch (11:25–26).

Here we see another important aspect of valuing and appreciating others. Barnabas is not only thinking strategically about the church in Antioch, since Saul would certainly be an asset in working with Gentiles. He is also thinking about the encouragement and development of Saul's strengths. What better laboratory for Saul to learn and grow with reference to Jewish-Gentile relationships than a Jewish church in Antioch with a growing Gentile minority?

> *Servant leaders who truly value people are concerned first and foremost with the growth and development of the people they lead.*

As leaders, we value people by learning about their strengths and gifts and finding opportunities for them to develop those gifts. Leaders seeking their own self-interest will channel followers into tasks that promote their own agenda. But servant leaders who truly value people are concerned first and foremost with the growth and development of the people they lead.

Valuing by Empowering Others above Personal Prestige or Position (Acts 13–14)

The work of Barnabas and Saul in Antioch not only honed their skills in working with Gentiles but also became a launching pad for the first great missionary outreach to the Gentiles: "While they were worshiping the Lord and fasting, the Holy Spirit said, 'Set apart for me Barnabas and Saul for the work to which I have called them.' So after they had fasted and prayed, they placed their hands on them and sent them off" (Acts 13:2–3).

Barnabas and Saul set out from Antioch and Syria and go first to the island of Cyprus, Barnabas's homeland. After a successful outreach there, they sail north to Perga and into the Roman province of Galatia, where they establish several churches. On returning to the church in Antioch after an enormously successful mission, they report "all that God had done through them and how he had opened a door of faith to the Gentiles" (Acts 14:27).

Several curious things happen on this journey. First, Luke, the author of Acts, begins using Saul's Roman name, Paul, in place of his Jewish one, Saul. Because his family has Roman citizenship (Acts 22:28), both names were likely given to Paul at birth. But he begins using the name Paul because of his ministry to Gentiles. Second, whereas prior to this trip Barnabas is clearly the leader and is always named first (11:26, 30; 12:25; 13:2, 7: "Barnabas and Saul"), in the middle of the journey the author suddenly switches order: "Paul and Barnabas" (Acts 13:42, 43, 50; 14:1, 3, 23; etc.). It seems clear that from this point on Paul assumes primary leadership of the group. Today we describe this as "Paul's first missionary journey," even though Barnabas clearly is the initial leader. Yet there is no indication that this produced conflict between the two. It seems that Barnabas recognized Paul's gifts and abilities and encouraged him to leadership.

It is not easy for leaders to relinquish their authority and leadership role to others. Yet a servant leader is one whose focus is primarily on equipping and empowering others, rather than achieving a personal agenda. We value those we lead by acknowledging, encouraging, and nurturing their gifts and abilities. This should be the case even if the promotion of their gifts and abilities undermines or downplays our own. This might mean giving the lead in a project to one of our coworkers, even though we enjoy the praise we have received for leading that project in the past. For a pastor, it might mean at times relinquishing the pulpit to an intern or associate, even if this means less authority over or respect from the congregation. Valuing others means keeping our egos in check and learning to appreciate and encourage the abilities of others.

Valuing by Seeking the Best in Others (Acts 15:39; 2 Timothy 4:11)

A final example of the value Barnabas places on people is seen in the case of John Mark, Barnabas's cousin, who went with Paul and Barnabas as an assistant on their first missionary journey (Acts 13:5). During that trip, Mark left the group and returned home to Jerusalem. Although the narrator does not tell us why Mark left, Paul clearly viewed it as a desertion (15:38). When Paul proposes to Barnabas that they return to visit the churches they started on their first journey, Barnabas agrees and suggests that they take John Mark. Paul refuses because of the desertion, and Luke tells us, "They had such a sharp disagreement that they parted company. Barnabas took Mark and sailed for Cyprus, but Paul chose Silas and left, commended by the believers to the grace of the Lord" (15:39–40).

Luke does not offer an opinion as to whether Paul or Barnabas is in the right here. And God uses this incident to double the missionary impact, with two groups instead of just one. Yet it is significant that Barnabas is again playing to character. He is putting people first, looking out for their best interest, promoting reconciliation, ready to give a second chance. It is also significant that Paul was ultimately reconciled with John Mark. In 2 Timothy 4:11, Paul writes to Timothy, "Get Mark and bring him with you, because he is helpful to me in ministry." Though previously a failure, Mark turned into a success; though once a deserter, Mark is now "helpful" for Paul's ministry. Of course, Mark has even more of a legacy than this, since church tradition tells us that he is the author of the Second Gospel, the Gospel according to Mark.

Barnabas was willing to see the best in Mark and so gave him a second chance. The chance paid off, and Mark turned out to be a great success. Leaders who value their team members do not consider individual mistakes or shortcomings to be disqualifying failures. They are rather part of the training process that leads to success. When Thomas Edison was criticized for the many failures in his attempts to create a light bulb, he is said to have replied, "I have not failed. I've just found 10,000 ways that won't work." Failure can be just one step on the road to success.

Though a relatively minor character in Acts, Barnabas turns out to be a remarkable example of a leader who values and appreciates people. When there is a potential rift between the rich and the poor in the Jerusalem church, Barnabas reaches out to meet the needs of the poor at great personal sacrifice. When the apostles refuse to be reconciled with Saul because of fear of betrayal, Barnabas takes a dangerous risk. For Barnabas, the power of reconciliation is worth the risk. When Gentiles respond to the gospel in Antioch, sparking confusion among the Jerusalem leadership, Barnabas heads to Antioch. There he looks past external ethnicity and culture and sees hearts changed by the grace of God. When Saul needs training and mentoring, Barnabas brings him alongside as his partner. And then when Saul/Paul begins to exceed Barnabas in effectiveness, Barnabas sets aside his pride and encourages Paul to leadership. Effective leaders don't let their egos get in the way of propelling others to success. Finally, when a young assistant named John Mark fails miserably, Barnabas is ready to give him a second chance. Leaders who value people consider failure to be just one step on the way to success.

Valuing and Appreciating in Contemporary Perspective

Contemporary theory and research build on these biblical perspectives by providing additional insight into the importance of leaders valuing and appreciating their followers. In my (Justin's) research on the topic, a follower who affirms that they "feel appreciated by a supervisor for what I contribute" was a statistically significant predictor of effective leadership practice.[5]

Leaders and followers alike have a natural desire for being valued and appreciated. In our discussion of these themes, we will emphasize two primary sides to this conversation. First, people desire to be valued not only for what they contribute but first and foremost for who they are as people. The leadership practice of valuing people begins with leaders valuing people for who they are as human beings created by God with value and dignity.

People desire to be valued not only for what they contribute but first and foremost for who they are as people.

Second, people also have a desire to be appreciated for the contributions they bring to organizations and teams. The leadership practice of appreciating people extends this inherent valuing of people to the next level of recognizing and affirming the contribution people bring to the team.

In light of this, we will organize our discussion of contemporary leadership theory and research for this section in the following areas: (1) valuing others and (2) appreciating others.

Valuing Others

Throughout the previous chapters we point to an important shift in the literature toward empowering approaches to leadership. At the foundation of this shift is an explicit call for leaders to value others. In an ultimate sense, people are valuable not primarily because of their contributions but because of their humanity.

From a Christian perspective, this valuing of others is grounded in God's creating people in his image with value and dignity. Additionally, God's gospel love for his people—a love that depends not on performance but on God's unmerited favor—provides a model for seeing, valuing, and loving people.

Business leader Max De Pree puts it this way: "We are created, I believe, in the image of God, a belief surrounded by enormous moral and ethical implications. Vital organizations don't grant their members authenticity; they acknowledge that people come already wrapped in authentic humanness."[6] As we emphasize the theme of valuing others, this principle that De Pree notes is essential. We value people based on this authentic humanness that each person has as an individual created in the image of God.

In this section, we engage the leadership practice of valuing people by highlighting the inherent value of people along with leadership practices that emphasize a concern for people and a commitment to followers.

THE INHERENT VALUE OF PEOPLE

One of the core themes found in the servant-leadership literature is valuing people. Jim Laub defines servant leadership as "an understanding and practice of leadership that places the good of those led over the self-interest of the leader."[7] Building on this definition, Laub's model of servant leadership begins with valuing people as the first and foundational dimension. Laub describes valuing people as trusting and believing in them, serving their needs before one's own, and listening to them in a receptive, nonjudgmental way.

Such leader behaviors provide a pathway for living out a commitment to treat followers not just as functional laborers but also as human beings deserving of dignity and respect. When leaders engage with followers in a manner that validates this human dignity, this behavior stands in stark contrast to more utilitarian models of leader-follower interaction.

Prioritizing people's value. In a study focused on the priority of valuing people, Mike McNeff and I (Justin) asked employees in a network of companies to share their perspectives on how senior leaders engaged—or did not engage—in valuing people in their company. Some of the responses of research participants highlight the importance of this leader practice for followers:

- "They never make you feel less. . . . They take interest in you and your family as people not just as an asset. They make decisions for the company with their employee's best interest in mind—not just the bottom line."
- "I have always been treated with great respect and always felt that my work was greatly valued."
- "[They] treat employees like valued family members."
- "Everyone is treated with respect."[8]

Reflecting on the overall findings from the study, we argue that valuing people had a disproportionately strong effect on the positive culture of the companies studied. The study findings also support the idea that valuing people is a foundation on which other empowering leadership behaviors may occur.

Leading with love. Another way to discuss this commitment to valuing people is with the language of love. Love may seem like an unconventional word to use when discussing leadership. Richard Daft observes, "Despite its power, the 'L' word is often looked upon with suspicion in the business world."[9] However, leadership scholars are pressing past this suspicion in order to study and affirm the importance of leaders showing love for followers in appropriate and meaningful expressions.

Leader love flows out of a commitment that leaders have to see people as inherently valuable—deserving of love and respect not because of what they do but rather for who they are. On this point, Kathleen Patterson writes, "Servant-leaders lead with love, are motivated by love, and serve their followers with love. . . . This love is a force, a force so intense that it changes lives—the lives of the followers, the life of the organization, and even the life of the leader."[10] Patterson affirms that while both fear and love will get results, the end gain is superior when followers are motivated by love.

Contrasting love and fear. Addressing these competing motivators, Jan Carlzon, former CEO of SAS Group, notes in an interview titled "The Art of Loving": "In my experience, there are two great motivators in life. One is fear. The other is love. You can manage an organization by fear, but if you do you will ensure that people don't perform up to their real capabilities. . . . But if you manage people by love—that is, if you show them respect and trust . . . in that kind of atmosphere, they dare to take risks. They can even make mistakes. Nothing can hurt."[11] While leadership by fear has the capacity to produce short-term gains for an organization, long-term effectiveness is better achieved through love as a motivator. For Patterson, this means a leadership atmosphere where respect, trust, and dignity are fostered.

In contrasting the benefits of love-based motivation to fear-based motivation, leaders must understand that fear diminishes trust and contributes to a lack of communication from followers. This is a significant problem, because effective leaders need honest and meaningful feedback. If something is not working, leaders need to hear about these challenges, not have challenges glossed over and filtered out of follower communication to leaders. When leaders motivate by fear, this type of honest feedback is shut down. Fear-based motivation destroys feedback and keeps leaders blind to potentially damaging realities in the organization.

Setting aside fear in favor of love opens the potential for leaders to motivate followers positively toward productive ends with a long-term perspective on organizational effectiveness. Daft writes, "If the job and the leader make me feel valued as a person and provide a sense of meaning and contribution to the community at large . . . then I will give you all I have to offer."[12] Leaders who value and love their followers open new pathways that help followers realize such meaningful contribution.

Lest we conclude this conversation seeing love as an option only for weak or passive leaders, Patterson reminds us that this approach to leadership actually must be quite tough. Patterson argues that this type of servant-oriented leadership is tough in love and tough in spirit and requires a willingness for leaders to "walk that extra mile, give of themselves, engage fully in the lives of the organization and the lives of their followers."[13] Leading with love does not mean being a pushover or viewing life through a Pollyannaish lens. It requires an intentional focus on seeing people as inherently valuable and then committing to love and care for people based on this inherent and God-given value.

CONCERN FOR PEOPLE

While contemporary leadership theories, like servant leadership, name the priorities of valuing and loving followers, earlier threads in the leadership literature emphasized the importance of leaders bringing a concern for people to their work. Two major sets of studies emphasizing this priority took place in the middle of the twentieth century at The Ohio State University and the University of Michigan.

In both sets of studies, task-oriented leadership behaviors were measured alongside people-oriented behaviors. The Ohio leadership studies measured initiating structure and consideration.[14] The Michigan leadership studies measured production orientation and employee orientation.[15] Several key findings emerged in these studies.

Although both types of leader behavior demonstrated some level of increased performance, some of the negative effects of leadership behavior that was task oriented are telling. Task-oriented leadership behavior resulted in increased levels of absenteeism, grievances, and turnover, and decreased levels of employee satisfaction. Conversely, relationship-oriented leadership behaviors resulted in lower levels of grievances and absenteeism and increased levels of satisfaction.

These studies provide an overall affirmation of the need for increased focus on employees and managers moving away from intensely structured supervision to more general levels of supervision that focus on meaningful feedback rather than what is seen as micromanagement.

Building on the findings from the Ohio and Michigan studies, Robert Blake and Jane Mouton developed a managerial grid that plots managerial style in light of concern for people and concern for production (see fig. 4.1). Their model describes people grouping around five styles of leadership, with the team management style characterized by both a high concern for people and a high concern for production. Blake and Mouton's work affirms the importance of both dimensions of the grid—a value and concern for both people and results.[16]

Figure 4.1
Management Style Grid

COMMITMENT TO FOLLOWERS

Building on these historic studies that emphasize concern for people, contemporary leadership theories such as transformational leadership and servant leadership help to provide additional balance in how the needs of leaders and followers are considered in organizations. For servant leadership specifically, an emphasis on follower focus is named as the core commitment for leaders wishing to empower followers to action and effectiveness.

Describing the essence of servant leadership, Greenleaf writes that "the servant leader is servant first" and is a person who takes care "to make sure that other people's highest priority needs are being served."[17] In other words, for Greenleaf a focus on followers and their needs is the distinguishing characteristic of servant leadership.

This distinguishing marker for servant-leadership practice is affirmed by others as well. For instance, Gregory Stone, Kathleen Patterson, and Robert

Russell note that servant leaders focus on followers, and the achievement of organizational objectives is a subordinate outcome.[18] This is not an argument for diminishing a focus on organizational goals and outcomes; we highlight the importance of navigating toward effectiveness in part 3 of the book. However, this is an argument for seeing focus on goals as secondary rather than primary. Servant-leadership theorists argue that the best way to achieve important organizational goals is to focus on serving the people who will deliver on those goals. "As followers become the focus of leaders, and are served by these leaders, followers become the primary agents by which organizational goals are met."[19]

In an effort to draw more attention to the importance of follower focus and provide a research instrument that may be used to measure a leader's focus on followers, I (Justin) developed the Purpose in Leadership Inventory.[20] The Purpose in Leadership Inventory is a tool that leadership researchers may utilize to study the following dimensions of leader focus: (a) follower focus, (b) goal orientation, and (c) leader purposefulness (see fig. 4.2).

Figure 4.2
Dimensions of Leader Focus

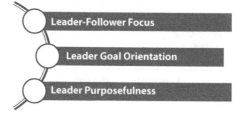

Each of these leader behaviors is positively related to overall leadership effectiveness and follower outcomes such as job satisfaction, organizational commitment, and person-organization fit. Comparing the relative importance of leader-follower focus, leader goal orientation, and leader purposefulness, leader-follower focus had the largest predictive effect on key organizational and follower outcomes. While the studies affirm the importance of leaders and followers working toward meaningful goals, this goal orientation stands alongside the first-order priority of leaders focusing on followers.

We would argue that leaders prioritizing goals over follower focus are more likely to achieve neither. The best way to honor the people of the organization and to maximize effective goal achievement is to prioritize a focus on the followers who will be the key agents by whom goal achievement will be accomplished.

Appreciating Others

Because people have inherent value as human beings, effective leaders begin their engagement with others in a manner that affirms the value and dignity of those with whom they work. While this is where leader collaboration with followers ought to begin, moving from valuing people to appreciating others for their contribution is also essential to human flourishing and organizational effectiveness in leader-follower engagement.

Leaders can value others without expressing it. However, appreciating others emphasizes the need for leaders to show their appreciation for followers. In this section, we explore the leadership behavior of appreciating others by considering the leader's engagement with followers as whole persons and the leader's recognizing followers for their contributions to important organizational objectives.

Encouraging the Whole Person

Contemporary leadership theories, such as transformational leadership, emphasize a holistic view of followers. In chapter 1 we highlighted the power of transformational leadership to move the focus of followers beyond themselves and to help followers begin to develop leadership capacity and skills. That discussion, related to the leadership practice of modeling what matters, highlighted Bernard Bass and Bruce Avolio's discussion of idealized influence.[21]

Transformational motivation. Building on idealized influence, Bass and Avolio note three additional factors in their Four I's of transformational leadership: inspirational motivation, intellectual stimulation, and individual consideration.[22] Collectively, transformational leadership theory emphasizes the need for leaders to pay attention to both the cognitive and affective dimensions of followers. A leader's work of valuing and appreciating followers likewise engages both of these dimensions, but there is a special focus on encouraging and motivating followers affectively. Inspirational motivation helps to provide intrinsic inspiration as people go about their work.

At its core, transformational leadership is about working well with people. This valuing of people involves building trust, fostering collaboration, and inspiring people in such a way that they see and appreciate the gifts they bring to the organization as their leaders value and appreciate them. Kouzes and Posner see this as leaders encouraging the hearts of followers. While extrinsic motivators can be meaningful to followers, Kouzes and Posner similarly emphasize the preference for intrinsic motivation. For instance, they note that rewards do not always need to be financial, because "in a situation that is already intrinsically rewarding, the addition of extrinsic rewards may reduce the effectiveness of the intrinsic rewards."[23]

Meaningful work. Consider your own work. What motivates you? While there are instrumental values to our work, such as providing income to meet diverse life needs, the most motivating forms of work also emphasize values and priorities that are intrinsic in nature. On this point, Eric Eisenberg and Harold Lloyd Goodall write, "Employees want to feel that the work they do is worthwhile, rather than just a way to draw a paycheck," and to see their investment in work and their organization as "a transformation of its meaning—from drudgery to a source of personal significance and fulfillment."[24]

While every minute of the workday may not tap into such a sense of deeper meaning, transformational leadership theory calls leaders to look for ways to appreciate the follower as a whole person and to draw out motivations that encourage the heart and inspire the follower toward a greater sense of meaning and purpose in their work on behalf of the organization.

Andy Pearson serves as an example of leaders inspiring others. Pearson, once known as a tough leader in his former CEO work with PepsiCo, came to realize that the need for recognition and approval is a fundamental drive in the human experience. Pearson saw the importance of leaders balancing the desire to get things done with consideration of follower needs. He notes that for leaders, "Your real job is to get results and to do it in a way that makes your organization a great place to work—a place where people enjoy coming to work, instead of just taking orders and hitting this month's numbers."[25] Such a work environment fosters a context where leaders encourage followers with inspirational motivation.

Positive expectations. When we consider the importance of inspiring others, educational theory provides a relevant lesson for managers and leaders. A concept known as the Pygmalion effect points to the power of expectations. The Pygmalion concept draws from an ancient Greek myth in which a statue is brought to life by a sculptor wishing for a bride in the likeness of a sculpted ivory girl. The Broadway musical *My Fair Lady* picked up on these themes as Eliza Doolittle, famously played by Julie Andrews, is transformed by Professor Higgins from a working-class, Cockney-speaking Londoner to a member of London's elite society.

One example of this in educational practice would be when teachers have high expectations of a particular student: this student often benefits from these positive expectations and performs at a higher level academically. Applying this to leadership practice, when leaders similarly have higher expectations of follower performance, these positive expectations tend to influence higher levels of follower performance.[26]

The Pygmalion effect is associated with what is known as self-fulfilling prophecy. While positive expectations are not the only, or the defining, factor influencing performance, diverse management studies point to the self-fulfilling prophecy dynamic surrounding the Pygmalion effect within managerial and leadership contexts.[27]

On this point, Kouzes and Posner note that leaders play Pygmalion-like roles in developing people, and the work of these leaders is not so much carving out a statue from the ivory as it is releasing the beauty that is already in it.[28] Knowledge, skills, and abilities significantly influence performance for followers, but research supports the role of leaders in providing additional support for followers through appreciation and positive expectation. Because people often behave in a manner consistent with expectations placed on them, leaders hold the power to influence followers positively when positive expectations are present in the leader-follower engagement.

Valuing and Appreciating for Contribution

As we discuss the priority of appreciating others, it is important to recognize that this appreciation extends to contribution as well. From a biblical perspective, we affirm the good nature of work as part of the human story. Although work is quickly associated with the story of humanity's fall into sin (see Gen. 3), work was first given as a good gift from God to humanity before sin entered the human story (see Gen. 2:15).

The gift of work. This gift of work given to humans is sometimes referred to as the creation mandate—God's call for people to work and care for the world. For us as human beings made in God's image, part of our image-bearing nature is to work and contribute to human flourishing in ways consistent with what God has done and continues to do. On this point, Timothy Keller and Katherine Leary Alsdorf write, "Work of all kinds, whether with the hands or the mind, evidences our dignity as human beings—because it reflects the image of God the Creator in us. . . . Work has dignity because it is something that God does and because we do it in God's place, as his representatives. . . . We were built for work and the dignity it gives us as human beings."[29] Based on such logic, leaders who recognize and appreciate the work of others may participate in honoring this core dimension of humans made in God's image.

We are wired to contribute value to the people and communities around us. Our work provides the context where we invest a majority of our waking hours in service of others, and this investment becomes even more meaningful when we are able to see progress in our work and goals. Some followers may find it easy to see where they are progressing meaningfully toward goals in their work; others may find recognizing such progress more difficult. In either case, followers benefit from leaders who recognize a job well done and provide meaningful affirmation when that is the case.

Paying attention and providing feedback. Supporting the importance of meaningful feedback, studies highlight the need for both feedback and the presence of clear goals.[30] In one study, although performance effort on the part of research participants increased by around 25 percent when either clear goals or clear feedback was provided, this percentage of increase in performance effort was nearly 60 percent when both clear goals and meaningful feedback were combined.[31] Reflecting on the principle from such studies, Kouzes and Posner summarize that "people's motivation to increase their productivity on a task increases only when they have a challenging goal *and* receive feedback on their progress."[32] Valuing and appreciating others goes alongside this work of providing meaningful feedback.

> We are wired to contribute value to the people and communities around us.

So how can leaders effectively engage in this work of appreciating follower contribution toward shared goals? Leadership theorists often point to the basic starting point of simply paying attention. Ken Blanchard refers to this as "one minute praising." On this point, Blanchard and Finch write, "Look around your organization and see if you can 'catch people doing something right.' When you do, give them a one minute praising that is immediate and specific and states your feelings."[33] Although we are wired to hear words of appreciation, it is often more intuitive to focus on catching people doing things wrong. Blanchard brings the spirit of positive thinking to his managerial advice; he calls leaders to make expectations clear and then do all they can to catch people doing things right.

Kouzes and Posner provide a similar encouragement: "One way of showing you care is to *pay attention* to people, to what they are doing, and to how they are feeling. . . . If you are clear about the standards you're looking for and you believe and expect people will perform like winners [think Pygmalion effect], then you're going to notice lots of examples of people doing things right and doing the right things."[34]

Valuing and Appreciating in Practice

In this chapter we have presented a case for the priority of leaders valuing and appreciating followers. Followers have inherent value as people created in God's image. Followers also have a drive to contribute meaningfully to a mission that is greater than themselves. Leaders have an opportunity to affirm both of these important follower dimensions.

In order to better illustrate what valuing and appreciating can look like in practice, we begin with sharing how one family engages in valuing and appreciating behavior in their businesses, and then we provide practical advice for those of you desiring to take the next step in valuing and appreciating your followers.

Valuing and Appreciating in Action: The McNeff Family

One unique example of business leaders valuing employees comes from a network of family-owned companies in Anoka, Minnesota. The companies—including SarTec Corporation, Ever Cat Fuels LLC, Mcgyan Biodiesel LLC, and ZirChrom Separations Inc.—are owned by Larry and Marie McNeff along with their son, Clayton McNeff.

Through a study focused on the leadership practices of these owners, the researchers highlight a particularly striking example of valuing people in action. Here's what Mike McNeff and I (Justin) wrote about the McNeffs' valuing of people in our research report:

> One of the reasons Larry McNeff left a large company to start his own company was because he felt that employees were not treated well. He said that he would see people get "tossed out just for the convenience of the company." He determined that when he started his own company, he would give people "more freedoms than they could have at a big company." Toward the end of the interview, Larry said, "Having a culture where you can treat people like a family is important. It makes it very difficult to part ways with family members. Occasionally we do have to part ways with an employee and that's not easy. And it shouldn't be easy. If it's an easy thing something is way wrong and most likely it's something wrong with management."
>
> The McNeffs have been very successful in creating community in their companies. Marie McNeff makes lunches every day for the 45 employees who work at the SarTec facility. Despite having been dean of faculty at Augsburg College she does not consider cooking for people a "menial" task. Rather she feels it is "one of the most important things you can do for people." This practice has also served to build community within the company as the employees sit around a table daily with one another. Clayton added that this practice sets them apart. He said, "We've gotten a lot of mileage out of it. There's almost like a folklore now about it." He then related a story about a local newscaster who came to the SarTec facility to interview the founders of the Mcgyan process. When the reporter stepped out of his car the first thing he said was, "Is this where the good meals are?"[35]

Although this example of personal care and fostering a family-oriented culture is likely not scalable in larger companies, the heart behind it should inspire others to consider how they might come alongside their employees and followers in a way that communicates the value of people. The McNeffs have done this well over the years with their employees.

Valuing and Appreciating: Insights for Practice

Although valuing and appreciating followers may feel obvious to some, leaders may face barriers to these leadership practices. In this section, we identify some of the barriers leaders commonly face, provide recommendations on how to address these barriers, and then give guidance for how to approach expressing and demonstrating your value and appreciation of followers.

ADDRESS BARRIERS TO VALUING AND APPRECIATING

This discussion of valuing and appreciating followers may raise several "yes, but" responses for readers. Consider these possible objections:

- "*Yes*, followers have inherent value, *but* sometimes it's difficult to express this value when as a manager or leader I have to hear a constant flow of problems and complaints from employees."
- "*Yes*, I want to provide regular affirmation of employees through rewards, *but* our division's budget is so tight; there is no margin for us to fund these rewards."
- "*Yes*, I want to recognize a job well done, *but* sometimes I worry that celebrating the work of one person will be perceived as showing favoritism in the eyes of others."
- "*Yes*, people desire having their contribution recognized and affirmed, *but* the reality is my schedule is so full of other work demands that I just don't feel like I have the time for this with my employees."

Of course, this list of responses could go on.

There is a common thread in all of these: the scarcity of resources. Whether a scarcity of time, money, personal energy, or supporting organizational structures, the issue of scarcity can hinder good intentions around valuing and appreciating. While these barriers are often real, the importance of valuing and appreciating followers is too great to allow a scarcity mind-set to rule the day.

In place of this scarcity mind-set, leaders must move to a mind-set that sees the assets, opportunities, and resources that are around them already. For example, while a company may not have the resources to provide lunch for employees every day like the McNeff family does, what resources are available to the organization that may be offered to employees? If money is not available for bonuses or incentives, how can thoughtful words and authentic celebration be regularized?

For those who feel that they just don't have the time, Finch and Blanchard, with their model of one-minute praising, remind us that affirming followers need not take massive amounts of time so long as feedback is provided that is specific, meaningful, and heartfelt. The key is for leaders to prioritize this work of valuing and appreciating, and then to look for what assets are available to deploy this vital work. Identify a situation at your institution where you could provide positive affirmation. Think through the time, place, and circumstances that will allow you to provide a significant and timely encouragement.

Express Value and Appreciation

Leaders and managers often rise to their roles because they work hard and intentionally contribute value to their organizations. This focus on getting things done is important. However, at times this attention to results can work against focusing on people. Connected to this is the sometimes implicit assumption that people know they are valued and don't need to hear it regularly.

The logic of assuming no news is good news when it comes to leader-follower relationships is not adequate. Finch and Blanchard name this as a managerial challenge: "[Managers] hire people, tell them what to do, and then leave them alone and assume good performance will follow. In other words, they abdicate."[36] Rather than abdicating, managers and leaders must press into the work of expressing their feedback and appreciation to followers on a regular basis.

Some people do this very well. One of our friends, and a graduate of Bethel Seminary, gets the importance of regularly expressing appreciation. Those who know Al Prentice well probably have several of his often-sent notes of encouragement and support. Al finds just about any excuse possible to provide an affirming word for a job well done.

Similarly valuing written communication, one church took time to print their logo on cards with a few words on the cover like: "Praying for you," "Thank you," and "A note from the Pastor." Of this church, Kevin Harney writes, "Every staff member keeps these cards in their desk and is expected to use them often. The cards are a reminder of the value of a handwritten note of encouragement."[37] In a day dominated by electronic forms of communication, it is amazing how meaningful it is to receive a brief handwritten note from someone who sees and celebrates a job well done.

The point is not so much about the mode by which value and appreciation for others is shared. The point is to take time to *express and communicate* these thoughts. As a leader, make sure that you are not merely assuming that the people with whom you work know they are valued and appreciated. Take time to express this. As Christians, we have so much for which we can be grateful. Because we have been loved by God, we have a reservoir of love from which to draw in loving others. Because we have so much for which we can be grateful, this spirit of gratitude can be shared with others. Christine Pohl reminds us, "For those of us transformed by grace, gratitude is not merely an act or an attitude; it is our identity."[38] Take time to embrace and live into this identity as you find ways to bring gratitude to others. For example, take some time in the week ahead to write a note of encouragement and appreciation to at least two people at your institution.

Demonstrate Value and Appreciation

Expressions of value and appreciation can take many forms. Whether spoken or written, taking time to verbalize or express our appreciation of followers matters. But it also matters that our words of value and appreciation align with our demonstration of this value.

There are two sides of this alignment. First, as with the leadership practice shared in chapter 1, we must model what matters when it comes to valuing and appreciating others. We shared that leaders don't just use words in their communication; leaders also communicate, for better or for worse, through their actions. When the words and actions of leaders properly align in the work of valuing and appreciating, this is a powerful combination. Conversely, misaligned expression and demonstration is counterproductive and often is either hurtful or harmful. Be sure that there is alignment between your words and actions when expressing and demonstrating your appreciation of followers. People want to know that your value and appreciation are authentic.

Second, as long as there is alignment between the expression and demonstration, find ways to celebrate creatively with your followers and team. Here are a few of our suggestions for demonstrating appreciation for followers:

- Offer a personalized gift that communicates that you know your employee well.
- Use formal award ceremonies on a regular basis along with something like a perpetual plaque.

- Use informal award ceremonies with a playful award or traveling trophy that can be passed from team member to team member, based on how the member lives out organizational values or exceeds goals.
- Utilize certificates of achievement to celebrate followers and a job well done.
- Offer perks that are meaningful to your context, such as an employee-of-the-month parking space.
- Provide impromptu time off.
- Encourage use of a departmental recognition board with supplies for posting notes of encouragement.
- Provide gift cards to pass along with notes of appreciation.

Choose two of these suggestions or create two of your own. Then identify a specific date and time on your calendar that you will actually do this.

When followers feel valued and appreciated by their supervisors and organizations, the extent that they will go on behalf of the team is amazing. Leaders must create a culture where people are valued because of their God-given human dignity. Leaders must also create a culture where people are appreciated for the time, effort, and attention they put into achieving important organizational goals. In contrast to an overemphasis on demanding perfection, Blanchard and Finch call leaders to go out of their way to catch people doing things right—even "approximately right."[39] Bring a spirit of gratitude and appreciation to your work with followers, and let them know about your appreciation through thoughtful expressions and demonstrations that recognize and celebrate their contributions to the team.

Next Steps

- Take some time to identify a situation at your institution where you could provide positive affirmation. Think through the time, place, and circumstances that will allow you to provide a significant and timely encouragement.
- Take some time to embrace and live into an identity of gratitude. Write a note of encouragement and appreciation to two people at your institution.
- Take some time to creatively celebrate team members. Identify a specific idea for celebrating a team member, along with a specific date and time you will actually do this.

Resources for a Deeper Look

Anderson, Leith, and Jill Fox. *The Volunteer Church: Mobilizing Your Congregation for Growth and Effectiveness*. Grand Rapids: Zondervan, 2015.

Blanchard, Ken, and Renee Broadwell. *Servant Leadership in Action: How You Can Achieve Great Relationships and Results*. Oakland, CA: Berrett-Koehler, 2018.

Kollmann, Bernd. *Joseph Barnabas: His Life and Legacy*. Translated by Miranda Henry. Collegeville, MN: Liturgical Press, 2004.

Nouwen, Henri. *In the Name of Jesus: Reflections on Christian Leadership*. London: Darton, Longman and Todd, 1989.

5

Creating a Place for Individuality

Introduction

We have previously highlighted the empowering leadership of Colleen Barrett of Southwest Airlines. Southwest's founder, Herb Kelleher, also understood empowering leadership and the priority of people.

Although most business executives see the general value of their employees, not all executives prioritize people as individuals. Herb sought do to this at Southwest for people at every level of the organization—whether fellow executives or those in line jobs such as baggage handlers and mechanics.

At one of the company's famous spirit parties, surrounded by hundreds of people circling Herb for attention, Barrett tells the story of Herb intently talking with a Southwest mechanic in worker's clothes for at least fifteen minutes—a long conversation by CEO standards. Barrett writes: "Herb never looked over the guy's shoulder to see who else might be there, and never diverted his eyes from this man while they were talking. Herb was courteous to everyone who was trying to shove the guy out of his space so that they could fill it, but he gave this man his time. It was clear . . . that Herb had no hierarchical concerns—he was completely interested in what the mechanic was trying to tell him."[1]

In this chapter we explore the priority of individuals and the associated leadership practice of *creating a place for individuality*. Over the years, leaders have often disagreed about the place of individual expression in service of organizational mission. For example, managerial theorists in the twentieth century often emphasized mechanistic models of organizational life in which the mission of the organization was seen as best accomplished by reducing the variability of individual expression and creativity among followers. These approaches viewed organizations through the metaphorical lens of organization as machine.

Contemporary researchers and theorists argue for more space for expressions of individuality and creativity in the organization. While organizational outcomes still matter to these researchers and theorists, the goal is not uniformity among organizational members but rather unity around the organization's mission. Rather than seeing expressions of individuality as a problem to be suppressed, contemporary theorists see the uniqueness of what individuals bring to organizations as essential for increasing the creativity and innovation necessary for a competitive advantage in the knowledge economy.

While creating a place for individuality in organizations likely will require more effort on the part of the leader than the mechanistic models of organizational life in previous years, this additional effort has the potential of reaping great rewards. In order to better understand the benefits and nature of creating a place for individuality, we will explore this topic through the following perspectives in this chapter: (1) creating a place for individuality in biblical perspective, (2) creating a place for individuality in contemporary perspective, and (3) creating a place for individuality in practice.

Creating a Place for Individuality in Biblical Perspective

One of the themes that the apostle Paul most emphasizes in his letters is the need for unity in the church. Several of his churches were plagued by divisions, and Paul calls them to get their act together. In Ephesians, a letter written to the churches in Asia Minor, he writes, "Make every effort to keep the unity of the Spirit through the bond of peace" (Eph. 4:3). To the church at Philippi, he writes, "Make my joy complete by being like-minded, having the same love, being one in spirit and of one mind" (Phil. 2:2).

As noted before, however, no church has greater difficulties in this area than the church in Corinth (see chap. 3). Paul says he has been informed "that when you come together as a church, there are divisions among you" (1 Cor. 11:18), and he urges them to unity (1:10–11). The problem is so severe at Corinth that Paul takes roughly a quarter of the letter (1 Cor. 1–4) to introduce it and then returns to the issue again and again throughout the letter (6:1–11; 8:1, 9–13; 11:18; 12:4–7). Paul knew that infighting, division, dissension, and strife are among the most destructive powers at work in the church and can cripple its effectiveness. He also knew that the means to this unity is not *uniformity* but rather a celebration of diversity.

Unity through Diversity

While unity is a critically important goal for the church (and for any organization), unity does not mean everyone thinks the same way or functions in the same manner. It especially does not mean that everyone has the same gifts, talents, and abilities. On the contrary, the church functions most effectively and in unity *only when the diversity of gifts and callings is acknowledged and encouraged.* Forced uniformity crushes creativity and individual contribution and so reduces the church's effectiveness.

> *The church functions most effectively and in unity only when the diversity of gifts and callings is acknowledged and encouraged.*

What is needed is unity around certain core values, including a shared mission, vision, purpose, and goals. Allegiance to these fundamentals gives the organization a common identity and a common direction, which is effectively implemented through the diverse gifts and abilities of individual members.

It is significant that the greatest emphasis on this kind of diversity comes in this same letter—1 Corinthians—which so strongly emphasizes the need for unity. No passage of Scripture places more emphasis on the importance of individual and diverse *spiritual gifts* than 1 Corinthians 12–14. Paul knows that the flourishing of these gifts will enable the church to be united, efficient, and effective in the world.

A word should be added here about what we mean by spiritual gifts. The New Testament speaks of "gifts" (*charismata*)[2] or "spiritual [gifts]" (*pneumatikoi*),[3] which the Holy Spirit gives to all Christians. These include such things as teaching, evangelism, prophecy, administration, wisdom, faith, encouragement, giving, showing mercy, serving, and so on (for others, see Rom. 12:6–8; 1 Cor. 12:8–10, 28–30; Eph. 4:11; 1 Pet. 4:11). These spiritual gifts may (or may not) be the same as a person's "natural" abilities or talents. Even when they do coincide, however, the Bible makes it clear that these gifts ultimately come from God and are empowered and energized by the Holy Spirit.

Diverse Gifts for the Common Good

Paul begins his discussion of spiritual gifts in 1 Corinthians 12 by focusing on diversity in the context of shared core values: "There are different kinds of gifts, but the same Spirit distributes them. There are different kinds of service, but the same Lord. There are different kinds of working, but in all of them and in everyone it is the same God at work. Now to each one the manifestation of the Spirit is given for the common good" (vv. 4–7). While there are many kinds of spiritual gifts, the church shares the same core allegiance to the Triune God—Holy Spirit, Lord Jesus, and God the Father. Without this common foundation, diversity would simply be people pursuing their own agendas.

The purpose of these diverse gifts is the benefit of the church as a whole—"for the common good." Spiritual gifts are meant to build up the church and improve its effectiveness. Paul says the same thing in Ephesians 4:11–13: "So Christ himself gave the apostles, the prophets, the evangelists, the pastors and teachers, to equip his people for works of service, so that the body of Christ may be built up until we all reach unity in the faith and in the knowledge of the Son of God and become mature, attaining to the whole measure of the fullness of Christ."

The purpose of distinct leadership gifts (prophet, evangelist, pastor, teacher) is for *equipping* and *edification*. Equipping means providing those you lead with the resources necessary to be successful. Edification means that as a result of this equipping, the church as a whole thrives and reaches its potential. The ultimate goal is threefold: "unity in the faith," "knowledge of the Son of God," and spiritual maturity—"attaining to the whole measure of the fullness of Christ." It is significant again that diversity—the celebration of individuality—has as its goal unity. The reason for this should be clear. The church has various purposes in the world: to evangelize, to pass on the teaching of Jesus and the apostles, to train or "disciple" believers in the faith, to guard the church against false teaching, to care for the poor and oppressed, to provide encouragement to those who are discouraged, and so on. To accomplish these diverse tasks requires individuals with a variety of spiritual gifts and abilities.

The Analogy of the Body

Paul draws on the analogy of the human body to illustrate the necessity of unity through diversity in the church: "Just as a body, though one, has many parts, but all its many parts form one body, so it is with Christ" (1 Cor. 12:12). "Now you are the body of Christ, and each one of you is a part of it" (12:27). Each part of the body is important, and each plays a crucial part in the functioning of the whole:

> Now if the foot should say, "Because I am not a hand, I do not belong to the body," it would not for that reason stop being part of the body. And if the ear should say, "Because I am not an eye, I do not belong to the body," it would not for that reason stop being part of the body. If the whole body were an eye,

where would the sense of hearing be? If the whole body were an ear, where would the sense of smell be? . . . As it is, there are many parts, but one body. (1 Cor. 12:15–20)

Paul introduces the absurd and comical picture of a whole body made up of a single eye or an ear. Such a body would be of very little use. Certain parts may seem to be inferior, but they play crucial roles. No body part can reject another as unnecessary. "The eye cannot say to the hand, 'I don't need you!' And the head cannot say to the feet, 'I don't need you!'" (1 Cor. 12:21). For the body to work properly, it needs all its diverse parts. In the same way, the diversity of gifts in the church enables it to fulfill its multifaceted mission in the world. Similar teaching appears in Romans 12:4–8.

What is true of the church, the body of Christ, is true of any organization. An ant colony functions with great efficiency because the ants are genetically programmed to fulfill *different and complementary* tasks, each of which benefits the colony as a whole. A corporation performs well only if all of its departments and individuals—managers, technicians, human resource personnel, and so on—perform their individual duties for the common good. Individuality and specialization—when directed toward a common purpose and for the common good—are an essential part to any organization.

The Leader's Role: Valuing Individuality and Encouraging Creativity

Of course, valuing individuality goes beyond simply acknowledging the variety of roles and functions in an organization. After all, each worker in a factory assembly line has a different role, but there is no necessary emphasis given to an individual's value and personhood or to their creative contribution. Servant leaders, by contrast, are *other-centered* and so focus on relationships. A servant leader knows each follower personally, including their strengths and weaknesses, and encourages the positive use of their gifts, with a goal toward that individual's personal and spiritual growth and development.

> *A servant leader knows each follower personally, including their strengths and weaknesses.*

Jesus, the epitome of a servant leader, consistently affirms the value and worth of individuals, especially those whom society has discounted as unworthy or irrelevant. For example, Jesus senses and responds to the touch of a woman who has languished with a blood disease for twelve years (Mark 5:25–34). He hears the cries of blind Bartimaeus, even as the crowd tries to silence him (10:46–52). Although Jesus's ministry is first and foremost for the Jews, he responds to a Gentile woman's desperate request for her demon-possessed daughter (7:24–30). He breaks societal norms by conversing with a Samaritan woman (John 4:1–42). In these and many other cases, Jesus affirms the inherent value of human beings.

A servant leader should encourage not only competence but also creativity. Human beings are created in the image of God (Gen. 1:26–27), and God's fundamental identity is as Creator. The creation of the heavens and earth and the remarkable diversity of earth's ecosystems testify to God's breathtakingly creative nature. As image bearers, human beings naturally share God's creative nature and fall short of their potential if they cannot exercise creative initiative.

The affirmation of individuality and creativity is not only healthy and nurturing for individuals; it is also beneficial to the organization as a whole. In 1 Corinthians 12–14, Paul makes it clear that the healthy practice of a variety of spiritual gifts will enrich the spiritual life of the Corinthian church. In the same way, the practice of diverse spiritual gifts among the Ephesians will "equip [God's] people for works of service, so that the body of Christ may be built up until we all reach unity in the faith and in the knowledge of the Son of God and become mature" (Eph. 4:12–13). Unity, knowledge of God, maturity—these attributes represent the epitome of a vibrant, healthy, and growing church.

Creating a Place for Individuality in Contemporary Perspective

Contemporary theory and research build on these biblical perspectives by providing additional insight into the importance of leaders creating a place for individuality among their followers. In my (Justin's) research on the topic, the following statements were statistically significant predictors of effective leadership practice: "People within this organization accept people as they are" and "People within this organization allow for individuality of style and expression."[4]

In light of these emphases, we will organize our discussion of contemporary leadership theory and research for this section around the following areas: (1) humanizing the machine, (2) considering individuals, (3) developing individuals, and (4) nurturing uniqueness and creativity.

Humanizing the Machine

CONTROLLING THE MACHINE

One of the persistent issues in organizational leadership is how the needs of both the organization and organizational members may be balanced. In early management theories, the solution to this issue seemed obvious: organizational needs were the priority, and management approaches that focused on control and order carried the day.

From such a perspective, organizations were seen as machinelike entities. Leaders of these organizations sought to reduce variation in the functioning of the organizational machine. The variation most often needing to be controlled in this machine was human behavior. The problem with this approach, however, is that in such organizations people are not valued for their creative potential; their work is treated merely as a factor of production—a factor that is expendable and interchangeable.[5]

Henry Ford is well known for his work in putting the first modern-day assembly line into operation in 1913. This move produced a replicable model for other organizations and gave rise to the main approach factories have used since then. Such a move allowed companies to increase production by controlling the human variable in coordinated work. Generally speaking, this allowed companies to see increased production on the factory floor.

Along with these benefits also came a dark side. In this model, people were viewed primarily as hired hands, valued only for their production value. Consider Ford's purported question raised earlier in this book: "Why is it that I always get the whole person when what I really want is just a pair of hands?" At its worst, this approach to work fosters the dehumanization of organizations and the people who work within these organizations.

Margaret Wheatley characterizes these machinelike approaches to leadership as the *old story* in organizations. The old story is all about creating better-functioning machines. To increase production and efficiency in these better-functioning machines, old-story managers had to emphasize control of unpredictable human behavior. Rather than celebrating individuality, old-story management sought to control human individuality. Wheatley notes, "In our machine-organizations, we try to extinguish individuality in order to reach our goal of certainty. We trade uniqueness for control and barter our humanness for petty performance measures."[6]

The problem, of course, is that humans do not behave or function like machines, and they never will. Wheatley observes that when old-story managers emphasize control over human individuality in these machinelike ways, we are led "to believe that we, with our unpredictable behaviors, our passions, our independence, our creativity, our consciousness—that we are the problem rather than the blessing."[7]

Managing organizations like machines has a lure of efficiency but at the end of the day works against human nature and works against the organization's need to tap into creativity and the human innovative spirit. Wheatley puts it this way: "When we conceived of ourselves as machines, we gave up most of what is essential to being human. We created ourselves devoid of spirit, will, passion, compassion, even intelligence."[8] While old-story management may have worked in the industrial age, in the knowledge economy the sacrifice of human creativity for the sake of control neither honors the image of God within humans nor produces the competitive advantage that today's organizations need.

NURTURING ORGANIZATIONS FIT FOR HUMANS

So what is the better way if managing organizations and people as machines has its limits? In a management talk titled "Reinventing the Technology of Human Accomplishment," Gary Hamel provides a call for designing and managing organizations that are fit for humans.[9] He argues that rather than asking how employees can better serve organizational goals, today's managers need to ask how we can create work environments that inspire everyone to give their creative best.

In contrast to Henry Ford just wanting a pair of hands rather than the whole person, people like Bruce Winston are providing a call to focus on hired hearts rather than just hired hands.[10] Making a similar point, Bill George notes that the shift in economies from production workers to knowledge workers necessitates a shift toward the whole person—engaging the hearts rather than just the heads and hands of followers.[11]

The priority [for effectiveness] is common purpose, not conformity.

As the hearts of followers are engaged in their work, a shift from control to empowerment may take place along with a shift from uniformity to uniqueness. Within healthy organizations today, effectiveness is not obtained by pressing people into a mold of uniformity. Rather, effectiveness is obtained by enabling unique individuals to bring their creativity to the work of a common mission and purpose. The priority is common purpose, not conformity.

Speaking to the value of leaders creating a place for individuality, research participants in my (Justin's) study noted the importance of setting strategic goals but allowing individuals to engage in creative processes to achieve them. Similarly, on the theme of how follower individuality coincides with organizational unity, research participants noted that commonality at the level of mission, vision, goals, and values provides "the glue that holds the organization together" and that "under this umbrella there is ample room for individuality."[12]

The old style of management sought not only unity at the level of mission and purpose but also uniformity in worker practice. In today's organizations, leaders seeking to create organizations fit for people understand that both unity and space for individuality are vital. In contrast to the old story of management, Wheatley describes the new story as a tale of life over machine—the organic over the mechanistic—and notes that as we set aside our machinelike perspectives we find a world that exhibits life's ebullient creativity and productivity.[13]

In such a world, organization still matters, but it looks much different and often uses messes to create and bring about organization.[14] In this process, unity of purpose—and people relating to one another around this shared purpose—is the key to organizing. Wheatley has this to say: "The process of organizing involves creating relationships around a shared sense of purpose, exchanging and creating information, learning constantly, paying attention to the results of our efforts . . . staying clear about our purpose."[15]

From this vantage point, leadership is more about facilitating and enabling than it is about directing and controlling. The key is for leaders to nurture a context or environment where creativity and connection foster innovation and productivity. Though it is tempting for leaders to want to take back the reins of control in working toward productivity, control alone is shortsighted. Lasting systems of productivity work with people and their creative impulse rather than against them and this creativity. As Thomas Bausch reminds us, "Leadership must begin with a deep understanding of the human person as the basis, and the only source of sustainable competitive advantage."[16]

Considering Individuals

As organizational managers and leaders come to terms with the shift away from machinelike systems of control, the priority of the individual in the organization rises to the surface. One contemporary leadership theory that explicitly speaks to the consideration of individuals is transformational leadership.

In chapters 1 and 4 we highlighted two of the Four I's of transformational leadership: idealized influence and inspirational motivation. Here we call attention to Bernard Bass and Bruce Avolio's discussion of *individualized consideration*. Bass and Avolio describe the individually considerate leader as one who listens effectively and pays attention to each individual's needs and desires as a developing employee or follower.[17] Rather than seeing and treating followers in an identical manner, the individually considerate leader understands that different followers need to be recognized for their uniqueness and given individualized and tailored leadership based on their uniqueness.

The simple fact is that people are different. Effective leaders learn to work with rather than against these differences. Avolio describes individualized consideration as "the type of leadership that focused on each individual being unique, whereby the leader assumed responsibility for developing his or her followers to their full potential, and ultimately to be leaders themselves."[18]

While mechanistic models of leadership tend toward a view of people as cogs in the organizational machinery, transformational leadership emphasizes consideration of followers as individuals rather than expendable units. Recognizing people as individuals, and affirming the uniqueness they bring to the organization, allows leaders to engage the work of developing followers to their full potential—what Bass and Avolio see as the outworking of effective transformational leadership and individualized consideration.

Developing Individuals

Transformational leadership is not alone in its emphasis on valuing and developing the uniqueness of others. Servant leadership theorists likewise emphasize this priority.

In describing the best test of a servant leader, Robert K. Greenleaf notes the following: "The best test, and difficult to administer, is this: Do those served grow as persons?" He continues, "Do they, while being served, become healthier, wiser, freer, more autonomous, more likely themselves to become servants?"[19] This emphasis on people growing is at the heart of Greenleaf's conceptualization of the servant leader.

Other servant-leadership theorists pick up on this point. In Jim Laub's work, themes such as valuing people, developing people, and building community are central to servant-leadership practice.[20] In his model of servant leadership, Laub notes that valuing the differences of others is a core leadership behavior connected to building community. Laub further notes that developing people involves providing followers with opportunities for learning and growth. These practices—valuing the differences of others and providing opportunities for learning and growth—exemplify what creating a place for individuality is all about in the organization.

When individuals in an organization are seen and recognized for their uniqueness, including their unique contributions, then developing people is a natural next step for the servant leader. This commitment to developing people is an outgrowth of leaders valuing and appreciating—the leadership practice engaged in the previous chapter.

Lest a commitment to valuing and developing people seems like mere charity work, Bausch reminds us of the priority of this work for organizations desiring a competitive advantage. Bausch puts it this way: "For any organization, for-profit, not-for-profit, or governmental, the only source of sustainable competitive advantage will be the commitment to and trust in the mission and vision of the organization by highly competent employees."[21]

Bausch argues that employee commitment to organization mission and vision is essential for organizational success, and he further notes that this commitment "depends on leadership that earns its legitimacy from within the organization, in part because of its commitment to the development of the full potential of each person."[22] A commitment to developing the people of your organization is not merely a strategy for increased employee job satisfaction; this commitment is also essential for maintaining a competitive edge in the knowledge economy—a context where we need people bringing their whole selves to work in order to engage complex problem solving with creative and innovative solutions.

Both leaders and followers must learn to own and invest in the developmental process. On this point, Ken Blanchard and his associates write, "While self leaders should be responsible for their own learning, they shouldn't bear the burden alone; management practices should support the development of knowledge and skills."[23] As a manager or leader in your organization, how are you investing in practices and systems that encourage people to see their own development as essential to the health of the organization?

Arguing that learning is a priority in the high-performing organization, Blanchard and his associates call leaders to treat people as appreciating assets—assets that grow more valuable with experience and knowledge. They see the skills of an organization as no greater than the skills of its people. Organizations cannot learn unless individuals learn.[24] Such a practice is consistent with great leaders throughout history.

Consider the leaders who have been judged well by history in American politics. Bausch notes that each political leader who has been judged great by history in some way was a servant leader releasing the creativity of the American people. He observes that these leaders found a way to engage the hearts of people and ultimately release potential.[25]

This is what developing others is all about—releasing creative human potential for the good of the organization and community. Leaders must learn to nurture systems that are oriented toward fostering people's desire to discover and implement innovated solutions.

The release of human creativity in organizations is essential for competitive advantage to be realized. This work requires the acceptance of some costs, however—costs such as the unpredictability and inefficiencies associated with human enterprise. On this point, Bausch notes that this type of inefficiency is a relatively low cost to pay for the tremendous release of human creativity—creativity that is the greatest of all assets but also the most unpredictable.[26] Leaders focused on developing followers and releasing this competitive advantage must be willing to tolerate mistakes and unpredictability. Through such leadership, creativity may be released as people develop their potential and move the organization toward the fulfillment of its vision and mission.

A commitment to developing the full potential of individuals in your organization becomes the foundation of releasing the creative uniqueness that each person has to offer the community. This is what leadership is all about: developing the potential of others and releasing them into service of a shared vision. As people are affirmed and developed, creative contribution becomes a possibility in healthy organizations.

Nurturing Uniqueness and Creativity

This process of developing potential must build on the uniqueness and strength of people as their individuality is creatively harnessed for the shared good of both the individual and the wider team.

Bill George highlights why tapping into the unique hearts of people matters for organizations: "Companies that link the passions of their employees to the generation of innovative ideas will have the capacity to sustain their growth for decades."[27] Passion, creativity, and innovation—in service of organizational growth—are fostered when leaders engage people in a manner that fosters rather than suppresses individuality. While such creative expression and individuality are less prone to control, sustained employee engagement in organizational mission depends on followers feeling not only free but also encouraged to contribute to the organization's mission out of their individual strengths.

On this point, positive psychologists and strengths-based theorists affirm the importance of team members understanding their personal strengths. Marcus Buckingham and Donald Clifton note that individuals using their strengths tend to be more productive, more fulfilled, and more successful in their work. They write, "Look inside yourself, try to identify your strongest threads, reinforce them with practice and learning, and then either find or . . . carve out a role that draws on these strengths every day."[28] Leaders must find ways to come alongside their people to help match roles and responsibilities to follower strengths.

Tom Rath and Barry Conchie note that effective leaders focus on surrounding themselves with the right people and then building on each person's unique strengths.[29] This leadership work is not just about helping people feel better about their contribution; it also is about facilitating follower engagement around the organizational mission. Rath and Conchie argue that such engagement at work is one of the key benefits of a strengths-based approach to leadership. For instance, when an organization's leaders do not focus on strengths, employee engagement is around 1 in 11, or 9 percent. In contrast to this, when an organization's leaders focus on strengths, employee engagement is around 3 in 4, or 73 percent.[30]

Leaders who provide space for follower individuality nurture a context within which followers may bring the best of themselves to work and so contribute to the wider organizational mission. Too often we try to capture the need for well-rounded strengths on our own. The problem is, no one individual can be well-rounded enough to be all that their organization needs. Here is where a focus on uniqueness and individuality provides a solution. As we tap into a diversity of gifts and strengths, providing space for creativity and individuality of expression, both the organization and individual employees win.

While creativity and employee innovation may have been viewed as a liability in the industrial age, these are essential in the knowledge economy for sustained organizational effectiveness. As an organization is connected and unified around strategic goals, individuals flourish when they are allowed to engage in creative processes to accomplish these common goals. These priorities emphasize bringing the threads of creativity and connectivity together. Rather than prescribing the end and the means, such organizations foster a context where creative contribution arising out of personal strength and relationships with others is encouraged.

Creating a Place for Individuality in Practice

In this chapter we have presented a case for creating a place for individuality. As we move away from machinelike mechanisms of organizational control, empowering approaches to considering and developing follower individuality and strength becomes a high priority.

As we examine what this leadership responsibility looks like in practice, it may be helpful to look at some of the associated strengths of this leadership approach. Consider just a few of these benefits to the employee and the organization:

- Increased employee engagement and contribution
- Increased employee job satisfaction
- Increased employee retention and reduced employee turnover costs

- Increased flexibility in work arrangements (work hours, location, décor)
- Increased capacity for sustained organizational innovation and growth

With an emphasis on creating a place for individuality, managers have less need to micromanage when a spirit of freedom within boundaries is emphasized. This is not about an absence of accountability but rather is about providing accountability on the things that matter most and freedom of expression on the more personalized dimensions of work life.

T. J. Addington uses the metaphor of a sandbox on this point in his book *Leading from the Sandbox*.[31] This metaphor emphasizes bringing creativity and fun into the sandbox of our work. It also emphasizes that this enjoyment is strengthened by shared values and mission, which provide the boundaries for the sandbox of work in community. In this model, accountability is provided at the bigger-picture level of shared mission and values, and freedom and individual expression of work can take place within the organizational or team sandbox. This approach is about majoring on the majors when it comes to accountability, while leaving room for freedom of individual expression and work as team members collectively move toward shared priorities.

Creating a Place for Individuality in Action: ServiceMaster

One example of creating a place for individuality comes from the years of William Pollard's leadership at ServiceMaster. Pollard joined the ServiceMaster Company in 1977 and served as the CEO on two different occasions—once from 1983 to 1993 and again from 1999 to 2001. In his time at the company, Pollard saw his success primarily measured by his fellow workers at ServiceMaster—the individuals delivering value to customers and shareholders on a daily basis.

Pollard reminds us of the importance of prioritizing and valuing people: "Let us not forget the people who are serving and making it happen—they are the soul of our organizations."[32] As the people of ServiceMaster were valued under Pollard's leadership, several priorities came about as an extension of this commitment.

First, people were recognized for their unique value and not simply the economic benefit they brought to the company. Pollard states, "People are not just economic animals or production units. Everyone has a fingerprint of personality and potential and desire to contribute."[33] He further states that when we "define people solely in economic terms, our motivational and incentive schemes tend to become mechanical and manipulative."[34] Even though the industry within which ServiceMaster operated could tend toward mechanical approaches to its labor force, Pollard resisted this tendency to see people merely for their production value.

Second, Pollard emphasized the whole person within training and development approaches at ServiceMaster. Pollard notes the following: "The scope of training must include more than teaching a person to use the right tools or to complete an assigned task within a defined period."[35] In contrast to these limited approaches, Pollard invites managers and leaders to engage with training in a way that includes how people feel about themselves, their work, and how they relate to others. Pollard lived out Winston's call to see people as hired hearts rather than just hired hands.

Third, Pollard valued employees as individuals. He notes that everyone has a distinct fingerprint of personality: we must remember that "people are different," and it is "a leader's responsibility to set the tone, to learn to accept the differences of people, and to foster an environment where different people can contribute as part of the whole and achieve unity in diversity."[36]

Pollard's call to unity in diversity is all about creating a place for individuality as unique individuals work together on a common mission. Pollard sees the organizational mission as an organizing principle that allows for a community of people to care for one another and those they serve. For Pollard, people are the soul of organizations, and when they can be valued for their individuality and unified in a common mission, great things can happen in and through people working together.

Creating a Place for Individuality: Insights for Practice

Creating a place for individuality may take on diverse expressions. In this final section of the chapter, we address three practical examples of how to put this leadership principle into practice.

PROVIDE SPACE AND EMPOWERMENT FOR PROBLEM SOLVING

First, we encourage leaders to provide space—and the associated empowerment—for followers to engage in direct problem solving in their roles. Every organizational context requires some level of problem solving. We each face challenges on the job that call for suitable solutions. At times these solutions are prescribed by the organization. Other times, when possible, leaders can create approaches that help to systematize creative problem solving on the part of individual employees or organizational members.

Two examples of this come from the Ritz-Carlton and Yum! Brands.[37] At Yum! Brands, rather than wait staff always having to talk to their managers when faced with a problem, team members are able to respond to customer issues directly and are empowered to use up to ten dollars to solve the issue. Similarly, at the Ritz-Carlton, frontline employees have a discretionary fund they may use to solve customer challenges directly without needing to check with a manager.

In your own organizational context, how can you as a manager or leader empower the individuals of your organization to engage in creative problem solving? How can you provide space for employees and organizational members to take ownership of their roles and associated responsibilities? Take some time in the week ahead to consider a specific problem your organization is seeking to address. Consider how you as a leader can empower your team members with the tools they need to address this problem.

PROVIDE SPACE FOR INDIVIDUAL EXPRESSION

Second, in contrast to organizational approaches that emphasize uniformity, the practice of creating a place for individuality emphasizes leaders' allowing for diverse expressions of style that take the individual into consideration.

When applying this principle, context matters. For instance, companies with storefronts may need to require uniforms at their stores while allowing for flexibility in clothing choices at the corporate headquarters. Where possible, though, followers express a strong preference for freedom and flexibility when reasonable.

The key is to maintain unity on the things that matter most.

In my (Justin's) study on the topic, research participants note the importance of simple expressions of individuality such as work style, clothing, and office hours. Participants also noted that flexibility for follower expressions of individuality is best supported through the avoidance of micromanaging leadership behaviors. The key is to maintain unity on the things that matter most—the organization's shared mission and achievement of goals associated with this mission—while providing flexibility on nonessential matters of life in the organizational community. Take some time this week to think through what expressions of individuality matter most to your team members. Consider how you as a leader can intentionally create space for these team-member priorities.

PROVIDE SPACE FOR PEOPLE TO DEVELOP THEIR CREATIVE POTENTIAL

Finally, we encourage leaders to take the development of followers and their creative potential seriously. As individuals created in God's image, we are wired with God's creative and creating characteristics. Bausch puts it this way: "The true meaning of work is *spiritual*. . . . We are called to be cocreators with our God or with each other in service of each other. It is through this inherently valuable work that we develop our potential."[38]

Creativity is not just a nice option to engage on occasion. Creativity is part of how we are wired as human beings, and it is core to how we add value to others through our work. Bausch notes that we will contribute directly and indirectly to the mission and vision of our organization to the degree that creativity is released. He argues that rather than just leaving this to employees to figure out, leaders seeking to serve their followers and their organizations work to translate this conceptual reality into operational reality.[39] So, how are you translating the release of creativity among your team members? Take some time in the week ahead to consider steps you may take to be more intentional in developing followers and their creative potential.

Leadership models of the past sought to minimize difference in order to treat their organizations and their workers as machines, but at the end of the day people were never designed to function like machines. Healthy and effective leadership models in our day emphasize the priority of unity of mission over uniformity of employee expression. Leaders must work hard to create organizations that are fit for human beings, and this necessitates creating a place for individuality in the organizational journey.

Next Steps

- Take some time in the week ahead to consider a specific problem your organization is seeking to address. Consider how you as a leader can empower your team members with the tools they need to address this problem.
- Take some time this week to think through what expressions of individuality matter most to your team members. Consider how you as a leader can intentionally create space for these team-member priorities.
- Take some time to consider what follower processes and practices may be adjusted to facilitate creative expression that will benefit both followers and your team.

Resources for a Deeper Look

Carson, D. A. *Showing the Spirit: A Theological Exposition of 1 Corinthians 12–14.* Repackaged ed. Grand Rapids: Baker, 2019.

De Pree, Max. *Leading without Power: Finding Hope in Serving Community*. San Francisco: Jossey-Bass, 1997.

Fee, Gordon D. *The First Epistle to the Corinthians*. New International Commentary on the New Testament. 2nd ed. Grand Rapids: Eerdmans, 2014.

Kouzes, James M., and Barry Z. Posner. *The Leadership Challenge: How to Make Extraordinary Things Happen in Organizations*. 2nd ed. San Francisco: Jossey-Bass, 2002.

Lencioni, Patrick. *The Ideal Team Player: How to Recognize and Cultivate the Three Essential Virtues*. Hoboken, NJ: Wiley, 2016.

6

Understanding Relational Skills

Introduction

For three and a half years I (Mark) served as the interim preaching pastor at a large church in San Diego. My role was almost exclusively teaching. We had an executive pastor who managed the staff and did most of the day-to-day administration. I just preached. This was essential for my sanity, since I was also a full-time professor. There were times, however, when I felt the need to get involved in pastoral issues.

One week I received a note from a senior member of the church. He was not at all happy with something I had said on Sunday. He thought I was fundamentally wrong and insisted I needed to recant publicly what I had said. In turn, I thought he was fundamentally wrong and should admit as much. I crafted a detailed email, step-by-step refuting his argument. (It was a beautiful piece of work!) This should end the matter, I thought.

But just before I pressed "send," I had second thoughts. Maybe this was not the best way to handle the issue. Instead, I picked up the phone and called him. He was clearly surprised to hear from me. I suggested we get together, so we arranged to meet that week.

At our meeting, things started off pretty tense. But instead of jumping into "the issue," I began asking him questions about himself and his family. He shared with me about his career, his family (especially the grandkids!), and his work with the church. We had a delightful conversation. To be honest, I can't remember how much we talked about "the issue" or whether it even came up. I do remember late in the conversation telling him how much

I appreciated his leadership at the church and the example of faithful service he had set for so many. We took some time to pray together before he left.

In the days and months following, this man became one of my greatest supporters. He would often reach out to encourage me, to check in on how I was doing, or to let me know if there were issues at the church he thought I needed to be aware of. He is still a dear friend.

I learned a lot about leadership (and relationships) that day. For one thing, understanding someone else's perspective is more important than making sure I'm understood. Proving my point is seldom a helpful goal, and "winning" an argument is almost never so. Affirming someone as a person and encouraging them in their strengths is mandatory; whether this affirmation is done together with some necessary critique is optional. Ultimately, relationships matter. People are more important than programs, and there can be no real institutional success if people are the casualties.

In this chapter we explore this leadership practice of *understanding relational skills*. People matter. Leadership, at its heart, is about relating well with people inside and outside your organization.

In the previous chapter we emphasized that the mechanistic nature of organizations is shifting to more organic and human-focused priorities. Leaders navigating these shifts recognize that a focus on effectively relating to the people of their organizations must be a top priority in the decades ahead.

As leaders work to shape organizations fit for human beings, the need for effective relational skills at every level of the organization is essential. Leaders foster collaboration, value and appreciate followers, and create space for follower individuality—all of this work necessitates effective relational skill.

In previous eras of coercive, top-down, and directive management, weak relational skills could be tolerated in some cases. In our day of team-oriented and network-style work environments, understanding and working well with others relationally is no longer an optional part of life in the workplace. Even in industries that arguably require high levels of technical skill, the trend is moving toward increased relational capacity and skill among the workforce.[1]

> Leadership is essentially a relational practice.

There is no getting around the priority of relational skills in today's organizations. While this is true for any organizational member, it is arguably even more of a priority for leaders. Leadership is essentially a relational practice. Although leaders need to pay attention to broader systems and structures in the organization and beyond, their core work is relational. Leaders set direction for people. Leaders align people and resources behind this direction. Leaders then motivate and inspire people toward shared goals. All of these core leadership responsibilities require effective relational skill.

In order to better understand the priority and practice of effective relational skills in the work of leadership, we will explore this topic through the following perspectives: (1) relational skills in biblical perspective, (2) relational skills in contemporary perspective, and (3) relational skills in practice.

Relational Skills in Biblical Perspective

The Bible places a high priority on maintaining strong interpersonal relationships. And the key to successful relationships is an attitude of love toward others.

Jesus on Relational Success: "Love One Another"

When an expert in religious law approached Jesus and asked him about the greatest of all God's commandments, Jesus responded with the Shema, the great Jewish confession of faith, taken from Deuteronomy 6:4–5: "The most important one is this: . . . 'Love the Lord your God with all your heart and with all your soul and with all your mind and with all your strength.'" Jesus then added a second, from Leviticus 19:18: "The second is this: 'Love your neighbor as yourself.' There is no commandment greater than these" (Mark 12:29–31). Loving God and loving others take precedence over all other priorities in life. In the parallel in Matthew's Gospel, Jesus adds, "All the Law and the Prophets hang on these two commandments" (Matt. 22:40). That's a pretty potent formula for success: keep these two commandments and all of life's imperatives will fall into place.

Although relational dynamics can be complicated and conflict an inevitable way of life, the key to successful relationships is presented as the simple formula: "Love one another" (John 13:34). On the last night of his life on earth, Jesus prepares his disciples to carry on after he is gone: "A new command I give you: Love one another. As I have loved you, so you must love one another. By this everyone will know that you are my disciples, if you love one another" (John 13:34–35).

Love is the defining character trait of an authentic Christian. But love is not defined as an emotional attachment, a feeling of affection, or a romantic longing. It is rather a conscious attitude and intentional actions that seek the best for the other person.

Throughout this book we have defined *servant leadership* in this same way. The goal of a servant leader is not to manipulate, control, direct, or persuade. It is to empower and enable others to be all that God has called them to be.

Of course, this was Jesus's mission on earth. He came to bring those who were spiritually dead back to life and to restore them to a right relationship with their Creator. The most famous verse in the Bible sums it up: "For God so *loved the world* that he gave his one and only Son, that whoever believes in him shall not perish but have eternal life" (John 3:16). Jesus's self-sacrificial life and his death on the cross for us were supreme acts of love (John 15:13) and were for the purpose of relationship, to reconcile us to God. "God . . . reconciled us to himself through Christ and gave us the ministry of reconciliation: that God was reconciling the world to himself in Christ, not counting people's sins against them. And he has committed to us the message of reconciliation" (2 Cor. 5:18–19). Reconciliation has as its goal a right relationship with others. The Christian life is about restoring and then deepening our relationships with God and with one another. That is what Jesus came to do.

Paul on Relational Success: "Put on Love"

The impression many people have of the apostle Paul is of a hard-driven, type A personality who tended to run roughshod over people in his zealous passion to accomplish the monumental task that God had given him: to take the gospel message to the ends of the earth. This stereotype of Paul is reinforced by an episode in Acts 15:36–41 (mentioned in chap. 4 above). When Paul and Barnabas decide to revisit the churches they started on their first missionary journey, Barnabas suggests that they bring his cousin John Mark, who accompanied them before. Paul refuses, since Mark "deserted" them on their first journey. Paul here seems more concerned about getting the job done than about maintaining his relationship with Barnabas or reconciliation with Mark.

Yet while Paul was certainly driven to fulfill God's calling in his life, a closer look at his letters confirms the remarkably high value he placed on relationships. Throughout his letters, Paul encourages church members to pursue the qualities necessary for healthy relationships.[2] As it was for Jesus, Paul's guiding principle for successful relationships was love (*agapē*). In Colossians 3:12–14, after encouraging the church to "put on" or clothe themselves with virtues like compassion, kindness, humility, gentleness, and patience, Paul adds, "And over all these virtues put on love, which binds them all together in perfect unity." These various virtues all have one thing in common: they are the outworking and expression of love.

Love for Paul is not a feeling or an attraction; it is an attitude and action that should characterize and motivate all of our relationships. Paul's great essay on love in 1 Corinthians 13:1–13 is set in the context of the Corinthians' infatuation with impressive spiritual gifts that brought pride, self-edification, and admiration from others. Paul asserts that the most dramatic and powerful gifts and abilities are worthless if not exercised with an attitude of love. And love, in essence, is people-centered, seeking the best for others: "Love is patient, love is kind. It does not envy, it does not boast, it is not proud. It does not dishonor others, it is not self-seeking, it is not easily angered, it keeps no record of wrongs. Love does not delight in evil but rejoices with the truth. It always protects, always trusts, always hopes, always perseveres. Love never fails" (1 Cor. 13:4–8).

Notice that everything love does is for the benefit of others. This is not an isolated thought in Paul's writings. In Philippians 2:3–4 he writes, "Do nothing out of selfish ambition or vain conceit. Rather, in humility value others above yourselves, not looking to your own interests but each of you to the interests of the others."

Notice too that, in describing the characteristics of love, Paul epitomizes a Christian leader. Replacing "love" with "Christian leaders" in 1 Corinthians 13 produces a strikingly appropriate description of servant leadership: "Christian leaders are patient, they are kind. They do not envy or boast; they are not proud. They do not dishonor others and are not self-seeking. They are not easily angered, nor do they keep a record of wrongs. They do not delight in evil but rejoice with the truth. They always protect, always trust, always hope, always persevere. They never give up" (1 Cor. 13:4–8 modified). The following are some of Paul's most important principles for leaders seeking to nurture and maintain healthy relationships.

Leaders Relate to Others with Honesty and Integrity

In Ephesians 4:25 Paul calls the church to honesty and integrity: "Therefore each of you must put off falsehood and speak truthfully to your neighbor, for we are all members of one body." A leader builds trust by living a life of authenticity. Saying one thing and doing another or making promises that are not kept erodes confidence and creates a toxic work environment. Relationships are built on trust, and the closer the relationship, the more important the trust.

Few things do greater damage to the church than hypocrisy. Older readers will remember the televangelist scandals in America in the 1980s, when several national Christian leaders were shown to be living lives of hypocrisy and immorality. Jim Bakker and his wife, Tammy Faye, were the heads of The PTL Club. Their message was the prosperity gospel. God wants you to be rich. Just name it, and claim it. And that's what they did. They had six homes, huge expense accounts, luxury cars, and extravagant jewelry. But in 1987 Jim Bakker was caught in a sex scandal with a church secretary. Then in 1989 he was convicted on twenty-four counts of defrauding the public and sent to prison. Bakker had sold his followers thousands of timeshare vacation units that were never built. While financially devastating for many, the damage was also spiritual and emotional. Millions of people had believed in this ministry. For many, their faith was shattered.

We aren't surprised when a Hollywood celebrity is caught in a scandal or when a politician is found to be skimming off public funds or having an affair. We have come to expect such corruption from the people of "the world." But when a Christian leader falls, it is devastating, because Christians claim to be God's agents of truth and reconciliation. Loving others means treating them with integrity and truth.

Leaders Pursue Kindness, Forgiveness, and Reconciliation

Conflict is inevitable in any relationship. The key to successful relationships is learning to resolve conflict in a positive and constructive way. Conflicts escalate when anger is met with anger, and a vicious cycle of retaliation and revenge begins. This is true of conflicts of all kinds, from a marriage in crisis to the quest for peace in the Middle East.

A wise leader recognizes that the only way to break this cycle of anger is to refuse to respond in kind but rather to repay evil with good. In Ephesians 4:31–32 Paul says, "Get rid of all bitterness, rage and anger, brawling and slander, along with every form of malice. Be kind and compassionate to one another, forgiving each other, just as in Christ God forgave you."

> *Intentionally choosing kindness and compassion opens the way for forgiveness.*

Bitterness and resentment, if allowed to fester, result in retaliation. Intentionally choosing kindness and compassion opens the way for forgiveness. Paul says that the incentive for forgiveness is the reality that "in Christ God forgave you." If God in his grace could forgive our debt of sin, we should see fit to forgive the much-less-significant sins committed against us. In Romans 12 Paul affirms the same truth: "If it is possible, as far as it depends on you, live at peace with everyone. Do not take revenge, my dear friends, but leave room for God's wrath. . . . Do not be overcome by evil, but overcome evil with good" (Rom. 12:18–21; cf. Eph. 4:26–27; Col. 3:12–13).

Again, the only way to break the cycle of evil is to refuse to retaliate, to respond with kindness rather than hatred. When hatred is met with hatred and violence with violence, the only winner is evil itself. The way to defeat evil is by responding with love.

Be Humble Rather Than Prideful

As just noted, conflict generally arises from wrongs committed against another person, sparking a cycle of anger, bitterness, and retaliation. The only way to stop this cycle is to avoid retaliation and, even more positively, to repay evil with good and hatred with love.

Yet to do this the wronged party needs to swallow their pride and even take a loss. In Romans 12:16 Paul writes, "Live in harmony with one another. Do not be proud, but be willing to associate with people of low position. Do not be conceited." Living in harmony often takes humility: being willing to say, "I'm sorry"; taking the first step toward reconciliation; swallowing your pride and taking the loss. Servant leaders will do this because they value the relationship more than they value always being right or gaining the advantage.

Relational Skills in Contemporary Perspective

Contemporary theory and research build on these biblical perspectives by providing additional insight into the importance of leaders understanding relational skills. In my (Justin's) research on the topic, the following statement was a statistically significant predictor of effective practice: "In general, people within this organization know how to get along with people."[3]

The features associated with getting along with other people may be difficult to specify at times, but for the most part we recognize getting along with others when we see it in action. Unsurprisingly, research supports the priority of this characteristic in effective leaders.

The image of the rugged, strong, silent, and individualistic leader—what popular culture saw as the Marlboro Man type in the latter half of the twentieth century—sometimes gets confused with leadership strength. Great leadership in our day is not about independence. Great leadership necessitates relationally engaged and network-style interactions with a diverse set of people both within and outside our organizations.

When research participants were asked about the nature of relational skills, several core themes emerged as central to relational skills and getting along with others as a leader. Among these themes are the priorities of self-awareness, empathy, and authentic listening—themes that intersect with the leadership practices of engaging in honest self-evaluation (chap. 2) and communicating with clarity (chap. 7). One participant noted that empathetic communication, personal connection, selective vulnerability, and attention to what motivates followers are all critical relational skills. Other participants emphasized the following items:

- A commitment to fairness and equality
- The importance of authentic listening
- The ability to tolerate and accept appropriate differences
- The importance of knowing oneself well in order to relate authentically with others
- The embodiment of confidence blended with the ability to see future possibilities and communicate the most appropriate path to get there
- The creation of a sense of safety and support for followers
- The demonstration of care and kindness
- The reinforcement of a commitment to the working relationship
- The maintenance of an open and approachable posture toward followers

All of these themes comprise key relational skills that help foster positive leader-follower relationships. Although leaders at times may like to work in the background, simply dealing with systems and structures, it is vital that they engage organizational members, team members, and direct reports with relational intelligence.

In light of these emphases, we will organize our discussion of contemporary leadership theory and research for this section around the following areas: (1) understanding people and their needs, (2) engaging people with relational intelligence, and (3) engaging people with intercultural intelligence.

Understanding People and Their Needs

In the 1950s Robert Katz wrote an important article in the *Harvard Business Review* titled "Skills of an Effective Administrator."[4] In his article, Katz argues that leaders need a mix of three primary skills to carry out their administrative responsibilities. These three skills are technical, conceptual, and human.

Katz notes that while leaders at various levels of organizational life—top, middle, and supervisory management—need all three of these skills, different leadership levels call on these three skills in diverse ways (see fig. 6.1). For instance, while direct supervisory managers need a high level of technical skill

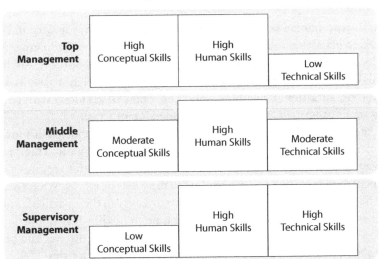

Figure 6.1
Management Skill Levels

related to those they lead, top-level managers do not need technical skills to the same extent. Complementing this, while top-level managers need a high level of conceptual skill, direct supervisory managers do not need this same level of conceptual skill.

In contrast to technical and conceptual skills, Katz emphasizes that human skill must be strong at every level of administrative leadership. This makes sense because the work of leadership and management is a relational practice. Organizations of various types and sizes are made up of people. To effectively lead in these organizations requires leaders to give attention to human skill at every level of leadership. Effective engagement with people is a priority at every level of leadership responsibility.

So how does Katz characterize human skill? Human skill involves

- Leaders possessing the capacity and competency needed to assist a group toward accomplishment of shared goals
- Leaders nurturing an atmosphere of trust
- Leaders encouraging followers
- Leaders helping followers feel secure and comfortable in their work even as leaders challenge them to excellence and productivity
- Leaders being aware of their own perspectives and the perspectives of others

- Leaders adjusting and adapting their own behavior in a manner that is responsive to the needs and perspectives of others

At its core, human skill is really about leaders having the capacity and skills needed to get along well with others—playing in a cooperative manner in the sandbox of organizational life and work. This is the focus of the research that stands behind this leadership practice of understanding relational skills. Leaders and organizational members who "know how to get along with people" are a significant predictor of effective leadership practice.

The human skills of getting along with people are supported in a foundational manner by leaders understanding the nature of people and their needs. As leaders nurture an understanding of relational skills, this requires a commitment to recognizing and responding to the needs of others. What are these core human needs? While individuals have diversity in their particular needs, some needs possess more of a universal human quality. It is important for leaders to understand these universal needs present in themselves and others. Ultimately, people need community, belonging, and relationship.

When such basic needs are met in our lives, these satisfied needs contribute to a person's overall experience of human flourishing and well-being. Although leaders do not directly meet all of these needs for their followers, they often do have the opportunity and stewardship responsibility to create contexts within which such needs can be addressed. Leaders often occupy roles that shape organizational cultures, systems, and roles that allow people to bring meaningful contributions in their work. This meaningful contribution in service of others can both provide a greater sense of purpose in one's work and allow the one working to provide meaningfully for their own needs and the needs of others. In other words, leaders are able to help their followers experience human flourishing in and through their work.

People need community, belonging, and relationship.

Such a vision of leadership and work is not fully realized, however, when leaders depersonalize or dehumanize the leader-follower relationship. Leaders must recognize the whole-life nature of their followers as spiritual beings with physical, rational, and emotional dimensions to their lives.

In their book *The Leadership Challenge*, James Kouzes and Barry Posner emphasize one aspect of this whole-person engagement for leaders through their practice of encouraging the heart.[5] While we might be tempted to have a "do it because I said so" approach to leadership, this misses the heart of healthy leadership practice.

One example Kouzes and Posner discuss is the need to maintain both an open door and an open heart. While open-door approaches to leadership physically depict leader accessibility, leaders also need to engage in open-heart approaches to leadership. Trust is built on appropriate openness and vulnerability. As a leader, are you showing both the rational and emotional sides of your life as a fellow team member? Are you engaging both open-door and open-heart practices in your leadership?

As you consider the followers you work with as a leader, take time to consider the holistic needs they have as people and how as a leader you can work with followers in a way that contributes to both organizational and individual flourishing. Modeling appropriate levels of emotional openness is one of the relational skills that invites a leader-follower relationship where leaders can speak into and encourage the hearts of their followers. By doing this, leaders can both affirm and help meet the needs of the people with whom they work.

Engaging People with Relational Intelligence

Based on our first point of understanding people and their needs, we now turn to the importance of engaging people with relational intelligence. Similar to other areas of leader intelligence, we argue that leaders must possess at least a functional level of relational intelligence.

Our colleague Mark McCloskey places relationships at the center of his leadership theory.[6] While leaders must move on to engage the necessary roles and responsibilities of leadership in the pursuit of organizational results and outcomes, the animating core of leadership begins with relationship.

For McCloskey, this relational core is characterized by virtue-oriented leadership capacity that provides a sufficient level of collaborative quotient. He notes that when leaders possess dynamic determination, intellectual flexibility, courageous character, and emotional maturity, collectively these dimensions of leader capacity provide a requisite core for effectively relating to and partnering with others in a common leadership venture.

McCloskey sees this capacity for colaboring with others to achieve common ends—collaborative quotient—as the expression of virtue-driven leadership. In his words, collaborative quotient is an honest and humble strength that "embraces the reality that no one person—no matter how talented—can go it alone."[7] Rather, leaders with this relational core and capacity invite others, including followers with leadership strength, to contribute to the welfare and flourishing of the overall community.

We would argue that this concept of collaborative quotient and a commitment to relationships at the core of leadership is consistent with emotional

intelligence in leadership as well. In chapter 2 we emphasized the importance of *self*-awareness and *self*-management in emotional intelligence theory.
Equally important is emotional intelligence in reference to others.

As leaders, are we paying attention to the emotional dynamics that are
happening both within ourselves and in our relationships with others? Some
label these dimensions as *intra*personal and *inter*personal intelligences.[8] Both
the intra- and interpersonal sides of intelligence are vital for effective relational
practice. For us as leaders, our self-awareness must translate into social and
relational awareness as well. Examples of this include paying attention to
both verbal and nonverbal emotional cues that followers provide and then
responding to these cues based on this awareness.

Travis Bradberry and Jean Greaves note several examples of practical leader
behaviors for effectively navigating social awareness and response.

- Watch body language.
- Practice the art of listening.
- Step into their shoes.
- Catch the mood of the room.
- Be open and curious.
- Avoid giving mixed signals.
- Have an open-door policy.
- Acknowledge the other person's feelings.
- When you care, show it.
- Explain your decisions; don't just make them.[9]

While the list could go on, these behaviors illustrate the relational intelligence we are calling for in this chapter. Relational awareness is key to recognizing and responding to the needs of others in leader-follower engagement.
Self-awareness leading to an awareness of and responsiveness to the needs
of others provides a platform on which effective leaders may appropriately
humanize the leader-follower relational engagement.

Engaging People with Intercultural Intelligence

Intercultural intelligence shares many of the features noted previously
about relational and emotional intelligence. As with emotional intelligence,
healthy intercultural intelligence does not begin with studying other cultures
but rather starts with first gaining awareness of one's own culture. This

self-awareness becomes the foundation for understanding and responding to people of other cultures.

This may sound like easy work, but an individual's engagement with their own culture is often similar to the experience of our atmosphere—we exist within the context of the air of our atmosphere but rarely take time to reflect on this context. Because culture is often just assumed—like the air we breathe—it takes intentionality for a person to pay attention to their own culture. But lack of reflection on our own culture works against effective cross-cultural engagement.

In his book *Close: Leading Well across Distance and Cultures*, Ken Cochrum notes that becoming more aware of their own cultural values and biases provides the basis for leaders to demonstrate cultural interest, sensitivity, and adaptability.[10] In order to gain the benefits of such cultural self-awareness, we need to resist a common tendency to see the culture differences that exist in others while being blind to our own cultural lenses.

In today's globalized world, effective intercultural engagement in leadership is a requirement of the job. Although engagement across culture has taken place for thousands of years, the realities of modern globalization heighten the need for intercultural intelligence. Globalization was propelled forward by key technological advances such as aviation, telecommunication, and the introduction of the internet to everyday use across the globe. Through such advances, the cultures of the world have been brought closer than ever before.

Lest we think globalization is relevant only for those traveling internationally, or for those in large metropolitan areas around the world, we must remember that globalization hits home at the local level in our organizations as well. Some have used the creative language of "glocalization" to talk about these local dimensions of globalization.

For leaders wishing to engage in effective intercultural practice in light of the realities of globalization or glocalization, what theories and tools can be a helpful guide along the way? In chapter 3 we introduced the Global Leadership and Organizational Behavior Effectiveness research project, known as the GLOBE studies.[11] Among other elements, the GLOBE studies examine what are known as modal values and practices in which research participants reflect on their culture in light of the *as is* (modal practices) and *should be* (modal values).

These analyses in the GLOBE studies provide key insight regarding how members of a cultural cluster view their culture across nine cultural dimensions: power distance, gender egalitarianism, uncertainty avoidance, assertiveness orientation, collectivism orientation (both institutional and in-group), future orientation, humane orientation, and performance orientation. As an example of findings from the GLOBE studies, while each cultural cluster is unique, there is a universal desire for higher levels of performance and humane orientation, along with a universal desire for lower levels of power distance or unequal sharing of power.

While projects like the GLOBE studies can provide useful insight into cultural clusters, other theories provide additional help as we engage cultural difference at an individual level. One tool on this front is the Developmental Model of Intercultural Sensitivity (DMIS).[12] Under the model, ethnocentric behaviors are characterized by denial, defensiveness, or minimization while effective cross-cultural behaviors are characterized by acceptance, adaptation, and integration.

Here is where more parallels are seen between emotional intelligence and intercultural intelligence. While emotional intelligence is about awareness and adaptation at the emotional level, intercultural intelligence is about awareness and adaptation at the cultural level. Effective intercultural leaders begin with awareness of their own cultural lenses. Then out of this awareness effective intercultural leaders see cultural differences in others, appreciate the cultural differences observed, and then learn to adapt their expressions in response to these differences. While intercultural engagement is complex, the core of what makes it work is not: learn to see difference, appreciate and accept what you see as valuable, and then work to adapt your behavior in a way that bridges this cultural difference.

Effective intercultural leaders begin with awareness of their own cultural lenses.

Relational Skills in Practice

In this chapter we have presented a case for understanding relational skills. Because leadership is essentially a relational practice, understanding people and their needs, and engaging people with relational and intercultural intelligence, is vital for sustained leadership effectiveness.

To illustrate what skills associated with relational and intercultural intelligence look like in practice, we begin with sharing the leadership example of one of our graduates and then provide practical advice for those of you desiring to take the next step in developing your own relational skills.

Relational Skills in Action: Dr. Saji Lukos

One of the joys of being a Christian is the reality that God's family crosses borders and cultures. One of the joys of working in the seminary environment is the pleasure we have of getting to know many of these family members—including passionate and effective ministry leaders who are making a profound impact through their work globally.

While we could highlight many individuals we've worked with over the years, we'd like to highlight one individual—Dr. Saji Lukos—who models well what it means to lead with relational wisdom and intelligence. Saji is a graduate of Bethel's Doctor of Ministry program and has devoted his life to seeing a transformational impact for Christ among the people of India.

Saji's relational skills began early in his life. Living in the Kerala region of southern India, he was the eldest of eight children. Saji notes, "In Indian culture, the oldest son is responsible for taking care of his younger siblings" as they emerge into the worlds of work and family life.[13] Saji felt this responsibility not only as a brother but also as a Christian. He desired for his siblings to see how his life had changed since he became a Christian so they too would come to know and love Jesus.

Out of these lessons early in life, Saji founded Reaching Indians Ministries International and later, Mission India Theological Seminary. Today, Saji leads this ministry of over fifteen hundred indigenous missionaries and thirty Bible schools connected to the seminary.

I (Justin) have had the pleasure of getting to know Saji and traveling to speak at the seminary in Nagpur, India. Anyone who knows Saji can attest to his sincere warmth and relational capacity. God has used Saji to build deep relationships with people throughout India, southern Asia, and North America. The challenge of leading this significant work could not take place without leaders with relational intelligence.

Through his smile and inviting presence, Saji gets to know the people with whom he serves and partners in ministry. I have been struck by simple gestures he brings to relationships—remembering names, asking about family members by name, and helping individuals across the globe see what their part can be as together they are developing "Christ-like global leaders for transforming communities in India and beyond."[14]

Among the many vital resources leaders like Saji bring to the table are relational and intercultural intelligence. In his work, Saji regularly has to engage cross-culturally. He and his wife, Mony, now live in Illinois. When Saji travels for ministry on the ground in India, he needs to shift his mind-set and practices from life in Illinois to life and ministry in the Indian context. Although having grown up in India provides him with a significant starting place, it still takes intercultural sensitivity to recognize when he must draw on different relational skills in new contexts.

Similarly, much of Saji's recent educational endeavors and fund-raising work have taken place in North America. He has had to learn how to translate his message and work across cultures in the North American context. Such translation is not primarily about language. It is about culture. Leaders like Saji working across cultures must be able to engage others quickly, recognizing the presence of cultural difference, and then respond to this difference with both appreciation and adaptation where needed.

The result of such intercultural wisdom and work is a thriving and fruitful ministry with both students and indigenous missionaries. It has been an honor to learn from Saji's skills as a transformational leader and to observe his application of relational and intercultural intelligence in the work of ministry leadership.

Relational Skills: Insights for Practice

Although engaging people with effective relational and intercultural skills is important for almost anyone in an organization, these skills hold particular importance for leaders in their work with people both inside and outside their organizations. In this section, we provide three recommendations—recognize, reflect, and respond—for leaders seeking to apply what we've discussed above.

Recognize with Availability and Awareness

As leaders work closely with others, relational skill often begins with simply recognizing. Consider the following questions: What do your followers care about? What motivates them? Why do they show up to their job or the role they serve in? What would inspire them to greater investment and service on behalf of the community?

Such questions involve seeing followers in a holistic manner and paying attention to the spiritual, emotional, physical, and intellectual needs they bring to their lives and work. To be able to nurture this awareness, leaders often have to both make themselves available to their followers and model what matters with courage and vulnerability.

Whether it is with emotional, relational, or intercultural intelligence, leaders model what matters by being aware of their own lives and being aware of the whole-person nature of their followers. Productivity still needs to take place in service of the organizational mission, but when leaders recognize that the people of their organizations are the primary ones delivering on this mission, then effectively engaging others with availability and awareness is a meaningful starting point. Take time for this work of recognizing in the week ahead. What needs are the people on your team bringing to their work? Consider spiritual and emotional needs that your team members have, and consider how you can increase your awareness of these needs in your daily work with team members.

Reflect with Openness and Curiosity

Beyond the work of recognizing, leaders must translate this recognition into reflection that is open and teachable. Among other things, leaders make themselves available for followers through simple acts like open-door policies. But open doors are not enough. Open hearts are also important. This translates into leaders caring about what they see in others and reflecting deeply on this. As you start to see the deeper needs that followers bring to their work, make sure to reflect on these needs with an open heart that truly cares for the well-being of those on your team.

In addition to caring, this type of openness also is accompanied by intellectual curiosity—an appropriately open mind. Rather than viewing themselves as having everything figured out on their own, effective leaders in the network-style organizations of our day invite and reflect on the perspectives of others with a spirit of creative curiosity. Take some time this week to consider the level of care you bring to relationships with followers. Consider how you may reflect more deeply on their needs as together you create a work environment that values human flourishing.

This type of reflective openness and curiosity communicates that the other person in the leader-follower relationship matters. It is a pathway to show care and build trust as leaders nurture a sense of safety and support. This type of openness exemplifies the teachable spirit of St. Francis of Assisi's famous prayer: "O divine Master, grant that I may not so much seek to be consoled as to console, to be understood as to understand, to be loved as to love. For it is in giving that we receive, it is in pardoning that we are pardoned, and it is in dying that we are born to eternal life."[15]

Respond with Adaptability

Finally, in addition to recognizing and reflecting, the final recommendation is to respond with adaptability. As leaders recognize what is happening in the interpersonal and intercultural leader-follower dynamics, individuals with relational intelligence seek to respond with a spirit that is willing to adapt and adjust.

But adaptability is not about mere accommodation and avoidance of issues. Adaptability is about responding in light of conviction. Leaders need to act with conviction based on what they believe is best for their followers and their organization. But conviction blended with biblical humility looks for ways to respond and adapt to others when it will serve the needs of followers and the organization. Rather than always expecting others to change, Christian leaders motivated by love look for ways to respond and adapt as well.

This pattern of recognizing and responding to follower need is at the heart of effective relational skill in leadership. This skill in relational intelligence parallels the skill needed in intercultural intelligence—learning to see cultural difference, and then responding and changing one's behavior in light of the difference seen.

In small and large organizations alike, the realities of globalization are all around us at the local level. While individual leaders cannot personally be experts in all the possible cultural differences they may encounter, they can raise their level of awareness, appreciation, and adaptive response to the differences they see.

As you recognize and reflect on the needs of your followers, what steps can you take in the week ahead to respond meaningfully to these needs? Becoming a skilled relational and intercultural leader often simply begins with taking an interest in the people you lead. Come to the leader-follower relationship with awareness, openness, and a willingness to make adjustments as you learn what will more effectively serve your followers' needs.

Next Steps

- Take some time this week to *recognize* the needs that the people on your team bring to their work. Consider the spiritual and emotional priorities your team members have in their daily lives and work.

- Take some time this week to *reflect* on the level of care you bring to relationships with followers. Consider how you may reflect more deeply on their needs as together you create a work environment that values human flourishing.

- As you recognize and reflect on the needs of your followers, take some time to consider how you should *respond* to these needs. Consider what steps you can take in the week ahead to respond meaningfully to your team members and their needs—vocationally, spiritually, emotionally, and so on.

Resources for a Deeper Look

Bradberry, Travis, and Jean Greaves. *Emotional Intelligence 2.0*. San Diego: TalentSmart, 2009.

De Pree, Max. *Leadership Is an Art*. New York: Dell, 1989.

McCloskey, Mark W. *Learning Leadership in a Changing World: Virtue and Effective Leadership in the 21st Century*. New York: Palgrave Macmillan, 2014.

Morris, Leon. *Testaments of Love: A Study of Love in the Bible*. Grand Rapids: Eerdmans, 1981.

Strauss, Richard L. *Getting Along with Each Other: Communication, Relationships*. San Bernardino, CA: Here's Life Publishers, 1985.

Part 3

Navigating toward Effectiveness

IN THE FIRST SIX CHAPTERS we highlighted the importance of beginning with authentic leaders and understanding the priority of people. In part 3 we turn our attention to navigating toward effectiveness. We start our discussion by emphasizing the importance of clear communication (chap. 7). Organizational members need to understand with clarity what is important in the organization and what is expected of them. Communication is therefore a top priority for leadership. All effective leaders are by necessity effective communicators.

Once goals and mission have been communicated with clarity in a manner that nurtures shared ownership, it is time for leaders to provide accountability (chap. 8). Although the leader's role in providing accountability is difficult work at times, it is important for empowering leaders to remember that their primary job is to be helpful to followers, not just be nice. Providing account-ability matters because empowering leaders want to see both followers and organizations flourish.

The final step in navigating toward effectiveness is for leaders to support and resource their followers (chap. 9). Models of leadership emphasizing service and empowerment recognize that the leader's number-one job is to work for those who work for them. This is not about responding to every whim and wish of followers but rather involves recognizing that the success of the team and organization depends on the success of every member. In this model, leaders focus on bringing the right people onto the team and then doing everything in their power to help them succeed.

7

Communicating with Clarity

Introduction

The list of Colin Powell's accomplishments is impressive. Among his many roles and responsibilities, Powell rose to the rank of four-star general and served as national security adviser, commander of the US Army Forces Command, chairman of the Joint Chiefs of Staff, and the sixty-fifth US secretary of state from 2001 to 2005.

During his work as a professional soldier and public servant, Powell learned powerful lessons about communicating as a leader. For instance, Powell learned that leaders must not only regularly communicate *to* followers but they must also nurture regular communication *from* their followers.

This is a communication practice Powell has emphasized. He writes, "The day soldiers stop bringing you their problems is the day you have stopped leading them. They have either lost confidence that you can help them or concluded that you do not care. Either case is a failure of leadership."[1] Nurturing pathways for communication that run in multiple directions is a leadership essential.

In this chapter we explore the leadership practice of *communicating with clarity*. If leadership is primarily about managing things (e.g., inventory, systems, structures, budgets, paperwork), then effective communication may not be essential. But if leadership is primarily about guiding and motivating people—which it is—then communication is absolutely essential for effective leadership practice.

Although effective communicators are not necessarily effective leaders, effective leaders are by necessity effective communicators. This does not mean that all leaders are great public speakers. It may be that their leadership practice draws on communication at the interpersonal or group level rather than speaking to large groups. But regardless of the level of a leader's communication, this communication must be done with clarity and effectiveness.

As we emphasized in the previous chapter, leadership is essentially a relational practice. It is about leaders engaging with effective relational skills and effective communication skills. Just as healthy relationships in our personal lives require clear and meaningful communication, so the communication between leaders and followers must also be characterized by health, clarity, and effectiveness.

Consider some of the core leadership responsibilities and how communication is central to this work. Leadership is about setting direction and communicating a compelling vision. Leadership is about aligning people around this direction and vision. Leadership is about motivating people along the way and inspiring them toward ownership of shared goals that must be accomplished together. In each of these responsibilities, clear and effective communication is central to the work of leadership.

As we seek to understand the priority of communicating with clarity in greater depth, we will look at this leadership practice from the following perspectives: (1) communication in biblical perspective, (2) communication in contemporary perspective, and (3) communication in practice.

Communication in Biblical Perspective

In the previous chapter we discussed the importance of relational skills in leadership. Here we zero in on one important factor in maintaining good relationships: effective communication skills. Any psychologist or marriage and family therapist will tell you that good communication is essential for good relationships. Couples, families, and leadership teams that don't communicate or that communicate poorly are prone to misunderstandings, anger, bitterness, and a failure to reconcile after conflict.

Clarity in communication is especially important for Christian leaders, who are responsible for motivating followers and carrying forward the mission of their organization.

Effective Communication Begins with a Compelling Message Clearly Expressed

To communicate effectively, the leader must have a clear and compelling message worth communicating. The apostle Paul kept his message simple.

Writing to the church at Corinth he says, "For what I received I passed on to you as of first importance: that Christ died for our sins according to the Scriptures, that he was buried, that he was raised on the third day according to the Scriptures" (1 Cor. 15:3–4). It was this simple message—"Christ died for our sins according to the Scriptures"—that was both the reason for Paul's mission and the content of his message. It was a simple message, so simple that it was sometimes dismissed as foolishness. In the same Corinthian context Paul writes, "Jews demand signs and Greeks look for wisdom, but we preach Christ crucified: a stumbling block to Jews and foolishness to Gentiles" (1:22–23). For some, the simplicity of the message of the cross was a liability. But for Paul, what truly counted was whether the message had the power to transform lives. Paul continues, "But to those whom God has called, both Jews and Greeks, Christ *the power of God and the wisdom of God*" (1:24). Elsewhere Paul writes similarly: "For I am not ashamed of the gospel, *because it is the power of God that brings salvation to everyone who believes*: first to the Jew, then to the Gentile" (Rom. 1:16). The message was worth communicating because it produced transformed lives.

> *To communicate effectively, the leader must have a clear and compelling message worth communicating.*

To be successful, leaders must have a clear and cogent message, which can be transmitted well and put into practice effectively. Slogans, mottos, or taglines can be useful if they are both accurate and applicable. I (Mark) work with a number of churches in the San Diego area, many of which have slogans or mottos that relate to their fundamental mission. One of these is "Save. Equip. Send," which succinctly describes the church's threefold mission as bringing people to Christ, equipping them as disciples, and sending them out to save and equip others. Another church has the mission slogan "Honoring God by living like Jesus," pointing to the ultimate goal of bringing glory to God by following the example set by his Son. A third has the simple slogan "Love will change the world." Less overtly Christian, this is meant to appeal to the broader culture. Those who are drawn to the church quickly learn that this "world-changing love" was demonstrated by God in sending his Son to save us, and it is now manifested through the church's self-sacrificial, Christlike love for people.

Effective Communicators Must Understand Their Audience

In addition to communicating well a church's mission, these slogans point to the need for the leader to "read" their audience in order to connect with them at their areas of greatest need. Jesus clearly understood his audience when he taught in the villages and countryside around the Sea of Galilee. This was an agrarian culture, and Jesus told parables and proverbs drawn from aspects of everyday life that people could relate to: sowing seed, harvesting crops, herding sheep, renting vineyards, attending wedding feasts, and so on. He also spoke in ways that connected to their deeply felt needs, addressing issues like poverty, injustice, piety, faithfulness to the law, hypocrisy, loving your enemies, daily sustenance, forgiveness, and reconciliation.

Paul also clearly "read" his audience when communicating the gospel. This is illustrated well by comparing two of Paul's sermons recorded in the book of Acts. When Paul teaches in the synagogue at Antioch Pisidia, his message is centered on the promises and covenants made to Israel and their subsequent fulfillment through Jesus the Messiah. It is a thoroughly Jewish message appropriate for the Jews and God-fearing Gentiles who attended the synagogue (Acts 13:13–52). Yet when Paul is invited to speak on Mars Hill in Athens, he gears his message to the Greek philosophers assembled there. He speaks not of Abraham and David and the Old Testament covenants but rather of the many altars to the "gods" of the Greco-Roman world and of the one true God who made the heavens and the earth (Acts 17:22–34).

Effective Communication Requires Good Listening Skills

Of course, to read your audience well you have to understand them. And the best way to understand them is to listen well. For this reason, one of the most important communication skills we can develop is becoming a better listener. The apostle James gives sound advice on listening in his New Testament letter. He writes, "My dear brothers and sisters, take note of this: Everyone should be quick to listen, slow to speak and slow to become angry, because human anger does not produce the righteousness that God desires" (James 1:19–20).

"Be quick to listen" seems at first an unusual command, since the speed of listening depends on the speed of the speaker! How can you listen quickly? But James is not asking for rapid listening. He is drawing a contrast to what we normally are, which is *quick to respond*. Too often we are not really listening to the other person; we are just waiting for our turn to speak. We may be nodding, but in our mind we are already formulating a response. Being quick to listen means focusing our attention on the other person and truly hearing what is being said.

Being "slow to speak" is similar. It means not talking or giving advice *until you know you understand*. One good way to do this is to consciously restate what the other person has just said, with a statement like, "So you're saying . . . ?" Or, "What I hear you saying is . . ." The person can then either affirm or correct your understanding. Too often we hear what we want to hear rather than what is actually being communicated.

Several years ago a student came into my (Mark's) office and asked me to sign a form for withdrawal from school. When I inquired why he was dropping out, he said, "Classes are just too hard. I can't handle the pressure." I was about to launch into my lecture on the need to persevere, but I sensed something else was wrong so I began to probe. I asked questions: What classes? Have you talked to the teachers? How are you spending your time? What other concerns do you have? Gradually it came out that

> *One of the most important communication skills we can develop is becoming a better listener.*

he was struggling with a serious moral issue. What he said was "Classes are too hard," but what he meant was "I need a good excuse to get away from this place, so I won't have to deal with this destructive behavior." We talked through the issue, and I was able to get him help. He ended up staying in school. I would have totally missed the message if I had been quick to speak— launching into my lecture.

James also tells us to be slow to anger. An important listening skill is to avoid reacting (or overreacting). It is easy for us to react and lose our temper, especially when we are facing criticism. An angry statement typically produces an angry response and escalation, and constructive dialogue can break down. Anger can be like feedback on a PA system, that shrieking sound caused when a microphone gets too close to its speaker and picks up its own sound, sending it back again to the speaker, which quickly escalates to shrieking. The solution is to turn down the volume or to separate the mic from the speaker. In the same way, when anger begins to escalate, both parties need to "turn down the volume" and answer calmly, or step back from the situation. As Proverbs 15:1 says, "A gentle answer turns away wrath, but a harsh word stirs up anger." When anger is kept in check, constructive dialogue can continue.

Good Communication Has as Its Goal the Benefit of the Listener

Ultimately, the goal of communication should be the same as our goal in all leadership functions: to choose words that *build others up rather than break them down*. As children growing up, we learn the impact words can have. Being called "ugly" or "stupid," especially by someone whose affirmation we crave, can be devastating to our self-image. Most of us remember the negative things our parents said to us even more than the positive.

In Ephesians 4:29 Paul writes, "Do not let any unwholesome talk come out of your mouths, but only what is helpful for building others up according to their needs, that it may benefit those who listen." The word translated "unwholesome" (*sapros*) often refers to food that is spoiled or rotten and so is unhealthy to eat. Some words are "unhealthy," doing damage by demeaning or humiliating. Others are "healthy," nourishing and building the other person up emotionally and spiritually. Paul says only ever to speak health-giving words.

This, of course, doesn't mean we never criticize or correct. But criticism should never be for the purpose of vindicating ourselves, or putting down or humiliating the other person. Its purpose should always be to help the other person grow closer to Christ. As we have seen in Ephesians 4:11–13, the apostle Paul affirms that the role of Christian leaders is "to equip his people for works of service" so that they mature and become more Christlike. Paul continues by discussing the way in which this maturity is expressed: "Speaking the truth in love, we will grow to become in every respect the mature body of him who is the head, that is, Christ" (4:15). "Speaking the truth" means being honest and straightforward about a person's shortcomings and areas of growth. "Speaking the truth *in love*" means the goal is always to benefit that person.

Along the same lines, Paul writes in Colossians 4:6, "Let your conversation be always full of grace, seasoned with salt, so that you may know how to answer everyone." Conversation that is "full of grace" means words spoken kindly, gently, tactfully, and for the benefit of the other person rather than to build up one's own ego or demonstrate superiority. Just as salt gives flavor to what is otherwise unpalatable, so careful speech encourages and uplifts even while instructing or correcting.

Effective leaders recognize the power of words. Words of commendation and encouragement should always follow work well done. And when criticism is necessary, it should be "healthy," accompanied by words of encouragement and always focused on the goal of benefiting the other person.

Communication in Contemporary Perspective

Contemporary theory and research build on these biblical perspectives by providing additional insight into the importance of leaders communicating with clarity. In my (Justin's) research on the topic, the following statement was a statistically significant predictor of effective practice: "Supervisors and top leadership in this organization communicate clear plans and goals."[2] Such insight should be no surprise to those in organizations. Goals and clear communication around these goals and plans matter.

This line of research is also supported by an additional set of studies that emphasize the priority of both follower focus and goal orientation.[3] Followers want their leaders to be goal oriented. But they want this goal orientation not to be devoid of heart; this expectation of goal orientation for leaders stands alongside leaders having a clear focus on followers. When leaders are both follower focused and goal oriented, great things can be accomplished through collaborative work.

If having clear plans and goals is a priority, then a leader should also possess the capacity to communicate these priorities to teams, organizations, and relevant stakeholders effectively and clearly. As noted in the previous chapter, leadership is essentially a relational practice. Therefore, like any healthy relationship, leadership depends on healthy communication.

Although one can be an effective communicator without being a leader, it does not work the other way. Effective leaders are effective communicators. The two cannot be separated in the work of leadership.

In light of the priority of communication for effective leadership practice, our discussion of contemporary leadership theory and research in this section is organized around two primary areas: (1) facing the complexities of leadership communication and (2) serving others through clear communication.

Facing the Complexities of Leadership Communication

Although it is easy to say leaders must be effective communicators, engaging in effective communication comes with significant complexity. Consider the diverse features associated with the communication process.

Communication takes place through distinct modes such as listening and speaking, reading and writing, observing and modeling. Communication must factor in that which is expressed intentionally and unintentionally, that which is expressed consciously and unconsciously, that which is expressed at the cognitive and emotional level, and that which is expressed both verbally and nonverbally—both through actions and inactions.

To further the complexities, leaders in organizations must pay attention to diverse levels of leadership communication. In his *Theories of Human Communication*, Stephen Littlejohn notes four major levels of communication: interpersonal communication, group communication, organizational communication, and mass communication.[4] Later in this section we'll mention at least seven levels.

So what are the core features in this complex process we call communication? Communication models emphasize diverse elements, but most models include elements such as the role of the *communicators* (each communicator functioning as a sender and receiver), the *filters* associated with the communicator that help and hinder the encoding and decoding of messages, the *message* itself, the *channels* used to communicate the message, the presence of *noise or interference* in the communication process, and the pathway of *feedback* that takes place between communicators.

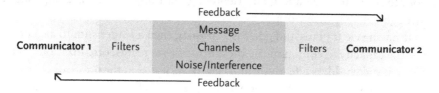

COMMUNICATORS

Whether the leadership-communication act involves two or more people, the role of communicators is central to the communication process. Early communication models provided single-direction models of communication where one person was viewed as the communicator and the other person was viewed as the receiver. In reality, every person in the leadership-communication process functions as both a sender and a receiver of information. As leaders we must press into this basic shift from monologue to dialogue, though this will look different at distinct communication levels. But even at the organizational and mass levels of communication, leaders must look for pathways for receiving input and feedback in order to know that their message is on point and clearly understood.

FILTERS

As we consider the role of communicators in the leadership-communication process, it is important to recognize there is no purely objective form of communication. Communication is always filtered through the lenses of the people involved. These lenses serve as filters as people encode and decode messages. For instance, in spoken or written forms of communication, communicators may also pay attention to the words used and the genre or rhetorical devices used for those words (e.g., humor or sarcasm change the meaning of the words used). Communicators may pay attention to the words that are absent in the communication process. What is assumed or what is left unspoken or unwritten can communicate as much as the spoken and written dimensions.

And communicators may pay attention to the point of view of communicators. This includes the emotions, perspectives, social locations, and histories that influence the various communicators and their point of view. Such filters may be conscious or unconscious. Communicators often benefit when unconscious blind spots surface, thus increasing understanding of the encoding and decoding filters that influence both the sending and receiving of messages.

Message

In the communication process, the message is the attempt to communicate meaning to others. For leaders, this is a reminder that there should be something that is both valuable and clear to call others to in the communication process. The contents of leader messages will be diverse and numerous, but leaders must be clear on a few key messages. On this point, Patrick Lencioni notes six vital questions for which organization leaders need to have answers: "Why do we exist? How do we behave? What do we do? How will we succeed? What is most important, right now? Who must do what?"[5] Although messages will always require encoding and decoding on the part of communicators, a leader who is clear on these messages provides a powerful starting point for organizational communication.

Channels

Leadership communication, like other forms of communication, includes channels that serve as the mediums for transmitting intended messages. Consider some of the common mediums for communication: spoken words, written text, nonverbal expression, and technologically mediated channels. Most communicative acts use multiple channels simultaneously. For instance, a communicator's message may be transmitted simultaneously through verbal and nonverbal expression. In today's geographically dispersed organizations, technology is regularly used to facilitate audio and visual channels for communication. Whether through conference calls or video conferences, diverse channels are available to organizational leaders today.

Noise or Interference

In each channel used for communicating are associated forms of noise or interference that can distort the intended and received message. In early models of telecommunication, this noise may have been literal static or voice distortion on a telephone line. In today's conference calls or video calls, this may be a challenge with bandwidth demands or internet connectivity that may distort the message received. But noise and interference extend beyond technology. They also include the physical environmental noise surrounding the communicators (e.g., a lawnmower passing by a classroom or a baby crying on the other side of a room). Further, noise can extend to the psychological dimensions of the communicators as they process their own intrapersonal dialogue associated with the thoughts and feelings occurring during the communicative process.

FEEDBACK

As noted above, single-pathway models of communication are yielding to multipath models. Because each communicator functions as both a sender and a receiver in the communication process, a recognition of the dialogical element of feedback is relevant for leaders. While leaders may have a preference for the directive leadership models of the past that emphasize command and control, these models are giving way to more participative and empowering models that necessitate dialogue and feedback. Effective leaders not only need to be clear on their message but also need to know if this message is understood by organizational members. Effective leaders are committed to authentic listening. Whether this is in dyadic, group, organizational, or mass forms of communication, feedback from the other participants in the communicative process is vital for leaders.

Serving Others through Clear Communication

Although communication is complex, leaders can prioritize core aspects of the communication process that help make the complexities a bit more manageable. One starting point to this is remembering whom leaders serve in their work. Healthy leadership is not primarily about serving the needs of leaders. Healthy leadership is about serving the needs of others—followers and those served by the organization.

Viewing leadership as primarily about serving the needs of others changes the way we look at leadership communication. Healthy and effective leadership communication is not primarily about leaders saying what they want to say, but rather it is about leaders ensuring that authentic communication is taking place—communication in which followers and stakeholders genuinely understand what matters most and provide meaningful feedback.

In his book *Tell It Often—Tell It Well*, Mark McCloskey presents what he calls the "road to other-centered communication."[6] He notes that other-centered communication is characterized by a commitment to relevance, listening, responsive sensitivity, and dialogue. This understanding of other-centered communication is contrasted to both self-centered and message-centered communication.

Diverse leadership models lean on these approaches in different ways. For instance, autocratic leaders will likely emphasize leader-centered models of communication that are highly directive in nature. This approach to communication is often one-way, downward in orientation, directive, and controlling. Transactional leaders will likely emphasize message-centered models focused on making sure contractual expectations are clear in the leader-follower relationship. And transformational and servant leaders will likely emphasize follower-oriented communication in a way that ensures leaders have not merely communicated information but that followers understand and are partnering with their leaders in the accomplishment of shared goals and aspirations.

This follower-oriented approach to leadership communication expresses the heart behind servant leadership. The goal is not speaking but understanding. The goal is not teaching but learning. The goal is not information transmission but insight and transformation.

In education theory, this shift would be viewed as the difference between teacher-centered and learner-centered models of education. Teacher-centered models emphasize students' passively receiving what the teacher wants to communicate. Learner-centered models emphasize the active role of students in the learning process and call teachers to view success not in terms of what was taught but rather in terms of what was learned.

Such learner-centered models of education are relevant for leaders desiring to be follower focused. For the transformational servant leader, the focus in communication is not on what leaders have said or written but rather on what followers understand and are implementing. The richest forms of leader communication engage followers in active and participative forms of relating with leaders. Are there authentic pathways for providing feedback? Are followers deeply understanding the clearly communicated message? Is this understanding translating into shared ownership of the common mission and strategy that leaders and followers are serving together?

In light of this other-centered commitment to leadership communication, we would like to share three priorities for leaders: (1) the need for a clear message, (2) the priority of competent communicators, and (3) the use of compelling channels.

Clear Message

It's difficult to overestimate the importance of communicating with clarity. In his book *The Trust Edge*, David Horsager emphasizes that "people trust the clear and distrust the ambiguous."[7] As a leader, is the message clear to you? Clarity starts with the initial communicator. Leaders must be clear on the message they wish to share if they want their message to be clear for those they lead.

Leaders must be ready to communicate messages that matter on a moment's notice. Sometimes this communication is planned and delivered through formal pathways like a speech given to a team, organization, or public audience. Other times communication is delivered through informal pathways like conversations with employees you pass in the hallway or impromptu discussions that arise during team meetings.

In both formal and informal paths for communication, it is the leader's job to make sure that the message is clear and not ambiguous. Here's where there is a bit of paradox in the work of leadership. While the work of leadership—for servant leaders—is ultimately about others and not the leader, leaders need to take time to clarify what they personally care about and want for their organization.

It is not sufficient simply to know what the message of the organization is. Leaders also need to find their voice and message in the midst of their leadership work. Why? Because if leaders do not know what matters to them in their work as a leader, then their communication will come off as inauthentic. Yes, leaders are stewards of what matters to their followers and their organization, but leaders must also know how this organizational message connects to a message that they authentically care about as well.

We recommend that leaders be clear on two or three core messages that guide their leadership. When you are clear on your core messages, then this clarity can guide your communication, whether this is planning a formal speech or engaging in an impromptu presentation at a moment's notice.

While we use the language of impromptu, when leaders know their core message, this impromptu communication becomes more extemporaneous—communication that appears impromptu and without notes but actually is informed by significant preparation. Although leaders can anticipate a lot, there will always be unexpected demands placed on leaders as the scope of their influence grows. How can we be ready for such impromptu demands? The key is to have clarity around the core messages so that impromptu moments become opportunities for extemporaneously sharing messages that matter.

So what is your core message? Are you ready to share about this core message thoughtfully on a moment's notice? In our concluding section of the chapter, we'll provide some practical advice on how you can identify your core leadership message.

COMPETENT COMMUNICATORS

As we note earlier in this chapter, communicators are both senders and receivers. This means that leaders must nurture a diverse set of competencies as leaders, including speaking and listening, being open to the ideas of others and having personal conviction, and seeking to understand while also being understood by others.

In my (Justin's) research on the topic, research participants identified several priorities associated with effective leadership communication. The priorities identified by participants include honesty, transparency, authenticity, clarity, listening, asking good questions, timeliness, confidence without arrogance, conciseness, regularity and appropriate repetition, ensuring congruence of verbal and nonverbal messages, paying attention to nonverbal communication from others, use of a diverse set of communication media, use of word pictures, and saying what you mean and meaning what you say (avoiding understatement and overstatement).

While a list like this can feel overwhelming, leaders do not need to be experts on every point. The goal is competent communicators, not perfect communication. On this point Horsager reminds us, "No two people ever perfectly communicate. However, the more clearly we communicate, the greater the ability to trust."[8]

So how are you growing your communication competence as a leader? Are you both authentically listening to followers and clearly speaking your priorities? Are you thoughtfully reading the written communication you receive and effectively expressing what matters most in your written communication? Are you paying attention to and observing the nonverbal communication coming your way and also being mindful of how your nonverbal actions and inactions communicate to others?

While the complexities of leadership communication are real, it is easy to recognize effective communication when we see it. In leadership, effective communication involves listening well; not manipulating; clearly stating one's thoughts, perspectives, and priorities; and coming to other members of the organization—fellow communicators—with openness and an authentic desire to develop shared understanding and mutual commitment.

COMPELLING CHANNELS

The core of effective leadership communication includes a clear message, competent communicators, and compelling channels. Channels are the mediums by which intended messages are shared among communicators. Basic channels include verbal, written, and nonverbal mediums. But each of these mediums can be used in either face-to-face or distributed pathways, synchronous or asynchronous pathways, or physical or digital pathways.

Consider the diverse options leaders have at their disposal today for communicating with organizational members and those beyond the organization. From long-standing forms of communication like written letters and telephones to the relatively newer forms of mediated communication like email and video conferencing, leaders today have many options from which they may draw.

The introduction of diverse channels for communication calls for leaders to grow in their understanding of how communication is facilitated rather than hindered by the channel selected. For instance, just because electronic forms of communication such as email or texting are available does not mean that all messages are best communicated through those pathways. When a complex conversation is needed at a distance, for instance, a video conference, in which nonverbal expression may be included, will be a superior communication channel in contrast to short-form and written-based channels like texting and email.

The point is not to excel at every communication level but rather to know the strengths and growth edges you bring to your role as a leadership communicator.

In addition to the many channels available to leaders today, leaders must also be aware of diverse communication levels. For instance, while some leaders excel at public forms of communication, such as plenary speaking or communication through mass media, others excel at interpersonal forms of dyadic and small-group communication. The point is not to excel at every communication level but rather to know the strengths and growth edges you bring to your role as a leadership communicator.

Elsewhere I (Justin) have presented seven levels of communication: intrapersonal, interpersonal, dyadic, small group or team, divisional or organizational, public or external, and mass communication.[9] As you consider your own tendencies as a communicator, what are your strengths? What are your growth edges?

As an example of how our personalities and strengths work with these seven levels, I (Justin) know that one of my growth edges is the need to assert my voice in groups or teams with ten or more people. Although I'm comfortable presenting to midsize and larger groups when I'm on the agenda or have the floor to speak, when important discussions are taking place in an open-ended and dialogical manner, I have to be intentional not to be silent in that type of group setting.

As you have a clear message and grow in your communication skills, take time to consider your strengths and growth edges when it comes to the levels and channels by which your leadership message may be effectively communicated. Remember that communication must primarily be about others rather than us as leaders; sometimes the call of a leader is to learn to communicate beyond their areas of comfort. If the message and those we serve are the priority, then nurturing our skills for communicating with clarity is also a priority.

Communication in Practice

Although communication is complex, in this chapter we have sought to bring clarity both to why clear communication is a priority for leaders and to what features are associated with communicating with clarity.

In order to better understand what effective leadership communication looks like in practice, we begin with a brief example of effective communication in action and then provide advice for leaders wishing to take the next step in their own journey with leadership communication.

Leadership Communication in Action: Rev. Dr. Martin Luther King Jr.

When it comes to leadership communication, there are many positive examples to which we could look. One of the most powerful visionary communicators of the twentieth century was the Rev. Dr. Martin Luther King Jr.

Earlier in this chapter we noted the priority of leaders knowing their core message. Being clear on this core message allows leaders to deliver their message extemporaneously with great clarity through both formal and informal channels.

John Blake notes that King delivered as many as 450 speeches a year.[10] Though he spoke hundreds of times a year, King had a core message that he returned to and communicated with conviction and clarity. This core message was not scripted and said in a rote fashion. He was able to call people to a core message of equality and justice, but he said this core message in a number of fresh and unique ways.

King also brought other powerful features to his communication. King not only knew how to present the logic for the case he was making but he also presented this logic in a way that captured the imagination of people by engaging their hearts and their minds.

One of our favorite speeches of King was delivered in Montgomery, Alabama, in 1965. In this speech titled "Our God Is Marching On!," King addresses the concern many had: "How long will it take?" To this question King moved into a powerful rhetorical pattern know as anaphora. Anaphora is about using intentional repetition at the first part of a sentence to emphasize the message. To this question "How long?" King made his point: "How long? Not long, because 'no lie can live forever.' How long? Not long, because 'you shall reap what you sow. . . .' How long? Not long, because the arc of the moral universe is long, but it bends toward justice."[11]

Of course, King's famous "I Have a Dream" speech called on similar patterns of communication. This pattern of repetition was used with numerous phrases: "One hundred years later," "Now is the time," "We can never be satisfied," "With this faith," "Let freedom ring," and, of course, "I have a dream."

We see in these examples how clarity and passion came together with both repetition and language that engaged the imagination of his hearers. And what powerful language it was: "The arc of the moral universe is long, but it bends toward justice," and "We refuse to believe that the bank of justice is bankrupt."[12]

Also embedded in these and other speeches by King is the power of vision and word pictures. As King cast a vision for equality and justice to diverse audiences, he intentionally used language that was visual in nature. His language awoke the imagination to "see" this arc of the moral universe. His language awoke the imagination to "see" freedom ringing across the United States, from the Northeast to the West Coast to the Deep South. His language awoke the imagination to "see" sons of former slaves and sons of former slave owners sitting down together at the table of brotherhood. His language awoke the imagination to "see" young black boys and black girls joining hands with young white boys and white girls as sisters and brothers.

This is the power of leaders using visionary language. Through their language, leaders help people to see and envision what a preferred future can look like. King used visionary language and rhetorical devices—his language engaged the whole person. King used personal authenticity—people knew he was an owner rather than a renter of the vision he was casting. And King used a message that was clear and focused—people knew what King stood for and how they could join him in this vital work of moving toward equality and justice.

While such a powerful model of communication is not something many, or any, can fully replicate, King's model of communicating with clarity should inspire current and aspiring leaders. Be clear on your message. Embody your message with personal authenticity. And learn tools of language and speech that can bring your message to life.

Communicating with Clarity: Insights for Practice

Embracing one's leadership message and learning to cast it with imaginative and visionary language is the call of leadership. As we consider practical recommendations for communicating with vision and clarity, we will end our chapter by focusing on three practical recommendations: (1) find your voice as a leader, (2) work for authentic two-way communication, and (3) make communication about those you serve.

FIND YOUR VOICE AS A LEADER

As leaders embark on their journey of setting visionary direction that helps align and motivate people, being clear and unambiguous is vital. This clarity does not simply come from parroting organizational mission statements or taglines. It comes from leaders who care personally and deeply about the message in such a way that it enables them to communicate as leaders with authenticity. This means that, as a leader, you need to find your own voice and use it in service of the community you lead.

As noted previously, we recommend that leaders be clear on two or three core messages that can guide their communication. Having clarity around these core messages prepares you for the work of leadership communication; it provides talking points that can be used for extemporaneous speaking, whether that is in passing hallway conversations, impromptu meetings, or formal speeches.

So what are your core messages, and how can you find your voice as a leader? We encourage people to look to their life story to find cues. What experiences and history inform why you are in your current leadership role? What transformative events or defining moments have taken place in your life and vocational story that add clarity to your voice as a leader? How has your context and environment—your social location—shaped your view on why the organization's story, mission, and vision matter? What animates you? What gets you out of bed in the morning and motivates you to serve your community? What theological values infuse your leadership work with meaning and purpose? What human values drive you to care about those you serve and with whom you work?

Answering such questions is hard work, but in these answers you will find the seeds of your core leadership messages. Find your voice, and then find ways to integrate your voice authentically with the work of your organization. Take some time to answer the questions listed above. Prioritize this process of planning your next steps and finding your voice as a leader.

WORK FOR AUTHENTIC TWO-WAY COMMUNICATION

As you find your voice, remember that the people with whom you work also have perspective and insight on the organization and its mission. Leaders who care about the success of the organization's mission must also care about authentic listening.

One of the challenges for leaders is finding ways to authentically hear what people are thinking. The larger the leadership platform in the organization, the more difficult it can be to access what people are really thinking about the organization, your leadership, and how you approach the people your organization serves. Over time, leaders can become isolated from reality if they are not careful. This is further complicated by the fact that while most leaders claim they are good listeners, often these leaders place a higher value on the speaking side of communication than the listening side.

Steven Sample, former president of the University of Southern California, calls leaders to practice *artful listening* in their role as communicators. He writes that a leader needs to be "an artful listener, not because it makes people feel good (which it does), but rather because artful listening is an excellent means of acquiring new ideas and gathering and assessing information."[13]

This work of authentic listening is about setting aside the leader's natural impulse to speak and being intentional in the work of listening well. Authentic listening recognizes that effective leader-follower communication must be two-way communication.

In their discussion of communication and dialogue, Eric Eisenberg and Harold Lloyd Goodall see dialogue as primarily associated with balanced communication in which both parties are able to speak and be heard.[14] They note that genuine dialogue is associated with equitable transaction, empathic conversation, and real meeting. This is particularly important for dyadic communication between two individuals, but it is also important to find pathways for authentic feedback and two-way communication at other levels.

For teams and groups, two-way communication means providing time for the group to speak into and authentically shape the work they are engaging. For larger divisions and organizations, two-way communication looks different. It may involve feedback coming through direct reports; it may take the form of in-person town hall meetings or listening sessions; or it may require using technologically mediated pathways for gathering insights and perspectives from others.

Regardless of the scope or pathway used, the key for leaders is to ensure that they are taking in this feedback sincerely and authentically. Although leaders should have their own convictions, two-way communication becomes authentic when the leader is honestly open to the feedback coming from others. If a leader is not open, then it is better not to ask for feedback. Followers and community members will know if the call for two-way communication is authentic or placating. While placating strategies almost always backfire, authentic two-way communication both helps organizational members feel involved and provides leaders with insight to better lead the communities they serve. As a leader, insist on authentic, two-way communication, whether at the dyadic, team, or broader organizational level. As you engage in a workplace conversation this next week, be sure to prioritize listening. Ensure that you are hearing the real message the people of your organization desire to share with you.

Make Communication about Those You Serve

Earlier in this chapter we contrasted leader-centered communication, message-centered communication, and other-centered communication. If we are committed to the values of biblical servant leadership, then our communication must be primarily about those we serve rather than us as leaders, or even the message.

The language we use in leadership communication matters. It communicates a lot about what, and who, we see as the focus of our leadership. For instance, Max De Pree challenges the language some leaders use when they refer to "my people." On this point, De Pree observes, "Even though such an expression may rise from the best of motivations and real concern, to the ear of a follower this language reveals a perception 180 degrees from reality. Leaders belong to their followers. A director should refer to employees as 'the people I serve.' What a different reality that is! And what a different effect on followers."[15] What a powerful reorientation for leaders and the way they communicate. Small adjustments like this, when authentically aligned with the commitments of a leader, speak volumes to followers.

Making communication about those we lead means adjusting the language we use, maintaining a commitment to valuing the people we lead, and finding pathways for meaningful feedback so that organizational members and those served by the organization feel heard and understood by those providing leadership.

Finally, leaders communicate a value for others by learning to be fully present whenever possible. The well-known missionary Jim Elliot, who became a martyr when sharing his faith in Jesus Christ in Ecuador, lived by the motto, "Wherever you are, be all there. Live to the hilt every situation you believe to be the will of God."[16] This motto motivated Elliot to go "all in" on the situations he believed to be from God.

This is a motto that can motivate Christian leaders as well. If God has called you to a role, to a responsibility, to an event, or to a conversation, this motto is a powerful reminder: "Wherever you are, be all there." Consider the demands of multitasking in our day. Researchers point to how multitasking almost always reduces rather than increases our retention and productivity. In an age of multitasking—something leaders and organizational members by necessity must sometimes engage—it takes intentional work to fight for focus and being present for the people we lead. The words and actions of leaders communicate. Leaders communicate that the people they lead are valuable when they focus on being fully present and fully engaged whenever possible.

> *Leaders communicate that the people they lead are valuable when they focus on being fully present and fully engaged.*

As a leader, consider the small steps you can take in this area. Learn to set aside, or limit, checking the time or your cell phone for messages. Engage in meetings without having other forms of communication—like email—open and available. Learn to focus mentally on what others are saying rather than diverting your attention in order to formulate your next addition to the conversation. By pressing into such steps, you will make progress in prioritizing those you serve, engaging in authentic two-way communication and effectively communicating the messages that matter most to them.

Next Steps

- Take some time to answer the questions listed in this chapter related to what you care most about as a leader. Consider what two or three core leadership messages animate you and compose the core of your voice as a leader.

- Take some time this week to listen authentically to the people with whom you work. Make sure you are hearing the core message they want to share with you. If there is wisdom in the message you are hearing, find meaningful ways to respond or make changes based on this important feedback.

- Take some time to evaluate your communication behavior this week. Consider whether you are fully focused on the other person with whom you are talking. Consider what distractions, like checking a cell phone, may be interfering with your focus on others as you communicate with them.

Resources for a Deeper Look

Baldoni, John. *Great Communication Secrets of Great Leaders*. New York: McGraw-Hill, 2003.

Horsager, David. *The Trust Edge: How Top Leaders Gain Faster Results, Deeper Relationships, and a Stronger Bottom Line*. Minneapolis: Summerside, 2010.

Lencioni, Patrick. *The Advantage: Why Organizational Health Trumps Everything Else in Business*. San Francisco: Jossey-Bass, 2012.

Nystrom, David P. *James*. NIV Application Commentary. Grand Rapids: Zondervan, 1997.

Snodgrass, Klyne. *Ephesians*. NIV Application Commentary. Grand Rapids: Zondervan, 1998.

8

Providing Accountability

Introduction

We have the pleasure of working with a great group of people in our university. This includes our many students—students like Saji Lukos, whose story we shared in chapter 6. It also includes working with great staff, faculty, administrators, and board members. One of the university's board members is Julie White.

Julie, a former executive vice president in the banking industry, now serves as president of Tapestry Solutions, which focuses on the areas of strategy, leadership, organizational culture, and people practices.

In Julie's years of leadership in multiple sectors, she has learned a lot about the importance of providing accountability and giving meaningful feedback. One of Julie's guiding principles with employees has been this: "I will care enough about you to tell you."[1] When leaders see follower behavior that is not consistent with shared values and expectations, it can be difficult for leaders to provide accountability. But communicating these observations is part of what caring about and being helpful to followers entails.

This is the focus of chapter 8—the leadership practice of *providing accountability*. Some individuals assume that leaders focused on serving and empowering others lack the nerve to make difficult decisions and hold followers accountable. Accountability and a focus on followers can feel at odds, and some may wonder, for example, if servant leaders ever fire people.

While servant leaders prioritize followers by focusing on them, valuing them, and developing them, this commitment to followers is also a commitment to seeing them and the organization flourish. Followers desire leaders who are both focused on followers and oriented around goals. This unique

blend of both follower focus and goal orientation is where providing accountability becomes an integral part of empowering leadership.

Leaders who empower followers are not content to see their followers remain ineffective. Leaders want to see followers realize their potential. Leaders
want to see organizations thriving as team members bring their very best to
the organization and those served by the organization. Turning a blind eye
to followers when expectations are not met and
potential is ignored is beneficial to neither the follower nor the organization.

Leaders who empower followers are not content to see their followers remain ineffective.

On this point, Richard Beaton and Linda Wagener write, "Accountability serves to protect both
individuals and the organization from mistakes
but also, stated more positively, allows them to
continue to develop and improve."[2] Here is where
providing accountability intersects with a commitment to serving followers.

In the leader-follower relationship, servant leadership is not just about being
nice to people. Servant leadership is primarily a call to help people—helping
people develop and holding people accountable to shared commitments that
matter to them and the organization. When such commitments are honored
and followers are growing, leaders must celebrate these successes with followers. When followers are stagnating in their professional engagement and
breaking expectations around shared commitments, leaders must be willing
to step up to direct conversations that provide needed accountability.

Although this is the side of leadership that most people find unpleasant
and difficult, it is one of the defining practices that separates average leaders
and organizations from exceptional leaders and organizations. Learning to do
this work well—in a way that honors the value and dignity of every member
of the team—is vital for effective leadership practice.

In order to better understand the importance and practice of providing
accountability in leadership, we explore this leadership practice from the
following perspectives: (1) providing accountability in biblical perspective,
(2) providing accountability in contemporary perspective, and (3) providing
accountability in practice.

Providing Accountability in Biblical Perspective

One of the most consistent principles throughout Scripture is the need for
responsible stewardship by God's people. Jesus tells a number of parables
that speak of an individual's responsibility and the consequences, positive

or negative, of fulfilling or not fulfilling that responsibility. In Matthew's parable of the talents (Matt. 25:14–30) and Luke's similar parable of the minas (Luke 19:11–27), the ruler or master of the household rewards those who invest his money wisely and receive a good return while he is away. But he condemns the one who simply hides the money and makes no profit. Jesus clearly expects faithful and responsible service from his followers and holds them accountable for the things he has taught. The best leaders are not only kind and compassionate but they also hold their followers to high standards and keep them accountable with constructive feedback.

This is a natural outgrowth of our model of servant leadership. Leadership, we have asserted, is not about power or control. It is about empowerment—equipping and enabling God's people to be all that God has called them to be. And equipping and empowerment include not only positive encouragement and affirmation but also critique and correction. A leader is not helping followers by overlooking low-quality work or condoning bad behavior. The helping community is well aware that consistently bailing out someone who has an addiction to alcohol, drugs, gambling, or sex is not helping them. It is "enabling" their sickness to continue. Not holding people responsible for their actions encourages further irresponsibility and greater immaturity. This is not loving; it is indifference and neglect. Accountability means holding others responsible for their actions with the goal of personal growth and maturity.

Jesus's model of discipleship included accountability.

Jesus's model of discipleship included accountability. We see this, for example, in the mission of the Twelve, when Jesus sends his disciples out to preach, heal, and cast out demons (Mark 6:6–13; Matt. 10:1–42; Luke 9:1–6; cf. Luke 10:1–23). When they return from this mission, they report to Jesus everything they have done and taught (Mark 6:30; Luke 9:10). In response, Jesus takes his disciples and withdraws from the crowds, saying, "Come with me by yourselves to a quiet place and get some rest" (Mark 6:31). Presumably the purpose of this retreat is not just to rest but to debrief, discuss successes and failures, and prepare for the next time.

The apostle Paul's discipleship training also involved accountability. He frequently sent his disciples on ministry tasks, expecting them to follow his guidance and report back to him. This hands-on training proved remarkably effective both for the advancement of the gospel and for the equipping of leaders. We mentioned earlier the example of Epaphras, who as Paul's disciple evangelized the city of Colossae and the Lycus Valley during Paul's time in Ephesus (Col. 1:7; 4:12). Those who carried Paul's letters were similarly carrying out delegated responsibility. Each letter was meant to represent the apostle's presence, and so the letter carrier was more than just a messenger. That person would also provide a report from Paul and pass on his instructions. Tychicus was apparently the letter carrier for both Ephesians and Colossians. Paul says to the Colossians, "Tychicus will tell you all the news about me. He is a dear brother, a faithful minister and fellow servant in the Lord" (Col. 4:7; cf. Eph. 6:21). Similarly, a woman named Phoebe apparently carried Paul's letter to the Romans. Near the end of this letter, Paul writes, "I commend to you our sister Phoebe, a deacon of the church in Cenchreae. I ask you to receive her in the Lord in a way worthy of his people and to give her any help she may need from you, for she has been the benefactor of many people, including me" (Rom. 16:1–2). Paul clearly had great faith in Phoebe to entrust her with the task of delivering this important letter.

Some of the best examples of delegated authority appear in two of Paul's later letters, 1 Timothy and Titus. Timothy and Titus are here functioning as apostolic delegates to resolve problems and train leaders in the church of Ephesus (Timothy) and the churches on the island of Crete (Titus). These letters are therefore full of encouragement, instruction, and the expectation that these two leaders will fulfill their responsibility to Paul and to the Lord.

Here are three principles for effective accountability, drawing examples from Jesus's mission instructions (Mark 6:6–13; Matt. 10:1–42; Luke 9:1–6) and from Paul's letters of 1 Timothy and Titus.

Accountability Begins with Clear Goals and Expectations

In the previous chapter we talked about the importance of good communication skills by leaders. Followers cannot effectively accomplish tasks unless they are aware of the goals and expectations related to those tasks.

In his mission discourse Jesus sets out specific instructions about how the disciples are to carry out their mission. For example, they are to take no provisions with them, depending fully on the hospitality of others. While they can carry a staff and wear sandals, they are to bring no additional food or clothing (Mark 6:8–9).[3] They are also to remain in one place during their stay in a town, rather than moving from house to house. The purpose of these commands is to prevent greed and materialism and to encourage the disciples to depend on God. The command to stay in only one home is likely meant to prevent them from taking invitations from people of higher and higher status, moving up the social ladder (and alienating the poor). Our point here is not how these commands apply to missionaries today (a complex question for another book) but rather the leadership Jesus shows in delegating and holding his disciples accountable.

Similarly, in both 1 Timothy and Titus Paul sets out clearly the goals and expectations for these two disciples. Paul writes to Timothy, "As I urged you when I went into Macedonia, stay there in Ephesus so that you may command certain people not to teach false doctrines any longer or to devote themselves to myths and endless genealogies" (1 Tim. 1:3–4). False teachers have begun to influence the church in Ephesus, and Paul sends Timothy to overrule these false teachers and to teach sound doctrine. He tells him to "guard what has been entrusted to your care" (6:20), meaning the apostolic gospel that Paul has consistently preached and passed on to his disciples. Titus too is given a clear mandate from Paul: "To Titus, my true son in our common faith. . . . The reason I left you in Crete was that you might put in order what was left unfinished and appoint elders in every town, as I directed you. . . . For there are many rebellious people, full of meaningless talk and deception. . . . Therefore rebuke them sharply, so that they will be sound in the faith and will pay no attention to Jewish myths or to the merely human commands of those who reject the truth" (Titus 1:4–5, 10, 13–14). As in Ephesus, the churches in Crete are being affected by false teachers. Paul delegates Titus with the authority to appoint new leadership and refute the false teachers. In both of these cases, Paul sets out clearly the tasks he wishes Timothy and Titus to fulfill.

Accountability Entails Honest and Helpful Feedback

Jesus's teaching included not only encouragement but also rebuke and correction. In Mark's Gospel in particular, Jesus's criticism of the disciples is severe. The disciples are criticized for their lack of faith (Mark 4:40), for failing to comprehend Jesus's miracles (6:52), for hard hearts and spiritual blindness (8:17), and for advocating Satan's perspective and thinking only of human interests rather than God's (8:33). Mark's theological purpose in this motif is to highlight the faithfulness of Jesus. While all others fall away, Jesus alone remains faithful to the task he has been given—to go to the cross.

Yet even taking into account this theological motif, Jesus's correction always has the goal of spiritual growth. By calming the storm, he calls the disciples to greater faith in his sovereign power (Mark 4:40). By rebuking Peter for his Satan-inspired response to Jesus's prediction of his own suffering, Jesus teaches the true meaning of cross-bearing service and its eternal rewards (8:34–37). While predicting that his disciples will all fall away in the coming crisis, he also predicts their restoration following his resurrection (14:27–28). In light of the paradigm-shifting, upside-down values of the kingdom of God—where the poor and humble are exalted, where strength comes from weakness, and where true life comes through Jesus's death—it is essential for Jesus to shake up his disciples' complacency with stern rebuke and correction.

Paul provides constructive criticism to his disciples as well. Hinting at Timothy's somewhat timid personality, for example, he tells his young disciple not to let anyone look down on his youth (1 Tim. 4:12); he tells him not to neglect his spiritual gifts (4:14), to be careful with his life and doctrine (4:16), to honor widows (5:3), and to relax his ascetic discipline for the sake of his health by drinking a little wine now and then (5:23). While not every command Paul gives Timothy necessarily reflects a deficiency on Timothy's part, Paul would likely not say these things if there were not some weakness or potential for failure. In short, a good leader holds followers accountable, looking for potential weaknesses and taking steps to strengthen those areas.

Accountability Has as Its Goal Both Personal Growth and Organizational Success

In the end, constructive accountability is a benefit both to the individual and to the organization. If an employee has anger issues and loses their temper regularly, the negative effects will be both personal and organizational. If another is careless and inefficient, the team or department will be affected as well as the individual. Effective leaders hold followers accountable as a means of *both* the well-being of the individual and the effectiveness of the organization.

The radical transformation that took place in the disciples' lives after the resurrection was certainly a result of the indwelling presence of the Holy Spirit (Acts 2). But it was equally a result of the impact Jesus had on them through his teaching and modeling a life of faith and dependence on God. Consider Peter's denial of Jesus (Matt. 26:69–75; Mark 14:66–72; Luke 22:56–62; John 18:15–27). Though perhaps the most traumatic event in Peter's life, it became transformative, as the rash and impetuous disciple became, through Jesus's correction and restoration, the Rock (*petros*) that Jesus had predicted he would become (John 1:42; Matt. 16:18). Jesus's threefold restoration of Peter, following Peter's threefold denial (John 21:15–17), transformed Peter from a hot-headed and prideful zealot (John 18:10) to a humble yet fearless proclaimer of the good news of the crucified Messiah. Peter's personal transformation in turn had a profound impact on the church. The metaphorical "keys" to the kingdom that Jesus gave to Peter (Matt. 16:19) were used to open the door of the gospel to the Jews (Acts 2), the Samaritans (Acts 8), and the Gentiles (Acts 10–11).

An even more radical transformation and course correction took place with the apostle Paul. While Paul's dramatic conversion on the road to Damascus is not typically thought of as an act of accountability, it could certainly be viewed this way. God intervened and called Paul to account for his misguided zeal against the church. And Paul's dramatic conversion was transformative, both personally and institutionally. It had a profound personal impact, radically changing his view of Jesus and his life direction (Phil. 3:7–11). It also had a profound impact on the church, as Paul became a leading advocate of the mission to the Gentiles. Paul's life is evidence that a leader's act of intervention and accountability can have a profound impact not only on an individual but also on the world.

Providing Accountability in Contemporary Perspective

Contemporary theory and research build on these biblical perspectives by providing additional insight into the importance of leaders providing accountability. In my (Justin's) research on the topic, the following statement was a statistically significant predictor of effective practice: "In general, people within this organization are held accountable for reaching work goals."[4] Goals matter. Clarity around these goals matters. And organizational members being held accountable to these goals also matters.

In our last chapter we emphasized the priority of goals and plans from a communication perspective. Leaders and followers alike need to understand what their team members and their organizations need from them. The leadership practice of communicating with clarity supports this clarification of goals. But having goals clearly communicated is not enough. Organizational members must also follow through on such goals, and this is where providing accountability comes into the leadership process.

Goals matter. Clarity around these goals matters. And organizational members being held accountable to these goals also matters.

Emphasizing the connection between communication and accountability, in my research the observation was made that "Honest and open communication that is regular and consistent at setting and reaching goals is very effective in developing accountability and building trust." For leaders seeking to empower their followers and build mutual trust, avoiding the potentially challenging accountability conversations is not the answer.

The nine leadership practices identified in this book bring such themes together. Beginning with authentic leaders, we are calling these leaders to prioritize people in the leadership equation and then help them navigate toward effectiveness. Effectiveness isn't merely about a financial bottom line. Effectiveness is paying attention to whatever bottom-line results matter for your community, whether these bottom-line results are observable quantitatively or qualitatively.

As leaders and followers learn to pay attention to these plans and goals, the importance of accountability rises to the surface. In light of this priority, we organize our discussion of contemporary leadership theory and research for this section around three areas: (1) collaboratively setting expectations, (2) communicating expectations openly and honestly, and (3) measuring what matters.

Collaboratively Setting Expectations

We began our discussion of core leadership practices in this book by engaging the priority of leaders modeling what matters. This makes it necessary for leaders to understand what matters most to them, their followers, and the organization. In order for leaders to model the right expectations of themselves and others, these expectations first must be determined and clarified.

Jim Laub identifies goal clarification as a core behavior of leaders, writing that the "servant leader provides leadership by envisioning the future, by taking initiative, and by clarifying goals."[5] But this work of providing leadership through clarifying goals is not done in isolation. In servant-leadership theory, providing leadership and sharing leadership stand alongside each other. While autocratic forms of leadership are driven by leader-centered models of setting expectations and goals, servant leaders prioritize the shared nature of this work.

A collaborative process in setting expectations is not simply a good idea, it also yields positive results because it increases the sense of ownership among both leaders and followers. James Kouzes and Barry Posner write, "No matter how grand the dream of an individual visionary, if others don't see in it the possibility of realizing their own hopes and desires, they won't follow."[6] Clear expectations and goals are not the only priorities. *Shared* expectations and goals are more important, particularly as predecessors to the work of accountability.

If you recall, this is one of the driving values we shared about transformational leadership theory. Transformational leadership involves leaders and followers becoming owners—rather than renters—of common aspirations and goals. If the goals and expectations are owned just by the leader, followers will likely treat their responsibilities as renters would. When goals and expectations are set and clarified by leaders and followers collaboratively, this renter mind-set shifts to an owner mind-set among followers.

Before actively enforcing expectations through accountability measures, the leader must nurture shared expectations among all team members. Shared expectation is about clarifying what matters most to the community. It is about connecting what matters most with clear goals and expectations. This is not about finding arbitrary standards to follow. It is about matters of great importance—finding out what matters most to employees, what matters most to the organization, and what matters most to those served by the organization.

When goals and expectations are set in light of what matters most, then organizational members understand the heart behind accountability. Accountability is not about leaders engaging in self-serving practices. Rather, accountability involves leaders ensuring a healthy and flourishing organization for all affected by the organization's success and performance. Flourishing organizations that nurture a culture where goals are clarified and reinforced through accountability benefit every person connected to them.

One final note on this point of collaboratively setting expectations: when expectations are set collaboratively—when they are rooted in shared values, goals, and aspirations—this guards leadership from degenerating into paternalism. When leaders are holding people accountable only to what they think is best without consideration of what the community of leaders and followers think is best, then accountability becomes a form of autocratic paternalism. However, when accountability flows out of setting shared expectations, then this form of accountability becomes a matter of stewarding shared commitments. Servant leaders are stewards of what matters to all connected to the organization. Rather than paternalistically setting the standard for everyone else, they serve as stewards of commonly set and owned expectations.

Communicating Expectations Openly and Honestly

Assuming expectations are clear and owned by all, why is it so hard to hold people accountable? Affirmation and encouragement of followers is easier to do than engaging in accountability conversations, especially when leaders are wired with a servant heart. In part, this is because we sometimes confuse the core of servant leadership.

Former CEO Ron Shaich notes, "Servant leadership isn't about being nice at all costs. *It's about being helpful at all costs.*"[7] This is a helpful correction for those who view servant leadership as just being pleasant to their followers. However, if servant leaders truly love their followers—if they truly value the people they serve and want what is best for them and the organization—then the leaders' love will translate into being helpful, even when this is the hard or unpleasant thing to do.

But why is holding others accountable so hard? In the book *Crucial Accountability*, the authors talk about the challenge of the mental math people calculate.[8] When people consider whether to confront someone else due to violations of expectations, the mental math they calculate often leads to the conclusion that it just isn't worth the effort. Their history with conflict encounters has often not effectively produced the results they wanted, and so silence, and at times violence, take over rather than finding a productive resolution.

Our personal conflict style and history weigh into these encounters. Though there are many styles from which to draw in conflict encounters, three major options include being confrontational, conflict avoidant, or collaborative. In his book *The Peacemaker*, Ken Sande refers to these options as "peace-faking," "peace-breaking," or "peace-making."[9] A key starting point for leaders seeking to press into critical or difficult conversations with their followers is to understand their own conflict-style tendencies. It is important to pay attention to one's default approach—confrontational, conflict avoidant, or collaborative—in order to pursue productive pathways in future conflict and accountability conversations.

When it comes to accountability, leaders and followers alike need to resist seeing silence and violence as the only options.[10] Rather, they need to see polite accountability as the reasonable and responsible approach to take. This work of accountability requires talking about expectations—and violations of these expectations—openly and honestly. Whether it is an employee engaging poorly on a performance issue over which they have control or an employee intentionally breaking from clearly understood expectations, leaders must be willing to wade into these waters for the sake of both the follower and the organization within which they serve.

Before beginning, though, at times we need to confront false narratives we can have as leaders. People are sometimes prone to make an attribution error in these situations. Our error in attribution goes something like this: When we make a mistake or error, we are prone to interpret the problem as our circumstances—that which is outside of our control. When others make a mistake or error, we are prone to interpret the problem as being due to the person, not their situation or circumstances.

Leaders need to take time to think carefully about the attributions they are making prior to an accountability discussion and whether they are dispositional or situational attributions. Taking time to pay attention to this pattern allows us to consider how very reasonable people could make what seem like very obvious errors or mistakes. Rather than the problem residing only with an individual's willingness or ability, it may also relate to other people or circumstances beyond their immediate control.

Taking time to consider these diverse attribution options can help a leader to pause, take a deep breath, and then enter into an accountability conversation in a more objective manner. *Crucial Accountability* notes several recommendations for when it is time to enter into the conversation, including creating a sense of safety in the conversation (e.g., helping the follower understand what you are saying and what you are not saying in this interaction), directly and objectively describing the gap between known expectations and observed behaviors, and then asking a question of the other person about this expectation violation.[11]

When expectations have been previously set in a collaborative manner, then it should not come as a shock to others when leaders politely ask about gaps between expectations and observed behavior. Because they are shared values, goals, aspirations, and expectations, leaders who have engaged previously in a collaborative manner are in a much better place when pursuing open and honest conversation about violations in expected follower behavior.

Of course, leaders need to do some appropriate mental math of their own. There are times when a leader is simply annoyed by something a follower has done. Leaders must be willing to differentiate personal preference from genuine performance concerns. Consider the words of Proverbs 19:11: "It is to one's glory to overlook an offense." Sometimes a personal offense should be overlooked. Other times, overlooking the offense or problem serves neither the offender nor the community.

> *Leaders must be willing to differentiate personal preference from genuine performance concerns.*

Max De Pree helpfully reminds us, "Leaders don't inflict pain; they bear pain."[12] There are times for leaders simply to bear a pain, offense, or annoyance. Other times, they need to confront this offense because the consequences of ignoring it will damage the leader-follower relationship, the culture of the team or organization, or the organization's capacity to carry out its mission effectively and serve others.

Just as leaders sometimes will bear pain by overlooking an offense, other times they will bear the pain by pressing into uncomfortable conversations that honestly and openly engage followers on the topic of violated expectations. Because the health and growth of followers and of the wider organization matter, servant leaders are willing to take on this unpleasant work. It matters too much to ignore. Servant leaders are about stewarding what matters most, even when it is hard work.

Measuring What Matters

Part of the story of accountability is learning to measure what matters as a community. When expectations are owned by leaders and followers alike, and when a culture of honest and open communication around expectations is present, then it is time to regularize the measurement of what matters.

The best accountability conversations do not come as a surprise to followers. Holding others accountable is an outgrowth of regular conversations that clarify expectations and help people see how they are performing in light of these expectations that followers also understand and own.

Consider these points that came out of my (Justin's) research on this theme of leaders providing accountability. First, "Leaders inspect what they expect." In addition, there is a preference for "honest performance evaluations—those which acknowledge both strengths and growth fronts and clearly set goals that can be reached quarterly and annually." Whether it is through formalized performance evaluations or ongoing conversation, the question of how one will "inspect what they expect" is a matter of knowing how to measure what matters most in your organization.

Engaging in direct and honest conversation with followers about outcomes that are important to followers and the organization provides an opportunity for meeting organizational goals and developing followers—a tangible factor associated with valuing and developing the people we lead. These outcome-based conversations are not single points in time but rather ongoing.

One executive noted to us his commitment never to bring up something in a formal annual review that the follower had not heard previously. This executive was committing himself to regularized conversations around performance expectations, not just engaging when a human-resource process compelled the conversation to occur.

But how do you decide what to measure and how to measure it? As De Pree reminds us, sometimes the things that matter most are not measured quantitatively.[13] Albert Einstein has been credited as saying, "Not everything that can be counted counts, and not everything that counts can be counted." Sometimes measuring what matters involves qualitative markers. Whether the markers are qualitative or quantitative in nature, leaders need to take the lead in helping a community regularize measures of what matters so that they and their followers may pay attention to common expectations around these priorities within their unique context.

Ryan Hardwig and Warren Bird argue, "Feedback is the breakfast of champions."[14] That's a fun way to say that feedback, based on clearly measuring what matters, helps organizations stay focused. When feedback and evaluation are provided, this opens up a pathway for recognizing positive performance and ensuring that additional opportunity and responsibility are given to those ready for such professional growth steps. Conversely, feedback and evaluation also help community members know that underperformance will be recognized and not allowed to harm the organization as a whole.

Addressing underperformance and broken expectations is not about leaders being punitive. Rather, it is about leaders taking their stewardship responsibility seriously on behalf of followers and the organization as a whole. On this point, Bob Briner and Ray Pritchard note, "Few things are more damaging to morale and to bottom-line results than failure of leadership to properly evaluate employees."[15] Such damage to morale and results is avoidable when leaders step into accountability conversations with courageous honesty.

If servant leaders are committed not only to being nice but also to being helpful, this will necessitate engaging in direct communication with followers about performance and expectations. Frank LaFasto and Carl Larson state: "Put simply, any management practice that leaves out accountability is useless. Lack of accountability—for some or for all—causes slippage in performance and impedes teamwork and collaboration."[16] This means that no one in the organization is exempt from accountability. From high-level executive leaders to front-line workers, everyone needs to be open to accountability based on mutually agreed-on expectations. Leaders who care about their organizations ensure that first and foremost they themselves are accountable. This accountability of leaders comes in diverse forms, including direct superiors, boards, and peers who are invited to speak into their lives and leadership. Leaders who genuinely care about their followers and the health of the organization will also take feedback and accountability of team members and followers seriously. Accountability matters. It matters for flourishing organizations. It matters for satisfied followers. It matters for those served by the organization.

Providing Accountability in Practice

While the leadership task of providing accountability may be one of the more difficult parts of the leader's role, when done well it has the potential not only to help the organization thrive but also to build trust in the leader-follower relationship.

In order to illustrate what providing accountability looks like in practice, we begin by briefly looking at an example—Ron Shaich and his leadership with Panera Bread.

Accountability in Action: Ron Shaich

When it comes to providing accountability, Ron Shaich says he had to learn the hard way what servant leadership with accountability involves. Shaich is the founder and current chairman of Panera Bread, and he has served as the company's CEO on two occasions—from 1984 to 2010 and again from 2012 to 2018. He notes that it wasn't until the last ten years in his career—after seasons of banging his head against a wall with some employees—that he realized what servant leadership is truly about.

We shared this quote from Shaich earlier in the chapter: "Servant leadership isn't about being nice at all costs. *It's about being helpful at all costs.*"[17] Shaich shares how he previously wrestled with several leadership errors in his desire to be nice to followers. For instance, as the company grew in its complexity from its early days, some jobs outgrew the skills of the individuals occupying those roles. When faced with this, Shaich would push these people and wait for them to step up, but he would never fire them from those roles. Instead of confronting the individuals, he would cover for them. He was willing to do the work needed—their work—but this covering hurt the organization.

While this type of above-and-beyond care for Shaich's employees was admirable, it ultimately helped neither the employees nor the organization. After years of this type of "nice" leadership, Shaich realized that the point of servant leadership is primarily about being helpful, not just being nice. This shift to "being helpful at all costs" means open and honest conversations are essential.

On this point, Shaich states, "A leader should be as brutally honest as possible—and you *can* do this in a kind and loving way. Let the chips fall where they may, and remember: Honesty is helpful."[18] Shaich goes on to explain that in being honest with employees, the key is not simply to tell them *that* they are performing poorly but rather to let them know *why* they are performing poorly. By doing so, Shaich argues, you are transferring the responsibility. With this information, they can change their course, improve, and go on to add significant value to the organization. Or they may choose to leave.

Shaich sees these brutally honest conversations—conversations that are direct, kind, and helpful—as empowering employees with the information they need. He argues that a leader creates space and opportunity for people to perform. After that, Shaich notes that each employee must own this opportunity as it relates to their career and choices.

Withholding relevant feedback from employees—especially feedback on poor performance—sets them up for failure. Armed with open and honest feedback, employees and followers can make the choices they need to succeed if they both desire to and are able to improve. Though sometimes unpleasant work for leaders, it is the kind, loving, and helpful thing to do. Servant leaders should be helpful at all costs, even when that work of providing accountability is hard.

Accountability: Insights for Practice

As we consider recommendations for providing accountability, we will end our chapter by focusing on two practical considerations. While usually it is helpful to focus on the proactive side of practice (what we should do rather than what we should not do), for this chapter we will address two leader behaviors to avoid: (1) don't delegate ultimate accountability, and (2) as you provide accountability, don't micromanage.

Don't Delegate Ultimate Accountability

While we highlighted Shaich above, we could have just as easily highlighted others, such as Max De Pree. De Pree provided leadership for Herman Miller as the CEO from 1980 to 1987 and was on the board from the early 1970s through 1995. In his work with the company, De Pree was committed to servant-leadership practices. One example of this was his commitment to keep his salary as CEO capped at twenty times the wage of an hourly worker.

But De Pree's commitment to servant leadership did not equate to an absence of accountability. De Pree emphasized that organizations are adrift at sea if they don't have a good idea of what is going to be measured. This is why De Pree held to the following philosophy of leadership: "The first responsibility of a leader is to define reality. The last is to say thank you. In between the two, the leader must become a servant."[19] Paying attention to what matters, defining this, recognizing when people are working toward this goal, and serving people along the way are all part of what the servant-leadership practice of providing accountability is all about.

But this important work of accountability cannot be ultimately delegated. On this point De Pree notes, "Leaders can delegate efficiency, but they must deal personally with effectiveness."[20] While there are many things in an organization that can and should be delegated, effectively attending to the overall goals and outcomes of the organization is something for which leaders are directly accountable. Because they are accountable as organizational stewards, this means leaders must engage in the work of providing accountability to others.

This work is essential. LaFasto and Larson remind us, "Accountability elevates all performance. Teams are more productive when team members know that the organization holds everyone to the same standard."[21] When leaders and followers alike know what is expected of them, and when they collectively nurture a culture of accountability, everyone connected to the organization benefits. Though followers are certainly part of the solution when it comes to accountability, leaders must stay engaged and not delegate ultimate accountability for what lies within their realm of stewardship responsibility. Take some time this week to ensure that you are prioritizing accountability surrounding the expectations that matter most to your followers and organization. Consider times where you have delegated accountability rather than owning a conversation you needed to have with an employee or team member.

As You Provide Accountability, Don't Micromanage

While leaders must not delegate ultimate accountability, this call must be blended with an awareness of the danger of micromanaging. One author uses the metaphor of tollways to communicate the problems that may accompany micromanagement. At least in the past, tollways in and near Chicago—one of the busiest transportation systems in the United States—created substantial frustration and inefficiencies for drivers. While designed to fund well-maintained roadways, tollways embedded inefficiencies within the systems these funds were designed to improve. Thankfully, many newer systems are using electronic means of collecting tolls that reintroduce efficiencies into the system.

Although simply a metaphor, such inefficient tollway systems provide a picture of what micromanaging brings about. While the best leaders find high-quality people to hire and then empower them to flourish on the metaphorical highways of organizational life, constant micromanaging leads to followers moving from freeway speeds to crawling congestion in their work.

As you provide accountability for followers, are you setting them on a course where they can productively move forward along the freeways on which they have been placed, or is your accountability becoming so burdensome and detail oriented that it turns the freeway of their work into a tollway parking lot? Accountability is essential but can quickly lead to too much of a good thing when micromanaging enters the equation.

Accountability structures prioritize the right things. Rather than constantly looking for things people are doing wrong—the tendency of micromanagers— healthy accountability picks the things that matter most and focuses on those areas. Leaders seeking this pathway find the right blend of light touch and large impact. Teddy Roosevelt purportedly made the following observation: "The best executive is the one who recruits the most competent men around, tells them what he wants done, and then gets out of their way so they can do it."

That is good advice. Who are the right people to have on your team? Once they are there, are you appropriately equipping and resourcing them to succeed? If you are, then the leader's job is primarily about empowering them to thrive in their work and occasionally providing the feedback followers need to know how they are doing in their work. This type of accountability avoids micromanaging while also courageously stepping into conversations about expectations and accountability when needed.

Next Steps

- Take some time to consider how you are prioritizing accountability surrounding the expectations that matter most to your followers and organization.
- Take some time to consider times when you have delegated accountability rather than owning a conversation you needed to have with an employee or team member.
- Take some time to consider when you have engaged in micromanagement. Consider how you could have approached this leadership responsibility in a healthier and more productive manner.

Resources for a Deeper Look

Kostenberger, Andreas J., and Terry L. Wilder, eds. *Entrusted with the Gospel: Paul's Theology in the Pastoral Epistles*. Nashville: B&H Academic, 2010.

Liefeld, Walter L. *1 and 2 Timothy/Titus*. NIV Application Commentary. Grand Rapids: Zondervan, 1999.

McCloskey, Mark W. *Learning Leadership in a Changing World: Virtue and Effective Leadership in the 21st Century*. New York: Palgrave Macmillan, 2014.

Patterson, Kerry, Joseph Grenny, Ron McMillan, Al Switzler, and David Maxwell. *Crucial Accountability: Tools for Resolving Violated Expectations, Broken Commitments, and Bad Behavior*. 2nd ed. New York: McGraw-Hill Education, 2013.

van Dierendonck, Dirk, and Kathleen Patterson. *Practicing Servant Leadership: Developments in Implementation*. New York: Palgrave MacMillan, 2018.

9

Supporting and Resourcing

Introduction

Steven Sample, former president of the University of Southern California, received some powerful advice early in his career. George Clement shared the following with him:

> Steve, let me give you some basic advice about leadership. You should spend a small amount of your time hiring your direct reports, evaluating them, exhorting them, setting their compensation, praising them, kicking their butts and, when necessary, firing them. When you add all that up, it should come out to about 10 percent of your time. For the remaining 90 percent of your time you should be doing *everything you can* to help your direct reports succeed. You should be the first assistant to the people who work for you.[1]

Sample sought to live by this advice, noting that if you're not firing someone, you should bend over backward to help that person get the job done. This is a call to actively serve, support, and resource those who work for you.

In this chapter we explore the leadership practice of *supporting and resourcing*. Effective leaders understand that their most important work is to get the right people on the team and then to do everything they can to help them succeed. After finding the right people, it is time for leaders really to go to work by coming alongside followers with needed support and resourcing.

As the final leadership practice engaged in this book, supporting and resourcing has a culminating priority among the others. This final practice maintains the goal orientation of leadership practices 7 and 8. Leaders must clearly communicate goals (practice 7). Leaders must hold followers accountable for shared goals (practice 8). But along with this clear communication and accountability is the culminating work of leaders supporting and resourcing (practice 9). If you, as a leader, have hired the right people, then it is time to stand with them as they work toward your shared goals and objectives. It is time to do everything you can to support and resource them for success.

In order to better understand the importance and practice of supporting and resourcing in leadership, we explore this leadership practice from the following perspectives: (1) supporting and resourcing in biblical perspective, (2) supporting and resourcing in contemporary perspective, and (3) supporting and resourcing in practice.

Supporting and Resourcing in Biblical Perspective

For years I (Mark) was a hardcore do-it-yourselfer (DIYer). It was probably because I was so cheap. I learned to work on my old cars to keep them running. I did just about everything around the house and the yard—from sprinkler systems, to drywall, to ceiling fans, to fixing running toilets. One thing I learned while doing all that DIY was that the right tool makes all the difference. Whether it's an oil filter wrench that reaches perfectly into a tiny engine compartment or the right drill bit to punch through a concrete slab, not having the right tool can be incredibly frustrating, time-consuming, and expensive (when you break something); having the right tool can turn a complex job into a simple one.

It is the same with any task and can be the difference between success and failure. Having the right support and resources can contribute to a healthy and profitable organization. Not being supported or having inadequate resources can be incredibly frustrating and morale killing. When approaching this topic from a biblical perspective, we can talk about general spiritual resources and specific or personal ones.

Spiritual Resources for the Task

THE HOLY SPIRIT

We might not normally think of the Holy Spirit as a leadership resource. But for *every* Christian—whether involving the work of Christians in the church or in the marketplace—the Holy Spirit should be our primary source of strength and guidance. While during the Old Testament period God's Spirit periodically empowered individuals to accomplish specific tasks, the

New Testament brought the permanent indwelling presence of the Spirit for believers (as promised in the Old Testament: Joel 2:28–32; Isa. 32:15; Ezek. 36:26–27; 39:29).

In the New Testament Jesus promised his disciples that after he left he would send another Helper (or Advocate, or Comforter, or Guidance Counselor)[2] who would remind them of what Jesus had taught them and would guide them into all truth (John 14:16–17, 26; 15:26; 16:7–15). Jesus was speaking here about the Holy Spirit. Before ascending to heaven, he told his disciples to stay in Jerusalem until they received "power from on high" (Luke 24:49; cf. Acts 1:7–8). Ten days later, on the Jewish day of Pentecost (ca. AD 33), the Spirit came powerfully on the disciples, and they began proclaiming the message of salvation in all the languages of those present in Jerusalem for the festival. The church of Jesus Christ was born (Acts 2:1–47)! From that point on, the church was filled, empowered, and guided by God's Spirit.

The Spirit is now the defining mark of a Christian. Every true believer has the Spirit (1 Cor. 6:19; 12:13). As we have seen, the Bible speaks about "gifts" of the Spirit, unique skills and abilities that every Christian receives from the Spirit (1 Cor. 12:7–11; Rom. 12:4–8). The Bible also talks about the "fruit" of the Spirit, meaning the evidence of the personal transformation that takes place through the work of the Spirit. The fruit of the Spirit is love, joy, peace, patience, kindness, goodness, faithfulness, gentleness, and self-control (Gal. 5:22–23). These are fundamental and essential leadership qualities.

Someone might ask why so many Christians act no differently from the rest of the world—selfish, greedy, unloving—if they have the Spirit of God. The answer is that while all believers have the Spirit, not all are "filled" with the Spirit, meaning that they haven't given God priority and authority in their lives (Eph. 5:18; Acts 4:8, 31; 9:17; etc.). Christians who do their own thing and ignore God's guidance will live no differently from those in the broken world around us. So the first critical resource for leaders to cultivate in their lives and to encourage in followers is the presence of God and the guidance that comes from the Holy Spirit.

THE BODY OF CHRIST

The second spiritual resource is closely related to the first. It is the body of Christ, that is, the church itself with all its resources. The Spirit works not only through individuals but also corporately through the church. Paul writes this to the church in Corinth: "Don't you know that you yourselves are God's temple and that God's Spirit dwells in your midst?" (1 Cor. 3:16). The temple represented the presence of God, so Paul is asserting that the church is a special place of God's presence. In the church we meet God in worship; we gain spiritual insight, counsel, and mentoring through those who are spiritually mature; we find support from our "family"—our brothers and sisters in Christ—in difficult and sorrowful times; we develop networks of relationships, which can help us in our marriages, our parenting skills, our spiritual disciplines, and our work habits. It is essential for all Christians to be part of a local church.

The Biblical Testimony

A third spiritual resource is the Bible itself. As God's Word, his message to us, the Bible teaches us about God's nature, character, and purpose for the world. We learn about who we are as human beings created in his image and how we are to live in light of his will and purpose.

Of course there is always a danger of misreading the Bible, of "proof texting"—reading the text apart from its context in order to support our own personal agenda. The way to avoid this is to tap into the other resources: (1) Pray for the Spirit's guidance while reading. (2) Always read the Bible *in context*, that is, taking into account its original meaning and purpose. (3) Read the Bible *in community*, together with the whole church. The reality is that there is strength in numbers, and errors we as individuals might make because of our limited perspective can be avoided by listening to the church as a whole. This means being part of a local church. But it also means being aware of the Great Tradition, the body of Christian doctrine that has developed through the centuries. We are less likely to fall into error if we learn the lessons of the past. Finally, it means recognizing that the church is not an American phenomenon; it is a global one. Listening to our brothers and sisters around the world—especially in cultural contexts that are closer to the ones in which the Bible arose—can give us greater insight into the message of the text and its application for us.

Personal Resources for the Task

In addition to these basic spiritual resources, leaders can provide followers with specific personal resources. To illustrate this from a biblical perspective, we return to the examples of Jesus and Paul. Here are various resources they provided for those they led.

Firsthand, in-the-Field Modeling and Training

As with Jesus, Paul's method of training was hands-on and on the ground. Paul wasn't a CEO in a top-floor office. As an itinerant preacher and church planter, he traveled with his associates on foot from place to place over hundreds and ultimately thousands of miles. They received food and shelter daily through the hospitality of others. They were harassed, often beaten, sometimes thrown in jail, and driven out of town. Paul was shipwrecked on several occasions. Difficult decisions, sometimes with life-and-death consequences, had to be made daily.[3] It is no wonder that John Mark, one of their early associates, deserted them midway through one journey (Acts 13:13; 15:37–39). This was no business for the faint of heart.

Assurance of support and loyalty in the face of hardship and trials—to know their leader has their back—is one of the best resources a leader can provide for followers.

This sort of life develops deep loyalty among individuals, no doubt resulting in the kind of "band of brothers" support that can compare only to wartime service. Assurance of support and loyalty in the face of hardship and trials—to know their leader has their back—is one of the best resources a leader can provide for followers.

DELEGATED AUTHORITY

Related to firsthand training is delegated authority. When Jesus sent out his disciples on their mission, he gave them his own power and authority to preach, to heal, and to cast out demons (Mark 6:7; cf. Matt. 10:1; Luke 9:1–2). As the Son of God, he had that authority to give.

Paul's delegated authority had a somewhat different shape. When he sent disciples on a particular task, he sent them with his full authority as an apostle. We see this in the case of Timothy and Titus, two disciples we have discussed before. Both men were sent on special tasks to represent Paul at the troublesome church in Corinth (1 Cor. 16:10–11; 2 Cor. 2:13; 7:13–14; 8:6, 16–17, 23; 12:18). Near the end of 1 Corinthians, Paul mentions to the church that he would like to come to them, but a great opportunity of ministry has opened up for him in Ephesus. So instead he's sending Timothy. About Timothy he says: "When Timothy comes, see to it that he has nothing to fear while he is with you, for he is carrying on the work of the Lord, just as I am. No one, then, should treat him with contempt. Send him on his way in peace so that he may return to me. I am expecting him along with the brothers" (1 Cor. 16:10–11).

As noted previously, Timothy seems to have been quite a sensitive and caring individual with strong pastoral-care skills, but perhaps he was not so assertive. Paul is apparently concerned that the Corinthian church, with its arrogance and meanness, will eat Timothy alive. So he warns them that if they do, they will have to answer to him! Timothy is acting with Paul's full authority.

In the same way Paul later sent Titus with a letter of restoration and reconciliation to the Corinthian church (2 Cor. 1:1–2:13; 7:13–14). At this point Paul had been alienated from the church because leaders there had rejected his authority. Titus had the challenging task of intervening on behalf of Paul to initiate this reconciliation. With that kind of responsibility, he needed to know that Paul was backing him up every step of the way.

Followers need to know that their leaders will back them up with both the resources needed and the authority necessary to accomplish their tasks.

Followers need to know that their leaders will back them up with *both* the resources needed and the authority necessary to accomplish their tasks.

LETTERS OF INSTRUCTION

Finally, Paul's letters themselves are resources for his followers. We saw this in the previous chapter. The letter we call 1 Timothy was sent to Timothy in Ephesus, to give him guidance and direction for dealing with problems in the church there. The letter is essentially an instruction manual for Timothy's ministry in Ephesus. The New Testament letter to Titus is the same thing, this time for Titus on the island of Crete. Its purpose is to give Titus instruction and direction. These kinds of specific guidance would be an invaluable resource for both men.

Effective leaders must not only choose and train their followers well but they also need to provide them with the support and resources necessary to be successful. In the last chapter we pointed to the importance of communicating a clear vision and instructions to followers in order to provide accountability. Such clarity of communication is equally essential as a resource and support when encountering challenging circumstances.

Supporting and Resourcing in Contemporary Perspective

Contemporary theory and research build on these biblical perspectives by providing additional insight into the importance of leaders supporting and resourcing followers. In my (Justin's) research on the topic, the following point was a statistically significant predictor of effective leadership practice: "Managers/Supervisors and top leadership in this organization provide the support and resources needed to help workers meet their goals."[4]

As addressed in the previous chapter through the example of Ron Shaich, effective servant leadership is not about being nice at all costs, nor is it about leaders covering for followers who are not doing what they need to do on the job. Effective leadership involves being clear on goals and holding followers accountable to those goals. Effective leadership also involves coming alongside followers and providing "the support and resources needed to help workers meet their goals."

What Shaich wrestled with was the difference between enabling and empowering as a leader. Enabling leadership provides support and resources in a manner that covers up for poor performance on the part of the follower. Empowering leadership provides support and resources in a manner that equips followers to excel all the more in their efforts to meet and exceed goals in service of the organization's mission. In contrast to the infamous example of Pharaoh demanding that the Israelites make bricks without straw (Exod. 5), empowering leaders are looking to what can be done, with the resources available to the organization, to support and resource followers authentically as they work to meet their goals.

In light of such a call to empowering leadership, we will organize our discussion of contemporary leadership theory and research for this section around the following areas: (1) finding your team, (2) supporting your team, and (3) resourcing your team.

Finding Your Team

Before diving into specific discussions around supporting and resourcing, we begin with emphasizing the priority of getting the right people on your organizational team. Jim Collins popularized this point in his book *Good to Great* by noting the "first who . . . then what" principle.[5]

We often want to begin with the what: *what* needs to get done, *what* the job description should look like, and *what* this job looks like in light of other positions in the organization. All of these are important considerations, but Collins notes that *what* questions are secondary to *who* questions. Sample makes a similar point, arguing that it is great people, not great job descriptions, that matter most for effective leaders and productive organizations.[6]

Finding the right people for your team is one of the most important roles you will engage as a leader. Complex organizations do not thrive based on the work of any single individual. We need to turn away from expectations of leaders like Wonder Woman or Superman, who will come in, save the day, and deliver results. Ultimately, leaders are not responsible for personally doing the work of the organization.

Leaders (especially executive leaders) meet goals primarily through the work of others. This is a vital concept for leaders to take in. While leaders often rise to their position from having produced significant outcomes for the organization, once they move into an executive leadership role the nature of their work shifts dramatically.

Rather than personally accomplishing goals, leaders primarily organize, support, and resource others who deliver on goals for the organization. Misunderstood, this emphasis on leading through others can result in leaders treating followers in a utilitarian manner—seeing people only in light of what value they bring to the organization. Appropriately understood, this emphasis on leading through others should raise the honor and value placed on members of the organizational team, since without the team the organization would fail in its work.

Finding the right people for your team is the first step, because leaders and followers are all in the work of the organization together. As team members thrive in their roles and meet their goals, so goes the success and flourishing of the leader and organization. As team members fail in their roles and miss their goals, so goes the failure of the leader and organization. This reality is not about saying that leaders are not needed. To the contrary, this reality highlights just how important it is for leaders to do their job well—to find the right people and then do everything possible to help their team succeed.

Supporting Your Team

The important work of leadership finds its fulfillment in standing with and supporting the members of the team. If the mission of the team and organization matters, then leaders have a responsibility to provide the support and resources necessary for followers to succeed in their mission-aligned work.

While some leaders take a passive approach to the work of supporting and resourcing, followers express the importance of leaders actively looking for ways to support the people who work for them. In my research on this theme, the special importance of a leader being active in the identification of follower needs can be expressed in this way: "The leader should be the first to ask 'what do we need to get the job done' versus being passive, waiting for requests to come to him/her and then trying to put the requests off as long as possible."

This posture of active responsiveness recognizes that leaders and followers are jointly working together toward common goals. As we consider the work of actively engaging and responding to follower needs, we will do so by considering both the supporting and resourcing dimensions.

The work of supporting builds off of follower-oriented practices previously identified in this book—practices such as valuing and appreciating followers and creating a place for follower individuality. Building on valuing people, supporting followers translates this inherent value of people into meaningful support as followers work to deliver on the organization's mission.

At its core, supportive leadership recognizes the whole-person nature of followers. People have spiritual, emotional, cognitive, physical, relational, and professional needs. Supportive leaders are actively paying attention to how these follower needs intersect with the ability of followers to engage their work goals productively. Drawing on emotional intelligence, supportive leaders will pay attention to when followers have needs that may be addressed by providing nurture, being approachable, listening well, and responding with care and compassion.

Such leaders go out of their way to make work rewarding and affirming for followers. But the point is not just to affirm, it is also about leaders seeing and responding to follower needs in order to help them rise to the demands placed on them by their work objectives. As leaders and followers navigate toward effectiveness, sometimes this work involves leaders encouraging, strengthening, emboldening, or empowering a follower.

Such supportive work aligns well with Victor Vroom's expectancy theory of motivation.[7] Here is one summary of the core of expectancy theory: "The underlying assumption of expectancy theory is that followers will be motivated if they think they are capable of performing their work, if they believe their efforts will result in a certain outcome, and if they believe that the payoffs for doing their work are worthwhile."[8] Leaders help to motivate followers in this way as they come alongside followers with supportive words and behaviors. This support both encourages followers and helps to raise their level of follower commitment. When followers face seasons of discouragement or lack of commitment, sometimes leaders simply need to come alongside followers with support and encouragement. Transformational leadership theory sees this supporting work as inspirational motivation and encouraging the heart. Through such supporting, leaders raise the level of follower belief in their capacity to act on the goals before them. Complementing the work of supporting, the work of leader resourcing is also vital.

Resourcing Your Team

Once leaders have found the right people, in addition to providing emotional support and motivation, leaders also need to come alongside followers with necessary resources. As goals are clarified and owned by followers, it is in the best interest of the organization as a whole, and leaders and followers alike, for leaders to do everything they can to help followers succeed and flourish in their work.

As we consider the resourcing dimension of this leadership work, path-goal theory provides relevant help and insight. Working together, leaders and followers need clarity on both where they are going and how they will get there. Clarity is vital both for goals and for pathways. But having this clarity is not enough. In most work regular obstacles arise along the way toward goal accomplishment. The leadership work of resourcing pays attention to such obstacles and then either removes the obstacles for followers or helps followers address these obstacles on their own.

Consider the resources that can either support or hinder people as they work toward goal accomplishment: time, money, staff resources, information, political capital, advocacy, training, empowerment, and individual or institutional cooperation. Of course, this list of resources could go on to other areas, but these represent categories that leaders must pay attention to as followers work toward accomplishing their goals.

Working together, leaders and followers need clarity on both where they are going and how they will get there.

Organizations do not have limitless resources, however. Leaders must regularly make strategic decisions about resource allocation within the bounds of the reality within which they work. When followers face obstacles along their path, it is not always reasonable for leaders to provide *more*. Leaders cannot always address obstacles with more money, more staff, or more material resources. At times, other pathways must be creatively identified.

In terms of achieving individual, team, and organizational objectives, many of the common hindrances are associated with a lack of resources. When facing lack of resources, whether material or immaterial resources, it is important for leaders and followers alike to recognize gaps that may or may not exist between perception and reality. Sometimes there are actually resource gaps that must be filled if an organization is to stay true to its mission. Other times there are perceived resource gaps that must be addressed but can be addressed in creative ways that get to actual needs rather than perceived needs.

For example, perhaps a team is experiencing a lack of resources in their travel budget as they work across diverse geographic regions. Budgeted dollars designated for travel are not keeping pace with the perceived demands placed on the team. Adding more to the travel budget may be the answer, but leaders attending to resource allocation may need to explore with this team how technology is being used, or not being used, to increase collaborative work across distance while limiting the amount of travel needed. When obstacles arise in such resource areas, leaders and followers may sometimes need to dig deeper to find the real need beneath the perceived need.

As noted earlier, sometimes leaders will remove obstacles for followers, and other times leaders will assist followers as they remove these on their own. This means that the work of resourcing your team adds a developmental dimension to the conversation. When an individual or team is new to a task, the direct intervention of the leader in addressing obstacles is often needed. Over time, however, the aim is for the leader to equip followers appropriately with the necessary tools for facing and addressing obstacles on their own. Like the developmental models noted in chapter 1 of this book, the aim is to move followers and teams from the stage of leaders doing and followers watching to the stage of followers doing and leaders watching. This is about using equipping and empowering strategies in an effort to prepare followers for their work of addressing obstacles along the path toward goal achievement.

Obstacles can take place at diverse levels. When an obstacle arises, leaders will want to work with followers to determine the nature of the obstacle, the level at which the obstacle is most at play, and whether the obstacle needs to be addressed now or simply monitored for potential action in the future.

Building on the levels of communication identified in chapter 7, when considering a problem or obstacle, there are several levels at which this problem may occur: Is it mostly about issues specific to the individual (intrapersonal)? Is it about substantive or relational difficulties between two individuals (dyadic)? Is it about issues specific to a single group or team (team or group)? Is it about issues arising between teams or departments (interteam)? Is it about broader issues within the organization (organizational)? Is it about obstacles raised in work between separate organizations (interorganizational)? Or is it about broader societal or global dynamics (societal and global)? While the levels of analysis for problems or obstacles can make the work of leadership complex, such analysis will help leaders and followers know if the issue raised is being paired with the appropriate intervention or solution.

When followers are new to their job, such a complex analysis cannot be expected of them. Early on their role is to learn their job and get to know the people with whom they directly and regularly need to work. When obstacles arise outside that scope, leaders need to serve as a protector, buffer, and resource provider engaging those external challenges. But empowering models of leadership do not just stop there—they call leaders to invest in followers in such a way that followers begin to take on leadership capacity and competence over time.

Bernard Bass and Bruce Avolio call this leadership work *intellectual stimulation*.[9] Intellectual stimulation is about helping followers engage in problem solving—equipping and empowering them to think things through on their own rather than always looking to the leader to problem solve for them. James Kouzes and Barry Posner call this leadership work *enabling others to act*.[10] Enabling others to act is about providing room for others to make thoughtful choices and then standing behind these follower decisions whenever possible.

Individual followers and teams need both support and resourcing as they work toward the achievement of goals. Once leaders have found the right people for their team, it is time to turn their leader energies to doing whatever is needed to help these people succeed. Supporting and resourcing your team is the key for this leadership work.

Supporting and Resourcing in Practice

In this chapter we have emphasized the priority of leaders finding the right people and then doing everything they can to support and resource these people. In this final section we consider what this emphasis on supporting and resourcing looks like in practice.

Supporting and Resourcing in Action: Steven Sample

Early in this chapter we introduced you to the advice Steven Sample received early in his career: "Ninety percent of your time you should be doing *everything you can* to help your direct reports succeed. You should be the first assistant to the people who work for you."[11] Throughout his career, including during his time as president of the University of Southern California from 1991 to 2010, Sample leaned into this advice in tangible ways.

One of these ways included his view of unfettered access. Sample notes that administrative staff members sometimes are used by leaders in an unhelpful manner—acting as a buffer between the leader and those reporting to the leader. While usually motivated by good intentions, such as protecting the time of the leader, these good intentions can get in the way of others being able to do their work effectively.

Observing those challenges over the years led Sample to take a different approach with his direct reports. Sample writes, "I make certain that the line officers who are my direct reports have unfettered access to me—twenty-four hours a day, seven days a week, no questions asked." How this works with Sample is that his support staff members were always instructed to do at least two things. First, tell the direct report where Sample was and what he was doing. Second, to say immediately, "If you need to talk with Steve right now, I'll be glad to get him for you."[12]

Notice what happens in this process. The work of determining whether Sample should be interrupted was taken out of the hands of the support staff and put into the hands of the direct report. For some leaders, such an approach to unfettered access sounds unmanageable. Wouldn't such access be abused?

Because Sample had regular meetings with his direct reports, in most cases the support staff's offer to interrupt Sample resulted in the direct report saying something like, "Oh, don't disturb him. Perhaps he could call me when he's free." The key to this, though, was that the direct report, not the support staff, decided whether the matter could wait.

If someone ever abused this access, Sample knew it was his job, not his support staff's job, to hold the direct report accountable for this. If they did it too often, Sample would provide the correction, or termination, needed to address the issue. The point was that Sample was accessible to his direct reports and would let them know if a line was crossed.

In our day of increasingly complex and accessible communication methods, this version of unfettered access requires intentionality when thinking through its application. But for Sample it communicated that direct reports had the access they needed for supporting and resourcing. They would generally wait for their regular meetings with Sample but understood that they were empowered to pursue the support and resources they needed to get their job done through Sample's approach to leader access.

Supporting and Resourcing: Insights for Practice

Sample's example of unfettered access is one insight for the practice of supporting and resourcing. We conclude this chapter with two additional insights for practice.

WORK FOR THOSE WHO WORK FOR YOU

First, we encourage leaders to view working for those who work for them as a top priority. This is what Sample was doing in his work of providing unfettered access to direct reports. Working for those who work for you is not about giving in to every whim and wish of team members. Rather, this is about recognizing that the top priority of leaders should be serving, supporting, and resourcing followers toward the successful completion of their work and goals.

Complex organizations do not run off the work of an individual. Leaders cannot guide the community to successful accomplishment of organizational mission without first guiding and supporting individuals toward the successful accomplishment of their part of the task. After bringing the right people onto the team, leaders must shift their work to support that team in whatever way they are able. Leaders and followers succeed together when there is a mutual commitment to supporting one another in the accomplishment of both individual work goals and the broader organizational mission. Do you view others as primarily working for you, or do you authentically view your job as a leader as working for those who work for you?

Hold Support and Openness Together

Second, we encourage leaders to hold both support of and openness with followers together. Emphasizing only the encouraging side of support will limit the growth of team members. We grow as people, and as organizational members, when faced with both support and challenge.

The previous chapter focused on providing accountability. Direct communication regarding areas of needed improvement will produce growth in followers when paired with authentic support. Followers need leaders who see both sides of this equation and hold them together with authenticity.

In Ephesians 4 Paul connects the growth and maturity of God's people with a willingness to speak the truth in love. Direct challenge of others without a spirit of love can lead to discouragement and emotional bruising. Warmth and encouragement of others without openness and truth-filled challenge can lead to immaturity and lack of growth. For Christians in general, and Christian leaders in particular, a willingness to bring truth and love—openness

> *We grow as people, and as organizational members, when faced with both support and challenge.*

and support—together is essential. This is the foundation for seeing organizational members grow and flourish together in service of the organization's mission. Take some time to consider how you can provide both support and challenge for your team members.

Next Steps

- Take some time to consider whether you tend to view others as primarily working for you or whether you authentically view your job as a leader as working for those who work for you.
- Take some time to consider how you can provide both support and openness—both love and truth—for your team members.

- Take some time to identify the one or two key resources your team members need to be successful in their work. Pick one of these resource needs in the week ahead and then develop a plan for meeting this need in partnership with your team members.

Resources for a Deeper Look

Blanchard, Ken, and Colleen Barrett. *Lead with LUV: A Different Way to Create Real Success*. Upper Saddle River, NJ: Pearson Education, 2011.

De Pree, Max. *Leadership Jazz: The Essential Elements of a Great Leader*. New York: Currency-Doubleday, 1992.

Sample, Steven B. *The Contrarian's Guide to Leadership*. San Francisco: Jossey-Bass, 2002.

Strauss, Mark L. *How to Read the Bible in Changing Times: Understanding and Applying God's Word Today*. Grand Rapids: Baker Books, 2011.

Notes

Introduction

1. James MacGregor Burns, *Leadership* (New York: Harper & Row, 1978), 2.

2. Colleen Barrett, "Treat Your People as Family," in *Servant Leadership in Action: How You Can Achieve Great Relationships and Results*, ed. Ken Blanchard and Renee Broadwell (Oakland, CA: Berrett-Koehler, 2018), 183.

3. Barrett, "Treat Your People as Family," 184.

4. Barrett, "Treat Your People as Family," 184.

5. Tacitus, *Life of Gnaeus Julius Agricola* 30 (Strauss's translation).

6. Recommended leadership resources: Peter G. Northouse, *Leadership: Theory and Practice* (Thousand Oaks, CA: Sage, 2018); Richard L. Daft, *The Leadership Experience* (Stamford, CT: Cengage Learning, 2015).

7. See Bernard M. Bass, *Bass and Stogdill's Handbook of Leadership: A Survey of Theory and Research* (New York: Free Press, 1990), for a helpful overview of trait-theory approaches to leadership study.

8. See historic works by Frederick Taylor: *Shop Management* (New York: American Society of Mechanical Engineers, 1903); *The Principles of Scientific Management* (New York: Harper, 1911).

9. See discussions of the Hawthorne studies: F. J. Roethlisberger and William J. Dickson, *Management and the Worker: An Account of a Research Program Conducted by the Western Electric Company, Hawthorne Works, Chicago* (Cambridge, MA: Harvard University Press, 1939); Elton Mayo, *The Human Problems of an Industrial Civilization* (Cambridge, MA: Harvard University Press, 1933).

10. See Robert L. Katz, "Skills of an Effective Administrator," *Harvard Business Review* 33, no. 1 (1955): 33–42.

11. See discussions in Bernard M. Bass, *Bass and Stogdill's Handbook of Leadership: A Survey of Theory and Research* (New York: Free Press, 1990); David G. Bowers and Stanley E. Seashore, "Predicting Organizational Effectiveness with a Four-Factor Theory of Leadership," *Administrative Science Quarterly* 11 (1966): 238–63.

12. See Robert R. Blake and Jane S. Mouton, *The Managerial Grid III* (Houston: Gulf, 1985).

13. See Douglas McGregor, *The Human Side of Enterprise* (New York: McGraw-Hill, 1960).

14. Kenneth H. Blanchard, *SLII®: A Situational Approach to Managing People* (Escondido, CA: Blanchard Training and Development, 1985).

15. Robert J. House, "A Path-Goal Theory of Leader Effectiveness," *Administrative Science Quarterly* 16, no. 3 (1971): 321–28; Robert J. House, "Path-Goal Theory of Leadership: Lessons, Legacy, and a Reformulated Theory," *Leadership Quarterly* 7, no. 3 (1996): 323–52.

16. For more on leader-member exchange theory, see Fred Dansereau, George B. Graen, and William Haga, "A Vertical Dyad Linkage Approach to Leadership in Formal Organizations," *Organizational Behavior and Human Performance* 13, no. 1 (1975): 46–78; Robert C. Liden, Sandy J. Wayne, and Dean Stilwell, "A Longitudinal Study on the Early Development of Leader-Member Exchanges," *Journal of Applied Psychology* 78, no. 4 (1993): 662–74.

17. Robert K. Greenleaf, *Servant Leadership: A Journey into the Nature of Legitimate Power and Greatness* (New York: Paulist Press, 1970).

18. See Bernard M. Bass, *Leadership and Performance beyond Expectations* (New York: Free Press, 1985); Bernard M. Bass and Bruce J. Avolio, *Improving Organizational Effectiveness through Transformational Leadership* (Thousand Oaks, CA: Sage, 1994).

19. See Daniel Goleman, *Working with Emotional Intelligence* (New York: Bantam, 1998); Travis Bradberry and Jean Greaves, *Emotional Intelligence 2.0* (San Diego, CA: TalentSmart, 2009).

20. Bill George, *Authentic Leadership: Rediscovering the Secrets to Creating Lasting Value* (San Francisco: Jossey-Bass, 2003); Bill George and Peter Sims, *True North: Discover Your Authentic Leadership* (San Francisco: Jossey-Bass, 2007).

21. Justin A. Irving and Julie Berndt, "Leader Purposefulness within Servant Leadership: Examining the Effect of Servant Leadership, Leader Follower-Focus, Leader Goal-Orientation, and Leader Purposefulness in a Large U.S. Healthcare Organization," *Administrative Sciences* 7, no. 2 (2017): 10, https://doi.org/10.3390/admsci7020010; Simon Sinek, *Start with Why: How Great Leaders Inspire Everyone to Take Action* (New York: Penguin, 2009).

22. Jim Laub, "The Servant Organization," in *Servant Leadership: Developments in Theory and Research*, ed. Dirk van Dierendonck and Kathleen Patterson (New York: Palgrave Macmillan, 2010), 105–17.

23. Eric M. Eisenberg and H. L. Goodall, *Organizational Communication: Balancing Creativity and Constraint*, 3rd ed. (New York: St. Martin's Press, 2001), 18.

Chapter 1 Modeling What Matters

1. Randall Wallace, dir. *We Were Soldiers*. Hollywood, CA: Paramount Pictures, DVD release date 2002.

2. Ken Blanchard, Scott Blanchard, and Drea Zigarmi, "Servant Leadership," in *Leading at a Higher Level*, by Ken Blanchard et al. (Upper Saddle River, NJ: Prentice Hall, 2007), 268.

3. Here and elsewhere, quotations pertaining to my research studies are drawn from participant observations collected during the data gathering process. For background on the research supporting the nine leadership practices identified in this book, see the following sources: Justin A. Irving, "A Model for Effective Servant Leadership Practice: A Biblically-Consistent and Research-Based Approach to Leadership," *Journal of Biblical Perspectives in Leadership* 3, no. 2 (2011): 118–28; Justin A. Irving and Gail J. Longbotham, "Leading Effective Teams through Servant Leadership: An Expanded Regression Model of Essential Servant Leadership Themes," *Proceedings of the American Society of Business and Behavioral Sciences* 14, no. 1 (2007): 806–17.

4. Don Page and Paul T. P. Wong, "A Conceptual Framework for Measuring Servant Leadership," in *The Human Factor in Shaping the Course of History and Development*, ed. S. Adjibolooso (Washington, DC: American University Press, 2000), 69–110.

5. Robert C. Liden, Sandy J. Wayne, Hao Zhao, et al., "Servant Leadership: Development of a Multidimensional Measure and Multi-Level Assessment," *Leadership Quarterly* 19 (2008): 161–77; Justin A. Irving and Julie Berndt, "Leader Purposefulness within Servant Leadership: Examining the Effect of Servant Leadership, Leader Follower-Focus, Leader Goal-Orientation,

and Leader Purposefulness in a Large U.S. Healthcare Organization," *Administrative Sciences* 7, no. 2 (2017): 10, https://doi.org/10.3390/admsci7020010.

6. Blanchard, Blanchard, and Zigarmi, "Servant Leadership," 261.

7. Kenneth H. Blanchard, *SLII®: A Situational Approach to Managing People* (Escondido, CA: Blanchard Training and Development, 1985).

8. Ken Blanchard, Margie Blanchard, Don Carew, et al., "Situational Leadership II: The Integrating Concept," in Blanchard et al., *Leading at a Higher Level*, 88 (emphasis in original).

9. Blanchard, Blanchard, and Zigarmi, "Servant Leadership," 265.

10. "The Leadership Square," accessed April 14, 2017, http://www.trinety.org/_literature_130126/Discipleship-Square.

11. Bernard M. Bass and Bruce J. Avolio, "Introduction," in *Improving Organizational Effectiveness through Transformational Leadership*, ed. Bernard M. Bass and Bruce J. Avolio (Thousand Oaks, CA: Sage, 1994), 3.

12. Richard Daft, *Leadership: Theory and Practice* (Fort Worth: Dryden, 1999).

13. Peter G. Northouse, *Leadership: Theory and Practice* (Thousand Oaks, CA: Sage, 2013), 200.

14. Francis J. Yammarino, "Indirect Leadership: Transformational Leadership at a Distance," in *Improving Organizational Effectiveness through Transformational Leadership*, ed. Bernard M. Bass and Bruce J. Avolio (Thousand Oaks, CA: Sage, 1994), 28.

15. Mark W. McCloskey, *Learning Leadership in a Changing World: Virtue and Effective Leadership in the 21st Century* (New York: Palgrave Macmillan, 2014), 41.

16. McCloskey, *Learning Leadership in a Changing World*, 42.

17. Yammarino, "Indirect Leadership," 28.

18. Daft, *Leadership*, 191.

19. Marc Ballon, "The Cheapest CEO in America," *Inc. Magazine*, October 1, 1997, 52, https://www.inc.com/magazine/19971001/1336.html.

20. Ballon, "Cheapest CEO."

21. Justin Irving, "Don't Confuse Motion with Progress," *Purpose in Leadership*, August 25, 2014, https://purposeinleadership.com/2014/08/25/motion-vs-progress.

22. Max De Pree, *Leadership Jazz: The Essential Elements of a Great Leader* (New York: Currency-Doubleday, 1992), 126.

23. Bill George, *Authentic Leadership: Rediscovering the Secrets to Creating Lasting Value* (San Francisco: Jossey-Bass, 2003), 37.

24. George, *Authentic Leadership*, 37.

25. James C. Collins and Jerry I. Porras, "Building Your Company's Vision," *Harvard Business Review* 74, no. 5 (September–October 1996): 65–77.

26. Daft, *Leadership*, 133.

27. James M. Kouzes and Barry Z. Posner, *The Leadership Challenge: How to Make Extraordinary Things Happen in Organizations*, 3rd ed. (San Francisco: Jossey-Bass, 2002), 93.

28. Justin A. Irving and Julie Berndt, "Leader Purposefulness within Servant Leadership: Examining the Effect of Servant Leadership, Leader Follower-Focus, Leader Goal-Orientation, and Leader Purposefulness in a Large U.S. Healthcare Organization," *Administrative Sciences* 7, no. 2 (2017): 10, https://doi.org/10.3390/admsci7020010.

29. Ken Blanchard, Margie Blanchard, and Pat Zigarmi, "Determining Your Leadership Point of View," in Blanchard et al., *Leading at a Higher Level*, 286.

Chapter 2 Engaging in Honest Self-Evaluation

1. Jim Dittmar, "Frances Hesselbein: To Serve Is to Live," in *Servant Leadership in Action: How You Can Achieve Great Relationships and Results*, ed. Ken Blanchard and Renee Broadwell (Oakland, CA: Berrett-Koehler, 2018), 171 (emphasis added).

2. Dittmar, "Frances Hesselbein," 172.

3. "σωφρονέω" in *Greek-English Lexicon of the New Testament and Other Early Christian Literature*, ed. Frederick W. Danker et al., 3rd ed. (Chicago: University of Chicago Press, 2000), 986.

4. Isaac Watts, "Alas! and Did My Savior Bleed."

5. For background on the research supporting the nine leadership practices identified in this book, see the following sources: Justin A. Irving, "A Model for Effective Servant Leadership Practice: A Biblically-Consistent and Research-Based Approach to Leadership," *Journal of Biblical Perspectives in Leadership* 3, no. 2 (2011): 118–28; Justin A. Irving and Gail J. Longbotham, "Leading Effective Teams through Servant Leadership: An Expanded Regression Model of Essential Servant Leadership Themes," *Proceedings of the American Society of Business and Behavioral Sciences* 14, no. 1 (2007): 806–17.

6. Peter Salovey and John D. Mayer, "Emotional Intelligence," *Imagination, Cognition and Personality* 9, no. 3 (1990): 185–211.

7. Samuel D. Rima, *Leading from the Inside Out: The Art of Self-Leadership* (Grand Rapids: Baker Books, 2000), 17.

8. Kevin Harney, *Leadership from the Inside Out: Examining the Inner Life of a Healthy Church Leader* (Grand Rapids: Zondervan, 2007), 17.

9. Edwin H. Friedman, *A Failure of Nerve: Leadership in the Age of the Quick Fix* (New York: Seabury, 2007).

10. Christopher S. Howard and Justin A. Irving, "The Impact of Obstacles Defined by Developmental Antecedents on Resilience in Leadership Formation," *Management Research Review* 37, no. 5 (2014): 466–78.

11. J. Robert Clinton, *The Making of a Leader* (Colorado Springs: NavPress, 1988). I rely heavily on Clinton's work for the concepts presented in fig. 2.3.

12. Bill George, *Authentic Leadership: Rediscovering the Secrets to Creating Lasting Value* (San Francisco: Jossey-Bass, 2003); Bill George and Peter Sims, *True North: Discover Your Authentic Leadership* (San Francisco: Jossey-Bass, 2007).

13. Bill George, "Why It's Hard to Do What's Right," *Fortune*, September 29, 2003, http://archive .fortune.com/magazines/fortune/fortune_archive/2003/09/29/349894/index.htm; A. J. Vogl, "The 21st-Century Leader," *The Conference Board Review* 44, no. 2 (March/April 2007): 54–60.

14. George, "Why It's Hard to Do What's Right."

15. George, "Why It's Hard to Do What's Right."

16. John Baldoni, *Lead with Purpose: Giving Your Organization a Reason to Believe in Itself* (New York: American Management Association, 2011), 3.

17. Baldoni, *Lead with Purpose*, 125.

18. Timothy Keller and Katherine Leary Alsdorf, *Every Good Endeavor: Connecting Your Work to God's Work* (New York: Dutton, 2012), 236–37.

19. Keller and Leary Alsdorf, *Every Good Endeavor*, 236.

20. Henry Cloud and John Townsend, *How People Grow: What the Bible Reveals about Personal Growth* (Grand Rapids: Zondervan, 2004).

Chapter 3 Fostering Collaboration

1. Miles McPherson was a former NFL player with the Chargers in the 1980s. God eventually got ahold of his life and led him to start Rock Church in 2000. See https://www.sdrock .com/pastormiles.

2. Miles McPherson, "How Servant Leadership Has Shaped Our Church Culture," in *Servant Leadership in Action: How You Can Achieve Great Relationships and Results*, ed. Ken Blanchard and Renee Broadwell (Oakland, CA: Berrett-Koehler, 2018), 212.

3. McPherson, "How Servant Leadership Has Shaped Our Church Culture," 213 (emphasis in original).

4. For background on the research supporting the nine leadership practices identified in this book, see the following sources: Justin A. Irving, "A Model for Effective Servant Leadership

Practice: A Biblically-Consistent and Research-Based Approach to Leadership," *Journal of Biblical Perspectives in Leadership* 3, no. 2 (2011): 118–28; Justin A. Irving and Gail J. Longbotham, "Leading Effective Teams through Servant Leadership: An Expanded Regression Model of Essential Servant Leadership Themes," *Proceedings of the American Society of Business and Behavioral Sciences* 14, no. 1 (2007): 806–17.

5. B. V. Moore, "The May Conference on Leadership," *Personnel Journal* 6 (1927): 124.

6. Robert K. Greenleaf, *Servant Leadership: A Journey into the Nature of Legitimate Power and Greatness*, 25th anniversary ed. (New York: Paulist Press, 2002), 24.

7. Frank LaFasto and Carl Larson, *When Teams Work Best: 6,000 Team Members and Leaders Tell What It Takes to Succeed* (Thousand Oaks, CA: Sage, 2001), 148.

8. Patrick Lencioni, *The Ideal Team Player: How to Recognize and Cultivate the Three Essential Virtues* (Hoboken, NJ: Wiley, 2016), 157.

9. Mark W. McCloskey, *Learning Leadership in a Changing World: Virtue and Effective Leadership in the 21st Century* (New York: Palgrave Macmillan, 2014), 42.

10. Jim Laub, "The Servant Organization," in *Servant Leadership: Developments in Theory and Research*, ed. Dirk van Dierendonck and Kathleen Patterson (New York: Palgrave Macmillan, 2010), 108.

11. E.g., Justin A. Irving and Julie Berndt, "Leader Purposefulness within Servant Leadership: Examining the Effect of Servant Leadership, Leader Follower-Focus, Leader Goal-Orientation, and Leader Purposefulness in a Large U.S. Healthcare Organization," *Administrative Sciences* 7, no. 2 (2017): 10, https://doi.org/10.3390/admsci7020010; Valorie C. Nordbye and Justin A. Irving, "Servant Leadership and Organizational Effectiveness: Examining Leadership Culture among Millennials within a US National Campus Ministry," *Servant Leadership: Theory & Practice* 4, no. 1 (2017): 53–74; Justin A. Irving and Gail Longbotham, "Team Effectiveness and Six Essential Servant Leadership Themes: A Regression Model Based on Items in the Organizational Leadership Assessment," *International Journal of Leadership Studies* 2, no. 2 (2007): 98–113.

12. James M. Kouzes and Barry Z. Posner, *The Leadership Challenge: How to Make Extraordinary Things Happen in Organizations*, 3rd ed. (San Francisco: Jossey-Bass, 2002), 148.

13. Kouzes and Posner, *Leadership Challenge*, 18 (emphasis in original).

14. John W. Gardner, "The Cry for Leadership," in *The Leader's Companion: Insights on Leadership through the Ages* (New York: Free Press, 1995), 5–6.

15. Bruce W. Tuckman, "Developmental Sequence in Small Groups," *Psychological Bulletin* 63, no. 6 (1965): 384–99.

16. Carl E. Larson and Frank M. J. LaFasto, *Teamwork: What Must Go Right, What Can Go Wrong* (Newbury Park, CA: Sage, 1989), 94.

17. Larson and LaFasto, *Teamwork*, 85.

18. Nordbye and Irving, "Servant Leadership and Organizational Effectiveness."

19. Robert J. House, Paul J. Hanges, Mansour Javidan, et al., eds., *Culture, Leadership, and Organizations: The GLOBE Study of 62 Societies* (Thousand Oaks, CA: Sage, 2004).

20. McCloskey, *Learning Leadership in a Changing World*, 42.

21. Jim Collins, *Good to Great: Why Some Companies Make the Leap . . . and Others Don't* (New York: Harper Business, 2001).

22. Dirk van Dierendonck and Inge Nuijten, "The Servant Leadership Survey: Development and Validation of a Multidimensional Measure," *Journal of Business Psychology* 26, no. 3 (September 2011): 249–67 (esp. 252).

Chapter 4 Valuing and Appreciating

1. Colleen Barrett, "Treat Your People as Family," in *Servant Leadership in Action: How You Can Achieve Great Relationships and Results*, ed. Ken Blanchard and Renee Broadwell (Oakland, CA: Berrett-Koehler, 2018), 184.

2. David Gergen, "Bad News for Bullies," *U.S. News & World Report*, June 19, 2006, 54.

3. James M. Kouzes and Barry Z. Posner, *The Leadership Challenge: How to Make Extraordinary Things Happen in Organizations*, 3rd ed. (San Francisco: Jossey-Bass, 2002), 335.

4. In Paul's letters "brother/sister" (*adelphos/adelphē*) appears 133 times, "co-worker" (*synergos*) appears 12 times, and "partner" (*koinōnos*) and "fellow soldier" (*systratiōtēs*) each appear 2 times.

5. For background on the research supporting the nine leadership practices identified in this book, see the following sources: Justin A. Irving, "A Model for Effective Servant Leadership Practice: A Biblically-Consistent and Research-Based Approach to Leadership," *Journal of Biblical Perspectives in Leadership* 3, no. 2 (2011): 118–28; Justin A. Irving and Gail J. Longbotham, "Leading Effective Teams through Servant Leadership: An Expanded Regression Model of Essential Servant Leadership Themes," *Proceedings of the American Society of Business and Behavioral Sciences* 14, no. 1 (2007): 806–17.

6. Max De Pree, *Leading without Power: Finding Hope in Serving Community* (San Francisco: Jossey-Bass, 1997), 106.

7. Jim Laub, "The Servant Organization," in *Servant Leadership: Developments in Theory and Research*, ed. Dirk van Dierendonck and Kathleen Patterson (New York: Palgrave Macmillan, 2010), 108.

8. Michael E. McNeff and Justin A. Irving, "Job Satisfaction and the Priority of Valuing People: A Case Study of Servant Leadership Practice in a Network of Family-Owned Companies," *SAGE Open* 7, no. 1 (January–March 2017): 5, https://doi.org/10.1177/2158244016686813.

9. Richard Daft, *Leadership: Theory and Practice* (Fort Worth: Dryden, 1999), 351.

10. Kathleen Patterson, "Servant Leadership and Love," in van Dierendonck and Patterson, *Servant Leadership*, 72.

11. George Gendron and Stephen D. Solomon, "The Art of Loving: An Interview with Jan Carlzon," *Inc. Magazine*, May 1, 1989, 35–46, https://www.inc.com/magazine/19890501/5635.html.

12. Daft, *Leadership*, 353.

13. Patterson, "Servant Leadership and Love," 76.

14. Ralph M. Stogdill, *Handbook of Leadership: A Survey of Theory and Research* (New York: Free Press, 1974).

15. David G. Bowers and Stanley E. Seashore, "Predicting Organizational Effectiveness with a Four-Factor Theory of Leadership," *Administrative Science Quarterly* 11 (1966): 238–63.

16. Robert R. Blake and Jane S. Mouton, *The Managerial Grid III* (Houston: Gulf, 1985).

17. Robert K. Greenleaf, *Servant Leadership: A Journey into the Nature of Legitimate Power and Greatness*, 25th anniversary ed. (New York: Paulist Press, 1977), 27.

18. A. Gregory Stone, Kathleen Patterson, and Robert F. Russell, "Transformational versus Servant Leadership: A Difference in Leader Focus," *Leadership Organization Development Journal* 25 (2004): 349–61.

19. Justin A. Irving and Julie Berndt, "Leader Purposefulness within Servant Leadership: Examining the Effect of Servant Leadership, Leader Follower-Focus, Leader Goal-Orientation, and Leader Purposefulness in a Large U.S. Healthcare Organization," *Administrative Sciences* 7, no. 2 (2017): 10, https://doi.org/10.3390/admsci7020010 (quote from §2).

20. Justin A. Irving, "Assessing Leader Goal-Orientation, Follower-Focus, and Purpose-in-Leadership: Development and Initial Testing of the Purpose in Leadership Inventory," *Servant Leadership Theory & Practice* 1, no. 1 (2014): 53–67; Irving and Berndt, "Leader Purposefulness within Servant Leadership."

21. Bernard M. Bass and Bruce J. Avolio, eds., *Improving Organizational Effectiveness through Transformational Leadership* (Thousand Oaks, CA: Sage, 1994).

22. Bass and Avolio, *Improving Organizational Effectiveness*, 3.

23. Kouzes and Posner, *Leadership Challenge*, 335. Also see Edward L. Deci and Richard Flaste, *Why We Do What We Do: Understanding Self-Motivation* (New York: Putnam, 1995); Alfie Kohn, *Punished by Rewards* (Boston: Houghton Mifflin, 1993).

24. Eric M. Eisenberg and H. L. Goodall, *Organizational Communication: Balancing Creativity and Constraint*, 3rd ed. (New York: St. Martin's Press, 2001), 18.

25. David Dorsey, "Andy Pearson Finds Love," *Fast Company* 49 (August 2001): 78.

26. Dov Eden, *Pygmalion in Management: Productivity as a Self-Fulfilling Prophecy* (Lexington, MA: Lexington, 1990); Xander Bezuijen et al., "Pygmalion and Employee Learning: The Role of Leader Behaviors," *Journal of Management* 35, no. 5 (2009): 1248–67.

27. E.g., Dov Eden, "Leadership and Expectations: Pygmalion Effects and Other Self-Fulfilling Prophecies in Organizations," *Leadership Quarterly* 3, no. 4 (1992): 271–305.

28. Kouzes and Posner, *Leadership Challenge*, 322.

29. Timothy Keller and Katherine Leary Alsdorf, *Every Good Endeavor: Connecting Your Work to God's Work* (New York: Dutton, 2012), 48, 49, 53.

30. J. E. Sawyer et al., "Analysis of Work Group Productivity in an Applied Setting: Application of a Time Series Panel Design," *Personnel Psychology* 52 (1999): 927–67; Adrian Gostick and Chester Elton, *Managing with Carrots: Using Recognition to Attract and Retain the Best People* (Layton, UT: Gibbs Smith, 2001).

31. Albert Bandura and Daniel Cervone, "Self-Evaluative and Self-Efficacy Mechanisms Governing the Motivational Effects of Goal Systems," *Journal of Personality and Social Psychology* 45 (1983): 1017–28.

32. Kouzes and Posner, *Leadership Challenge*, 319.

33. Ken Blanchard and Fred Finch, "Essential Skills for Partnering for Performance: The One Minute Manager®," in *Leading at a Higher Level*, by Ken Blanchard et al. (Upper Saddle River, NJ: Prentice Hall, 2007), 154.

34. Kouzes and Posner, *Leadership Challenge*, 327 (emphasis in original).

35. McNeff and Irving, "Job Satisfaction and the Priority of Valuing People," 4. Mike McNeff's cousin and his family were the focus of this study.

36. Fred Finch and Ken Blanchard, "Partnering for Performance," in Blanchard et al., *Leading at a Higher Level*, 128.

37. Kevin Harney, *Leadership from the Inside Out: Examining the Inner Life of a Healthy Church Leader* (Grand Rapids: Zondervan, 2007), 101.

38. Christine D. Pohl, *Living into Community: Cultivating Practices That Sustain Us* (Grand Rapids: Eerdmans, 2012), 25.

39. Blanchard and Finch, "Essential Skills for Partnering for Performance," 157.

Chapter 5 Creating a Place for Individuality

1. Colleen Barrett, "Treat Your People as Family," in *Servant Leadership in Action: How You Can Achieve Great Relationships and Results*, ed. Ken Blanchard and Renee Broadwell (Oakland, CA: Berrett-Koehler, 2018), 187.

2. Rom. 1:11; 11:29; 12:6; 1 Cor. 1:7; 7:7; 12:4, 9, 28, 30, 31; 1 Tim. 4:14.

3. Rom. 1:11; 1 Cor. 12:1; 14:1, 37; cf. 1 Cor. 14:12.

4. For background on the research supporting the nine leadership practices identified in this book, see the following sources: Justin A. Irving, "A Model for Effective Servant Leadership Practice: A Biblically-Consistent and Research-Based Approach to Leadership," *Journal of Biblical Perspectives in Leadership* 3, no. 2 (2011): 118–28; Justin A. Irving and Gail J. Longbotham, "Leading Effective Teams through Servant Leadership: An Expanded Regression Model of Essential Servant Leadership Themes," *Proceedings of the American Society of Business and Behavioral Sciences* 14, no. 1 (2007): 806–17.

5. Thomas A. Bausch, "Servant-Leaders Making Human New Models of Work and Organization," in *Insights on Leadership: Service, Stewardship, Spirit, and Servant-Leadership*, ed. Larry Spears (New York: Wiley, 1998), 241.

6. Margaret J. Wheatley, "What Is Our Work?," in Spears, *Insights on Leadership*, 343.

7. Wheatley, "What Is Our Work?," 343.

8. Wheatley, "What Is Our Work?," 342.

9. Gary Hamel, "Reinventing the Technology of Human Accomplishment," University of Phoenix, The Phoenix Lecture Series, accessed September 5, 2018, http://www.garyhamel.com /video/reinventing-technology-human-accomplishment.

10. Bruce E. Winston, *Be a Leader for God's Sake* (Virginia Beach: Regent University, School of Leadership Studies, 2002).

11. Bill George, *Authentic Leadership: Rediscovering the Secrets to Creating Lasting Value* (San Francisco: Jossey-Bass, 2003).

12. Irving, "Model for Effective Servant Leadership Practice," 125.

13. Wheatley, "What Is Our Work?," 344.

14. Wheatley, "What Is Our Work?," 347.

15. Wheatley, "What Is Our Work?," 347.

16. Bausch, "Servant-Leaders Making Human New Models," 231.

17. Bernard M. Bass and Bruce J. Avolio, eds., *Improving Organizational Effectiveness through Transformational Leadership* (Thousand Oaks, CA: Sage, 1994), 1–9.

18. Bruce J. Avolio, "Pursuing Authentic Leadership Development," in *Handbook of Leadership Theory and Practice* (Boston: Harvard Business Press, 2010), 748.

19. Robert K. Greenleaf, *Servant Leadership: A Journey into the Nature of Legitimate Power and Greatness*, 25th anniversary ed. (New York: Paulist Press, 1977), 27.

20. Jim Laub, "The Servant Organization," in *Servant Leadership: Developments in Theory and Research*, ed. Dirk van Dierendonck and Kathleen Patterson (New York: Palgrave Macmillan, 2010), 108.

21. Bausch, "Servant-Leaders Making Human New Models," 231.

22. Bausch, "Servant-Leaders Making Human New Models," 231.

23. Susan Fowler, Ken Blanchard, and Laurence Hawkins, "Self-Leadership: The Power behind Empowerment," in *Leading at a Higher Level*, by Ken Blanchard et al. (Upper Saddle River, NJ: Prentice Hall, 2007), 105.

24. Fowler, Blanchard, and Hawkins, "Self-Leadership," 105.

25. Bausch, "Servant-Leaders Making Human New Models," 240.

26. Bausch, "Servant-Leaders Making Human New Models," 241.

27. George, *Authentic Leadership*, 134.

28. Marcus Buckingham and Donald Clifton, *Now, Discover Your Strengths* (New York: Free Press, 2001), 21.

29. Tom Rath and Barry Conchie, *Strengths Based Leadership: Great Leaders, Teams, and Why People Follow* (New York: Gallup, 2008), 21.

30. Rath and Conchie, *Strengths Based Leadership*, 2.

31. T. J. Addington, *Leading from the Sandbox: How to Develop, Empower, and Release High-Impact Ministry Teams* (Colorado Springs: NavPress, 2010).

32. C. William Pollard, "Mission as an Organizing Principle," in *Beyond Integrity: A Judeo-Christian Approach to Business Ethics*, ed. Scott B. Rae and Kenman L. Wong (Grand Rapids: Zondervan, 2012), 278.

33. Pollard, "Mission as an Organizing Principle," 277.

34. Pollard, "Mission as an Organizing Principle," 278.

35. Pollard, "Mission as an Organizing Principle," 278.

36. Pollard, "Mission as an Organizing Principle," 278.

37. Blanchard et al., *Leading at a Higher Level*, 82–83.

38. Bausch, "Servant-Leaders Making Human New Models," 241 (emphasis in original).

39. Bausch, "Servant-Leaders Making Human New Models," 241.

Chapter 6 Understanding Relational Skills

1. Valerie Strauss, "The Surprising Thing Google Learned about Its Employees—and What It Means for Today's Students," *The Washington Post*, December 20, 2017, https://www.wash

ingtonpost.com/news/answer-sheet/wp/2017/12/20/the-surprising-thing-google-learned-about-its-employees-and-what-it-means-for-todays-students.

2. While all of Paul's letters contain these exhortations, the most extensive discussions are found in Rom. 12:9–21; 14:1–15:13; 1 Cor. 13:1–13; Gal. 5:13–6:10; Eph. 4:1–5:9; and Col. 3:1–4:1.

3. For background on the research supporting the nine leadership practices identified in this book, see the following sources: Justin A. Irving, "A Model for Effective Servant Leadership Practice: A Biblically-Consistent and Research-Based Approach to Leadership," *Journal of Biblical Perspectives in Leadership* 3, no. 2 (2011): 118–28; Justin A. Irving and Gail J. Longbotham, "Leading Effective Teams through Servant Leadership: An Expanded Regression Model of Essential Servant Leadership Themes," *Proceedings of the American Society of Business and Behavioral Sciences* 14, no. 1 (2007): 806–17.

4. Robert L. Katz, "Skills of an Effective Administrator," *Harvard Business Review* 33, no. 1 (1955): 33–42.

5. James M. Kouzes and Barry Z. Posner, *The Leadership Challenge: How to Make Extraordinary Things Happen in Organizations*, 3rd ed. (San Francisco: Jossey-Bass, 2002).

6. Mark W. McCloskey, *Learning Leadership in a Changing World: Virtue and Effective Leadership in the 21st Century* (New York: Palgrave Macmillan, 2014).

7. McCloskey, *Learning Leadership in a Changing World*, 131.

8. Howard Gardner, *Frames of Mind: The Theory of Multiple Intelligences* (New York: Basic Books, 2011).

9. Travis Bradberry and Jean Greaves, *Emotional Intelligence 2.0* (San Diego, CA: TalentSmart, 2009), 138, 179.

10. Kenneth Lee Cochrum, *Close: Leading Well across Distance and Cultures* (North Charleston, SC: CreateSpace Independent Publishing, 2013), 43.

11. Robert J. House, Paul J. Hanges, Mansour Javidan, et al., eds., *Culture, Leadership, and Organizations: The GLOBE Study of 62 Societies* (Thousand Oaks, CA: Sage, 2004).

12. Milton J. Bennett, "Towards Ethnorelativism: A Developmental Model of Intercultural Sensitivity," in *Cross-Cultural Orientation: New Conceptualizations and Applications*, ed. R. M. Paige (New York: University Press of America, 1986), 27–70.

13. Ava Bergman, "Doctor of Ministry Alum Leads Transformational Indian Ministries," Bethel University News, Oct. 21, 2017, https://www.bethel.edu/news/articles/2017/october/saji-lukos.

14. Mission India Theological Seminary homepage, http://www.mits-india.org/aboutus.html.

15. "Peace Prayer of St. Francis," Loyola Press prayer page, https://www.loyolapress.com/our-catholic-faith/prayer/traditional-catholic-prayers/saints-prayers/peace-prayer-of-saint-francis.

Chapter 7 Communicating with Clarity

1. John Baldoni, *Great Communication Secrets of Great Leaders* (New York: McGraw-Hill, 2003), 59.

2. For background on the research supporting the nine leadership practices identified in this book, see the following sources: Justin A. Irving, "A Model for Effective Servant Leadership Practice: A Biblically-Consistent and Research-Based Approach to Leadership," *Journal of Biblical Perspectives in Leadership* 3, no. 2 (2011): 118–28; Justin A. Irving and Gail J. Longbotham, "Leading Effective Teams through Servant Leadership: An Expanded Regression Model of Essential Servant Leadership Themes," *Proceedings of the American Society of Business and Behavioral Sciences* 14, no. 1 (2007): 806–17.

3. Justin A. Irving, "Assessing Leader Goal-Orientation, Follower-Focus, and Purpose-in-Leadership: Development and Initial Testing of the Purpose in Leadership Inventory," *Servant Leadership Theory & Practice* 1, no. 1 (2014): 53–67; Justin A. Irving and Julie Berndt,

"Leader Purposefulness within Servant Leadership: Examining the Effect of Servant Leadership, Leader Follower-Focus, Leader Goal-Orientation, and Leader Purposefulness in a Large U.S. Healthcare Organization," *Administrative Sciences* 7, no. 2 (2017): 10, https://doi.org/10.3390 /admsci7020010.

4. Stephen W. Littlejohn, *Theories of Human Communication* (Belmont, CA: Wadsworth Learning, 2002), 14–15.

5. Patrick Lencioni, *The Advantage: Why Organizational Health Trumps Everything Else in Business* (San Francisco: Jossey-Bass, 2012), 77.

6. Mark McCloskey, *Tell It Often—Tell It Well: Making the Most of Witnessing Opportunities* (Nashville: Nelson, 1995), 227.

7. David Horsager, *The Trust Edge: How Top Leaders Gain Faster Results, Deeper Relationships, and a Stronger Bottom Line* (Minneapolis: Summerside, 2010), 48.

8. Horsager, *Trust Edge*, 62.

9. Justin Irving, "7 Levels of Leadership Communication," *Purpose in Leadership* (blog), July 17, 2014, https://purposeinleadership.com/2014/07/17/7-levels-of-leadership-communication.

10. John Blake, "The Greatest MLK Speeches You Never Heard," *CNN*, January 20, 2014, https://www.cnn.com/2014/01/19/us/king-speeches-never-heard/index.html.

11. Martin Luther King Jr., "Our God Is Marching On!," speech given March 25, 1965, transcript available at https://kinginstitute.stanford.edu/our-god-marching.

12. Martin Luther King Jr., "I Have a Dream," speech given Aug. 28, 1963, transcript available at https://kinginstitute.stanford.edu/king-papers/documents/i-have-dream-address-deliver ed-march-washington-jobs-and-freedom.

13. Steven B. Sample, *The Contrarian's Guide to Leadership* (San Francisco: Jossey-Bass, 2002), 21.

14. Eric M. Eisenberg and H. L. Goodall, *Organizational Communication: Balancing Creativity and Constraint*, 3rd ed. (New York: St. Martin's Press, 2001).

15. Max De Pree, *Leading without Power: Finding Hope in Serving Community* (San Francisco: Jossey-Bass, 1997), 71.

16. Jim Elliot, *The Journals of Jim Elliot*, ed. Elisabeth Elliot (Grand Rapids: Revell, 2002), 278.

Chapter 8 Providing Accountability

1. Julie White, "Ministering to the Wounded, Weary, and Wary in the Workplace," presentation at the Work with a Purpose Initiative hosted by Bethel Seminary, May 1, 2018, https:// www.youtube.com/watch?v=uz8gl6tCimE.

2. Richard Beaton and Linda M. Wagener, "Building Healthy Organizations in Which People Can Flourish," in *Beyond Integrity: A Judeo-Christian Approach to Business Ethics*, ed. Scott B. Rae and Kenman L. Wong (Grand Rapids: Zondervan, 2012), 284.

3. There are some differences between the Synoptic Gospels here. E.g., in Matthew and Luke the disciples can't even take a staff or sandals. For possible solutions, see Mark L. Strauss, *Mark*, Zondervan Exegetical Commentary (Grand Rapids: Zondervan, 2014), 251.

4. For background on the research supporting the nine leadership practices identified in this book, see the following sources: Justin A. Irving, "A Model for Effective Servant Leadership Practice: A Biblically-Consistent and Research-Based Approach to Leadership," *Journal of Biblical Perspectives in Leadership* 3, no. 2 (2011): 118–28; Justin A. Irving and Gail J. Longbotham, "Leading Effective Teams through Servant Leadership: An Expanded Regression Model of Essential Servant Leadership Themes," *Proceedings of the American Society of Business and Behavioral Sciences* 14, no. 1 (2007): 806–17.

5. Jim Laub, "The Servant Organization," in *Servant Leadership: Developments in Theory and Research*, ed. Dirk van Dierendonck and Kathleen Patterson (New York: Palgrave Macmillan, 2010), 108.

6. James M. Kouzes and Barry Z. Posner, *The Leadership Challenge: How to Make Extraordinary Things Happen in Organizations*, 3rd ed. (San Francisco: Jossey-Bass, 2002), 148.

7. Ron Shaich, "The Founder of Panera Bread: 'I Wish I'd Fired More People,'" *Entrepreneur*, March 2018, https://www.entrepreneur.com/article/308427 (emphasis added).

8. Kerry Patterson, Joseph Grenny, Ron McMillan, et al., *Crucial Accountability: Tools for Resolving Violated Expectations, Broken Commitments, and Bad Behavior*, 2nd ed. (New York: McGraw-Hill Education, 2013).

9. Ken Sande, *The Peacemaker: A Biblical Guide to Resolving Personal Conflict*, 3rd ed. (Grand Rapids: Baker Books, 2004), 28.

10. Patterson, Grenny, McMillan, et al., *Crucial Accountability*, 7.

11. Patterson, Grenny, McMillan, et al., *Crucial Accountability*, 73–103.

12. Max De Pree, *Leadership Is an Art* (New York: Dell, 1989), 11.

13. Max De Pree, *Leading without Power: Finding Hope in Serving the Community* (San Francisco: Jossey-Bass, 1997), 47–67.

14. Ryan T. Hardwig and Warren Bird, *Teams That Thrive: Five Disciplines of Collaborative Church Leadership* (Downers Grove, IL: InterVarsity, 2015), 238.

15. Bob Briner and Ray Pritchard, *The Leadership Lessons of Jesus* (Nashville: Broadman and Holman, 1997), 104.

16. Frank LaFasto and Carl Larson, *When Teams Work Best: 6,000 Team Members and Leaders Tell What It Takes to Succeed* (Thousand Oaks, CA: Sage, 2001), 169.

17. Shaich, "Founder of Panera Bread" (emphasis added).

18. Shaich, "Founder of Panera Bread" (emphasis in original).

19. De Pree, *Leadership Is an Art*, 11.

20. De Pree, *Leadership Is an Art*, 19.

21. LaFasto and Larson, *When Teams Work Best*, 170.

Chapter 9 Supporting and Resourcing

1. Steven B. Sample, *The Contrarian's Guide to Leadership* (San Francisco: Jossey-Bass, 2002), 121 (emphasis in original).

2. The Greek word Jesus uses (*paraklētos*) can mean any of these things.

3. Here is Paul in his own words:

I have worked much harder, been in prison more frequently, been flogged more severely, and been exposed to death again and again. Five times I received from the Jews the forty lashes minus one. Three times I was beaten with rods, once I was pelted with stones, three times I was shipwrecked, I spent a night and a day in the open sea, I have been constantly on the move. I have been in danger from rivers, in danger from bandits, in danger from my fellow Jews, in danger from Gentiles; in danger in the city, in danger in the country, in danger at sea; and in danger from false believers. I have labored and toiled and have often gone without sleep; I have known hunger and thirst and have often gone without food; I have been cold and naked. Besides everything else, I face daily the pressure of my concern for all the churches. (2 Cor. 11:23–28)

4. For background on the research supporting the nine leadership practices identified in this book, see the following sources: Justin A. Irving, "A Model for Effective Servant Leadership Practice: A Biblically-Consistent and Research-Based Approach to Leadership," *Journal of Biblical Perspectives in Leadership* 3, no. 2 (2011): 118–28; Justin A. Irving and Gail J. Longbotham, "Leading Effective Teams through Servant Leadership: An Expanded Regression Model of Essential Servant Leadership Themes," *Proceedings of the American Society of Business and Behavioral Sciences* 14, no. 1 (2007): 806–17.

5. Jim Collins, *Good to Great: Why Some Companies Make the Leap . . . and Others Don't* (New York: Harper Business, 2001), 13.

6. Sample, *Contrarian's Guide to Leadership*, 125.

7. Victor H. Vroom, *Work and Motivation* (New York: McGraw-Hill, 1964).

8. Peter G. Northouse, *Leadership: Theory and Practice* (Thousand Oaks, CA: Sage, 2016), 116.

9. Bernard M. Bass and Bruce J. Avolio, eds., *Improving Organizational Effectiveness through Transformational Leadership* (Thousand Oaks, CA: Sage, 1994), 1–9.

10. James M. Kouzes and Barry Z. Posner, *The Leadership Challenge: How to Make Extraordinary Things Happen in Organizations*, 3rd ed. (San Francisco: Jossey-Bass, 2002), 3–22, 241–314.

11. Sample, *Contrarian's Guide to Leadership*, 121.

12. Sample, *Contrarian's Guide to Leadership*, 130.

Scripture Index

Subject and Name Index